On the Shoulders of Giants

Cambridge Feb. 5. 1675.

Sr

At y^e reading of y^r letter I was exceedingly well pleased & satisfied wth y^e generous freedom, & think you have done what becomes a true Philosophicall spirit. There is nothing wch I desire to avoyde in matters of Philosophy more then contention, nor any kind of contention more then one in print: & therefore I gladly embrace ye proposall of a private correspondence. What's

done before many witnesses is seldome w^thout some further concern then that for ye truth: but what passes between friends in private usually deserves ye name of consultation rather then contest, & so I hope it will prove between you & me. Your animadversions will be therefore very welcome to me; for though I was formerly tired with this subject, & have not yet nor I believe ever shall recover so much love for it as to delight in spending

time about it; yet to have at once in short ye strongest or most pertinent Objections that may be made, I could really desire, & know no man better able to furnish me wth them then y^r self. In this you will oblige me. And if there be any thing els in my papers in wch you apprehend I have assumed too much, or not done you right, if you please to reserve your sentiments of it for a private letter, I hope you will find also that I am not so much in love wth philosophicall productions but y^t I can make them yield to equity & friendship. But, in ye meane time you defer too

much to my ability for searching into this subject. What Des-Cartes did was a good step. You have added much severall ways, & especially in taking ye colours of thin plates into philosophicall consideration. If I have seen further it is by standing on ye shoulders of Giants. But I make no question

Yo^r humble Servant

Is. Newton

The Vicennial Edition

On the Shoulders of Giants

A Shandean Postscript

Robert K. Merton

WITH AN AFTERWORD BY Denis Donoghue

AND A PREFACE BY the author

Harcourt Brace Jovanovich, Publishers
San Diego   New York   London

Library of Congress Cataloging in Publication Data
Merton, Robert King, 1910–
    On the shoulders of giants.

    Reprint. Originally published: New York: Free Press, 1965.
    I. Title.
PS3525.E717305 1985   816'.54   85-848
ISBN 0-15-169962-3

Printed in the United States of America
Vicennial edition
  B C D E

Picture credits:
2. Photographie Giraudon.
3-6. Marburg—Art Reference Bureau.

AN EXPLANATORY NOTE by the German translator of this book drawn from an account requested of its author: " 'As you supposed, the dedication is indeed to my three children, listed in order of birth, and then, as you could not easily surmise, to their fifteen cats (not, as you understandably inferred, to fifteen grandchildren). The allusion would be understood at once by close friends. Still, others can find a clue in the antonymic "Effable Three . . . and Their Ineffable Fifteen." For those paired adjectives of course echo T. S. Eliot's "The Naming of Cats" in his unforgettable *Old Possum's Book of Practical Cats* (Harcourt, Brace & World, Inc., 1967, twenty-first printing), which was read successively and often by each of The Effable Three. A further clue is provided by my confession, in the note on page 71, that in my middle years I became "a confirmed ailurophile." ' "

Incidentally, I now confess to having coined that much-needed term *ailurophile* to designate, in strongly scientific language, what laymen describe by the Anglo-Saxon construct, "cat-lover." Without for a moment implying that the incomparable *Oxford English Dictionary* is prejudiced against that "well-known carnivorous quadruped (*Felis domesticus*) which has long been domesticated, being kept to destroy mice, and as a house pet," I must report that the 1972 *Supplement* to the *OED* has an entry for *ailurophobia* (morbid fear of cats) and *ailurophobe* (a person so afflicted) but nary a mention of my loving coinage *ailurophile* (and, as an obvious derivative, *ailurophilia*). Can it be that the well-nigh omniscient editor of the *Supplement*, for whom I retain the highest regard, has not yet scanned *On the Shoulders of Giants*?

Preface to The Vicennial Edition

THE FIRST EDITION of this epistolary book has no preface, and for the best of reasons. Letters are not generally prefaced (although some colleagues-at-a-distance complain that mine often are). However, my publisher informs me that the appearance of this new edition imposes a distinct obligation of writing a preface to tell something of what has become, to one's surprise, a thrice-published book. I comply rather more out of obedience than conviction. But at the least, I can be mercifully brief.

The confessional subtitle signalizes the determining ancestor of this prodigal brainchild of mine now approaching adulthood. As I now reconstruct its origins, I adopted the non-linear, advancing-by-doubling-back Shandean Method of composition at the same time I was reflecting that this open form resembles the course taken by history in general, by the history of ideas in particular, and, in a way, by the course taken in scientific inquiry as well. For a lifelong addict to *The Life and Opinions of Tristram Shandy, Gentleman*, this complex hypothesis inexorably brought to mind the graphic depiction, in Book VI, Chapter XL, of the eccentric trajectories followed by the first four of its pathmaking volumes along these exact lines:

The diligent reader of this little book might in retrospect attempt to chart its divagating course in like manner; I dare not. But I can bear witness that once I elected to trace the complex course of the aphorism commonly ascribed to Newton—"if I have seen farther, it is by standing on the shoulders of giants"—the temporal pattern became altogether clear: both the history of the aphorism and my history of that history would have to move forward and backward in social time, just as the author's private time would have to interact with the reader's private time. As the deep-sighted historiographer Siegfried Kracauer rightly observed,* *On the Shoulders of Giants* (*OTSOG* for short) attends to discontinuities as well as continuities in tracing the vicissitudinous history of the aphorism. In doing so, it gives us to understand that history is contingent. Thus it is that the *OTSOG* history provides intimations of what did *not* happen along with its faithful account of what *did* happen. Yet it must be said, in all candor, that many an academic mind, failing to recognize that historical interpretation perforce assumes this kind of thought-experiment, will proceed to stigmatize the otsogian conception as mere self-indulgence in counterfactual history.

Be it also confessed that this otsogian historiography was not entirely a matter of design. It was only when the search into the travels and adventures of the Newtonian aphorism had moved well along that one discovered one was thinking and writing in the Shandean mood, a mood continually reinforced by what one was serendipitously finding en route. It was only at that belated moment of discovery that, in self-exemplifying fashion, I recalled the canonical passage

* Intimated in his posthumously published *History: The Last Things before the Last* (New York: Oxford University Press, 1969), pp. 189-90, and said more directly in a letter dated March 16, 1966, which remains memorable to its recipient.

in the Shandean Scripture:

> That of all the several ways of beginning a book which
> are now in practice throughout the known world, I am
> confident that my own way of doing it is the best.—I'm
> sure it is the most religious,—for I begin with writing the
> first sentence,—and trusting to Almighty God for the
> second. (Book VIII, Chapter II)

An evident case of cryptomnesia since, for a brief moment of
Joycean epiphany, I actually believed that *I* had discovered—
not, of course, invented—the method. It was something of a
relief to be brought back to my senses.

That syncopated synopsis of the Shandean Method that
is not a method has of course reverberated ever since it was
first formulated, not least in our own time. I instance only
Forster, Gide, and Claudel, who confine their musings on
'the creative process' to its workings in the domain of the
arts. Thus it is plain to me that Forster was putting the
Shandean method in the form of a parable when he wrote of
"that old lady in the anecdote" who exclaimed: " 'How can
I tell what I think till I see what I say?' "

That, of course, is purest Shandean doctrine of the kind
adopted throughout this little book of mine. Nor need its
import be confined to the arts. As I strongly affirmed almost
twenty years ago—doubtless benefiting from a miscellany of
Shandean insights—work in the sciences also commonly
proceeds in anything but inexorably linear style. Since it
bears on much that follows in this book, I provide a specimen
passage to this effect from *Social Theory and Social Structure*
(1968), choosing compressed selective quotation in prefer-
ence to roundabout and risky paraphrase as I refer to

> the rock-bound difference between the finished versions of
> scientific work as they appear in print and the actual
> course of inquiry followed by the inquirer. The differ-

ence is a little like that between textbooks on 'scientific method' and the ways in which scientists actually think, feel, and go about their work. The books on methods present ideal patterns: how scientists *ought* to think, feel and act, but these tidy normative patterns, as everyone who has engaged in [such] inquiry knows, do not reproduce the typically untidy, opportunistic adaptations that scientists make in the course of their inquiries. Typically, the scientific paper or monograph presents an immaculate appearance which reproduces little or nothing of the intuitive leaps, false starts, mistakes, loose ends and happy accidents that actually cluttered up the inquiry. (p. 4) *

If this preface is to provide otherwise inaccessible personal context for the pages that follow, I cannot drop this theme here. For only now, after years of discontinuity, do I realize that its essentials appear in my doctoral dissertation of almost half a century ago, in these words:

> . . . scientific theories and laws are presented in a rigorously logical and 'scientific' fashion (in accordance with the rules of evidence current at the time) and *not* in the order in which the theory or law was derived. This is to say, long after the theory has been found acceptable by the scientist on the basis of his *private* experience he must continue to devise a proof or demonstration in terms of the approved canons of scientific verification present in his culture. As Poincaré has indicated, most important scientific discoveries have been divined before they have

---

* Not having the Third Programme of BBC readily accessible and not being a subscriber to its publication, *The Listener*, I did not know that, some five years before, my later good friend, Peter Medawar, had made much the same observations in his published talk, "Is the scientific paper a fraud?" (*The Listener*, September 12, 1963). But then, as the pages of this book amply attest, the phenomenon of 'the anticipatory plagiarist' is commonplace in the history of science and learning.

been demonstrated. But intuition, howsoever powerful an instrument of invention it may be, is never a sufficient basis for a doctrine to become incorporated as a part of science. Demonstration is still necessary. (pp. 220–1) *

In other, more compact words, the difficult trick in the art and craft of science is to exercise discipline while still obeying one's daimon—a subterranean theme that will be readily identified by the dedicated reader of this book. Even more accessible themes and themelets need no explicit word here. I should note, however, that the book supplies a veritable nosography and *materia medica* of closely identified ailments endemic among scholars and scientists: denigrating adumbrationism (or the practice of finding seeming anticipations in times long past of ideas or findings newly discovered in the present); the correlative anatopic or palimpsestic syndrome (the covering over of earlier versions of an idea by ascribing it to a comparatively recent author in whose work the idea was first encountered); an honest cryptomnesia ("submerged or subliminal memory of events forgotten by the supraliminal self" as in forgetting the source of an idea one takes to be newly one's own); the obscurantist grimgribber (the art of gobbledegook); *insanabile scribendi cacoëthes* (the excruciating itch to publish, an ailment remedied only by scratching words down on paper); the humbling Parvus-complex or nanism (diminishing the scholarly merits of one's own work by ambitiously contrasting it to the towering work achieved by giants of science and learning); the parochial peregrinosis (the subliminal fear of foreign learning); and, to extend this prefatory list no further, the

---

* That 1938 dissertation, *Science, Technology and Society in Seventeenth-Century England*, has been reprinted from time to time; most recently, in hardcover by Howard Fertig, Inc. and in softcover by Humanities Press.

defensive *tu quoque* (thou also), first generally identified in the seventeenth century and specified here as meeting a charge of plagiarism by retorting that the accuser has himself plagiarized. Throughout, the physician of the soul cherishes the thought that by thus diagnosing the ailment, a first step is being taken toward prophylaxis or cure.

Long since diagnosed by the eighteenth-century master-observer, Richard Steele, as proceeding "from much Reading and little Understanding," the endemic scholarly ill known as pedantry requires no further diagnosis, for its transparent arid dignity without substance effectively lampoons, saddens, and, in the end, ennobles itself by paying tacit tribute to that authentic scholarship which blends the amateur's passion for learning with the professional's commitment to formal and substantive discipline.

To report the other themes of the book at this place would only be preemptive, not to say subversive. But another word about mood is indicated. Without reading too much into the book, thus saddling it with an excess of interpretation, I refer once again to its Shandean mood and now propose that this take its proper syntactical place alongside the indicative, subjunctive, and imperative moods. (And to these, of course, we must also add the 'of-course mood,' as the careful reader will soon discover.)

Plainly enough, the Shandean mood calls for a comic perspective on serious matters. In that mood, and appearances notwithstanding, the truly comic is far removed from the merely frivolous. It far transcends mere jokiness. This, of course, is scarcely a radical claim. As one knows, quite a few others—in the broad sweep from, say, Aristotle, to, say, Elder Olson—have perceived this before me. To be sure, Auden may have overstated the general case in his *obiter dictum* that "only through comedy can one be serious." But he is wholly right in joining with Cassirer and others to recognize the liberating character of the comic. On this theme with its several variations, I seize upon only a luminous sentence from Ernst Cassirer's memorable *Essay on Man* (1953) and spare the reader similar observations by many another. In a comic work, he writes, "Things and events begin to lose their material weight; scorn is dissolved into laughter and laughter is liberation." This is surely a truth which Cassirer speaks. Else, what is *Tristram Shandy* for? Yet to give the comic sense its full due, that aesthetic and psychological truth must be joined with the sociological truth that comic writings confront, with licensed irreverence, the irony inherent in socially established ways of thinking, feeling, and acting. And this, in its turn, reminds us that it is not at all the case that whatever is, is right, or, for that matter, that whatever is, is wrong. Rather, it is only the case that whatever is, is possible.

For reasons that will become progressively evident, this book has no Table of Contents. But toward its close, it does set forth an Otsogal glossary and at its very close, an "Onomasticon OR A Sort of Index," first of "Persons and Personages," and then, of "Places, Things, and Non-Things."

Lastly, I gladly acknowledge my debt to William Jovanovich for having instituted, to Peter Jovanovich for having directed, to Jacqueline Decter for having engineered, and to Denis Donoghue for having concluded this coming-of-age edition of *OTSOG*.

R.K.M.

New Year's Day, 1985

Foreword

WHAT A PLEASURE, to write a foreword for this brilliant, crazy, riotous Shandean Postscript, all two hundred seventy-seven pages of it, including more footnotes than any letter to a friend has carried before or since.

The book is a romp, a frolic, a frisk, a ball — an impossible mad excursion into scholarship and round about and out again, but boasting a plot with a beginning and an ending (one cannot guarantee a middle). I laughed all the way through and often I laughed out loud. Here is a college professor of sociology who spoofs the college professors, who makes fun of himself and his brethren by indirection, yet ends by earning our profound respect for his own learning. In fact he earned mine on page 2, where he tosses off his first easy reference to Didacus Stella (in Luc. 10, tom. 2).

The book purports to be a letter to a colleague, tracing the origin of the famous phrase attributed to Sir Isaac Newton: "If I have seen farther, it is by standing on the shoulders of giants." Actually, the thing started as a letter from Dr. Merton to a friend. I first saw it in that form, and it was not written for publication. But how has anybody time to write such a letter, time to read all those books and then laugh them off, time to collect such a vocabulary? I thought Sir Francis Bacon had the oddest repertory of words ever printed. But even Bacon never spoke of cryptomnesia or minimifidianism. If this is a sample of the letters Professor Merton writes to his colleagues, I ask humbly, What about his students, his sociology majors at Columbia? Where do they fit in, and what else does he do with his life?

It takes a little while to find one's way into this book, discover what on earth the Professor is doing, where he is going and why. But once in, it is impossible to stop. One wants to stop. These digressions, asides, preambles, excursions bring on hiccoughs, hysteria and high blood pressure. Nevertheless one reads on. Dazed and groping, one holds desperately to the thread Professor Merton has dropped. One follows him to the end.

I have not met Robert K. Merton, nor have I seen him. What manner of man is this, who darts under rocks like a minnow after his prey and comes up spouting like an erudite whale? How is he, at home with his family, what is he like around the house? How is he with his daughter Vanessa, of whom he tells us nothing save her enchanting name (and as Merton himself would say, everybody knows where *that* came from). Oh yes, he tells us that Vanessa does not say "again and again"; she says again and again and again and again and again. Are all the Mertons so deliciously discursive? Do they all talk as fast as Merton *père* writes — galloping, shouting, whispering, stumbling, recovering, gasping for breath but always cheerful and assured?

There is wisdom in this book as well as fun. "Follow your bent where it leads," says Merton, "for there is no better road to the writing of a history." From this he goes into what he calls the gist of the Shandean method. "In making this strong statement," Merton says (it does not matter apropos of what) — "in making this strong statement, *unweakened by carefully insinuated reservations*" (my italics) "I lay myself open to the charge of unscholarly conduct." Professor Merton on unscholarly conduct is marvelous; he is a breath of fresh air where fresh air is needed. "If only," he mourns, "authentic scholarship were not such a series of anti-climaxes."

Perhaps one loves Dr. Merton most when he is apologizing because some abstruse reference book is not at hand in his library (this happens about every three pages). As for instance *The Edinburgh Review* for October, 1838, or the copy of an item bearing the reference "in *Cod. Corpus Christi Oxon.* 283 fol. 147ra."

Here is one piece of scholarship, at any rate, which is not a series of anti-climaxes. More power to you, Professor, in all your searches and seizures!

Catherine Drinker Bowen

On the Shoulders of Giants

Nov. 8

Robert K. Merton
Dept. of Sociology
Columbia University

Dear Bob:

Many, many thanks for sending me a copy of
your presidential address . . .

. . . The paper rings all sorts of bells, as you
can see; many thanks. By the way, I haven't read the
Koyré article you cite in ftnote 34; maybe he goes over the
history of the epigram you mention re Newton; but that
saying appears to have a rather impressive antiquity. I
came on it twice, in Gilson and in Lavisse, as a remark of
Bernard of Chartres in the early 12th century. But Thales
probably said the same thing, only vaguely remembering
where he had got it from . . .

Bud

Professor Bernard Bailyn
Department of History
Harvard University

Dear Bud,

I sit here working away on a series of lectures I am
doomed to give next spring on the sociology of science. In
them, I shall extend some of the observations made in my
paper on priorities. And since I am this very moment
trying to decide whether to do much, little or nothing
more at all with the dwarf-on-the-shoulders-of-giants
aphorism, my thoughts naturally enough turned to your
question about its history.

Here is what I now have in hand. So far as I can tell
from printed evidence, it all started for me as a Johnny-
come-lately in 1942, when I published a paper entitled
"A note on science and democracy," (with the note
running, typically enough, to eleven labyrinthine pages of
print). In it, I refer to "Newton's remark – 'if I have seen
farther, it is by standing on the shoulders of giants' " –
and add in the inevitable footnote: "it is of some interest
that Newton's aphorism is a standardized phrase which
has found repeated expression from at least the twelfth
century." To support this, I cite, rather cryptically, "*Isis*,
1935, 24, 107–9; 1938, 25, 451–2." All this was reit-

erated when the paper was reprinted in *Social Theory and Social Structure*.

Like so many before me, I pounced upon the aphorism as soon as I first encountered it — it says much in little and says it graphically rather than only picturesquely. Between 1942, when I first wrote the note, and 1949, when I reprinted the allusion without further comment, I had been industriously collecting, like the squirrel in your own backyard but without his presumably assured knowledge of why he is doing what he is doing, every little nut of an allusion to the epigram and providently storing it away. Like that furry rodent, I didn't always remember where I had put the things.

The story, at least those small parts of it that I am able to reconstruct this morning, goes something like this.

⟪ *i*

EVERYBODY knows, of course, that the aphorism goes back to Didacus Stella (in Luc. 10, tom. 2) and may even have originated there — who can say? Everybody knows because Robert Burton, that squirrel-like collector of innumerable good things to learn, reports that it does.*

* But who or what is "Didacus Stella in Luc. 10, tom. 2," one might ask? Burton writes in the text, page 8 of his book, that he, Burton, can "say with Didacus Stella" and then footnotes his citation, thus: "in Luc. 10, tom. 2." That undeniably great historian of the Scientific Renaissance, Alexander Koyré, faithfully reports that Burton uses the sentence "as a quotation from Didacus Stella, In Luc. 10, tom. 2," urging us to "Cf. [L. T.] More, *Isaac Newton*, 177, note 28." L. T. More, it turns out (just as Koyré said it would), refers to Burton who "quotes Didacus Stella, In Luc. 10, tom. 2" as his source for believing that this "celebrated saying" goes back to a time much earlier

He does more, does Burton. He even quotes intact: *"Pigmei Gigantum humeris impositi plusquam ipsi Gigantes vident."* This is a little different from the form in which it appears in Bartlett's *Familiar Quotations* (at least, as it appears in my copy of the 1939 printing of the eleventh, *i.e.*, the 1937, edition). They — that is, either Bartlett himself (and this could easily be checked) or perhaps his posthumous coeditors, the sprightly Christopher Morley and the indefatigable Louella D. Everett — they have Burton omit the pair of capitalized Gs in *Gigantum* and *Gigantes,* though they permit the capitalized P in *Pigmei* to remain unscathed, possibly because it had the good fortune to come at the beginning of the sentence. The same one, two or three compilers I have just mentioned also do what Burton himself had done; they translate the Latin into English. The compact Latin is transformed into this rather literal shape: "Pigmies placed on the shoulders of giants see more than the giants themselves." The saying seems to lose a little of its force in the transition. Indeed, it seems to deny the truth of what Burton had had the wit to suggest as an addition to the aphorism, a non-epigrammatic addition but one informed with wit and understanding, nevertheless. Burton quotes the sentence in English and then reflectively says: "I may likely add, alter, and see farther than my predeces-

than Newton. But as we move from scholars to compilers, and turn to one of the most enduringly popular compilations of sayings ever put together — you have by now spotted this roundabout route to Bartlett's *Familiar Quotations* — when we turn to this "source," we find the entire citation italicized, so: *"Didacus Stella in Lucan 10, Tom. II."* Who, then, is Didacus Stella or what is *Didacus Stella in Lucan 10, Tom. II.?* Lucan I can vaguely identify; he was one of that crowd of ancient Latin writers much admired in the Middle Ages; of a piece, say, with Statius and Frontinus. But does Burton speak of him or is there an even more extraordinary fellow, Didacus Stella?

sors." Burton might, but evidently not the compilers of
Bartlett's *Quotations*. For in their translation of the *mot*
into English, they evidently did not see farther than *their*
predecessor Burton when they altered his Englished version of the sentence from the elusive Didacus Stella. In
this version, you will notice, the force of the alleged
original in Latin suffers very little, if at all:

> A dwarf standing on the shoulders of a giant
> may see farther than a giant himself.

So, in the form that all this comes down to us citizens
of the twentieth century through the ubiquitous Bartlett,
the epigrammatic quality of the original and Burton's
instructive addendum are both lost. This is a pity for, by
his addition, Burton achieved what few can: combining
a decent humility with forthright acknowledgement of his
own merit. What is more, by excising what they did, the
compilers of Bartlett have deprived Burton of his fairly
sound and enviably succinct theory of how the growth of
knowledge comes about.

This is not the sort of thing that should be done to a
writer like Robert Burton. True, he was a man of essentially one book, but what a grand, tumultuous and
companionable book it is (with quotations so diverse and
apt as to become original again with the borrower):
*The Anatomy of Melancholy, What It is, with All the
Kinds, Causes, Symptoms, Prognostics and Several Cures
of It* [all this] *in Three Partitions, with their several
Sections, Members and Subsections, Philosophically,
Medically, Historically Opened and Cut Up* which, you*
will recall, is pseudonymously ascribed on the title page to
"Democritus Junior" with later editions being rectified
and expanded, suitably enough, by "Democritus Minor."
(This is all as it appears in the 1867 printing of the

1651/2 edition; for a moment, but only that long, I take no responsibility for how it might look in other editions and other printings.)

Now it is all very well for Koyré and More, for Bartlett-Morley-and-Everett, to cite Burton as having cited Didacus Stella as the source of the aphorism whose origin we are in quest of. But surely the modern scholars, if not the compilers, should have noted the context in which Burton sets the aphorism. On this, they are strangely silent. And yet, as is almost ever the case, it is the context that supplies much of the meaning of the text. I must tell you, then, that Burton introduces the aphorism very early on in the book; in a sense, before the book itself begins. It appears on page 8 of the 74-page introduction entitled "Democritus Junior to the Reader," an introduction designed to acquaint the reader with the philosophy and tactics adopted in the book and, above all, to guard in a most cautious, prophylactical way against the presumed charge that he, the author, had unconscionably either borrowed to excess (and not always with due acknowledgement) from the anterior writings of others or, even worse, that he had adopted the practice of what I believe George Sarton once described as "ghost-writing in reverse" (though as I now learn from Burton, one that Aulus Gellius had eighteen centuries before, described in these words:

> later writers and impostors . . . broach many absurd and insolent fictions, under the name of so noble a philosopher as Democritus, to get themselves credit, and by that means the more to be respected;

a practice about which the pseudonymous Democritus Junior is quick to say, " 'Tis not so with me").

So much for the general context of the Aphorism; it is

5

part of Burton's apology for his book. But the more immediate context is even more revealing: Burton is engaged in defending his decision to draw without stint upon the learning of the past, explaining that "I have only this of Macrobius to say for myself, *Omne meum, nihil meum*, 'tis all mine, and none mine." Still much on the defensive, the harvester Burton goes on to explain that

> I have laboriously collected this Cento out of divers writers, and that *sine injuriâ*, I have wronged no authors, but given every man his own; which Hierom so much commends in Nepotian; he stole not whole verses, pages, tracts, as some do now-a-days, concealing their author's names, but still said this was Cyprian's, that Lactantius, that Hillarius, so said Minutius Felix, so Victorinus, thus far Arnobius: I cite and quote mine authors (which, howsoever some illiterate scribblers account pedantical, as a cloak of ignorance, and opposite to their affected fine style, I must and will use) *sumpsi, non surripui* . . .

and achieves in this last bit of Latinity a pretty phrase that denies its own substance since it is, of course, only a compact extraction from Cicero's view of plagiarism.

In his prolonged defense against the charge that he is at best only a gatherer of the fruits of other men's wisdom and at worst a thief who stealthily pilfers the gems of other men's wit, Burton carefully approaches the one passage, from Didacus Stella, in which you and I have our abiding interest.

> . . . I do *concoquere quod hausi*, dispose of what I take. I make them pay tribute, to set out this my Maceronicon [this last, being, I take it, a nonce-word derived from the well-known friend of Virgil and Ovid, Aemilius Macer], the method only is mine own,

I must usurp that of *Wecker è Ter. nihil dictum quod non dictum prius, methodus sola artificem ostendit,* we can say nothing but what hath been said, the composition and method is ours only, and shows a scholar. [And now he rises to the theme of a practice become legitimate by ample precedent] Oribasius, Æsius, Avicenna, have all out of Galen, but to their own method, *diverso stilo, non diversâ fide.* Our poets steal from Homer; he spews, saith Ælian, they lick it up. Divines use Austin's words *verbatim* still, and our story-dressers, do as much; he that comes last is commonly best . . . [And only then is Burton ready to introduce The Aphorism, carefully quoted] Though there were many giants of old in Physic and Philosophy, yet I say with Didacus Stella . . .

You will say, no doubt, that I am being a bit hard on Bartlett for not having reported this self-justifying context for the Aphorism. You will say that Bartlett did, after all, quote a few snippets from the passage I have just given you entire. But your defense only aggravates the offense. For nowhere does Bartlett so much as hint at the question — let alone supply the answer — of how it was that Burton came to bring the mysterious *Didacus Stella in Luc. 10, tom. 2* and the Aphorism into the picture. For note this well, and ponder its implications, *in the first edition of the Anatomy, there is not a word about Didacus Stella or the Aphorism!* But the second edition, appearing three years later in 1624, has it all. The great significance of this universally neglected fact can surely not escape your notice — or mine. Burton was calling upon Didacus Stella as an impartial expert witness to testify that he, Burton, was neither plagiarist nor mere compiler; that he was, instead, standing upon the shoulders of his predecessors to see much farther than they and

7

that this was a practice long since hallowed by the Aphorism.

As we know, the *Anatomy* was read religiously by generation after generation of literate readers, ever since its first appearance in 1621 (*not* as Dr. John Ferriar — that commentator now remembered chiefly for his memorable mistake, — not as Dr. Ferriar erroneously says somewhere, in 1617). It was then reprinted again and again (or, as my ten-year-old daughter, Vanessa, would say, and indeed has said) and again and again and again and again and again in 1624, 1628, 1632, 1638, 1651/2, 1660 and 1676.

In his book, Burton-Democritus established a bridgehead that enabled the old Aphorism to move into the seventeenth century. Ever since, it could be periodically trotted out by all manner of men, those of genuinely big minds with a right to this kind of combined humility-and-self-confidence and those of at best middle-sized minds, for whom that right is at least disputable. Burton-like, the *Anatomy of Melancholy* looks two ways: toward the ancients for wisdom that should be transmitted to his own day and toward the moderns who, drawing upon that wisdom, could proceed to broaden and deepen it.

⸿ *ii*

AMONG the seventeenth-century giants who modestly described themselves as standing on the shoulders of the giants who have gone before, the greatest, of course, was Newton. This he did by personalizing the old saying a bit, leaving it open whether he was only a dwarf raised to an eminence from which he could see farther than others and also leaving it problematical whether in fact he had seen farther. These subtle changes result in the sentence reading this way:

> If I have seen further it is by standing on ye sholders of Giants.

Before going on to explore the historical context of Newton's very personal version of the Aphorism, we should pause to examine some obscure aspects of his early life if only to understand the better how he came to modify the Aphorism as he did.

Every great man inevitably becomes the lauded subject of an elaborate hagiology — and properly so. Now, like Ecclesiasticus, I too think we should be quick to praise famous men. But I am prepared to go only so far. Let me then dispose at once of that story about Newton's birth recounted by Edward J. Wood (appropriately enough, in his treatise, *Giants and Dwarfs* — a book which, although it was published as recently as 1868, remains, in spite of its title, strangely silent about our Aphorism). On page 285, you will find Wood calmly reporting that "Sir Isaac Newton, who was born in 1642, is said to have been a posthumous child, his father dying at the age of ninety-six years." I don't know what to make of this. As a genuine scientist must, I try to keep an open mind about seeming miracles, knowing that even the most remote probability has a finite chance of becoming realized. Yet, as we shall in due course see, even Jonathan Swift,* in his profound analysis of gerontology, never ascribed such progenitive powers to a near-centenarian — and I am inclined to go along with him.

Quite another kind of story about Newton's birth

* Swift was also a posthumous child but his father died long before becoming a nonagenarian.

9

(recorded by his devoted biographer, Brewster) * not only has the ring of authenticity about it but enjoys the further merit of forging a close symbolic link between that giant among scientists and the Aphorism. The story (in a nutshell of a sentence) is this: "The infant . . . ushered into the world was of such a diminutive size, that, as his mother afterwards expressed it to Newton himself, he might have been put into a quart-mug . . ." Surely never before has so small a beginning had so grand a conclusion.

But it is time to move from tales of Newton's birth to the story of his truncated use of the Aphorism. It is of some interest, as was recently noted again in the publication by Alexander Koyré, in *Isis*, December 1952, of "An unpublished letter of Robert Hooke to Isaac Newton," that Newton's paraphrase of the Aphorism appeared in a conciliatory letter to that contentious genius, Hooke, who was then challenging Newton's priority in having arrived

---

* More exactly: Sir David Brewster, K.H., A.M., D.C.L., F.R.S., Vice-Pres. R.S. Edinburgh, and M.R.I.A., and we should add, a scientist of significance in his own right, having turned, in the course of his eighty-seven years of life, from a career as a Presbyterian minister because, as they say in the *Dictionary of National Biography*, "he never preached without severe nervousness, which sometimes produced faintness," first to a career as tutor, in "the family of General Diroon of Mount Annan in Dumfriesshire," and only a year later, in 1805, standing as a candidate for the chair of mathematics in the university at Edinburgh only to have "Mr. (afterwards Sir John) Leslie" get the chair instead – this, even though Brewster had received firm promises of support from the great astronomer Herschel, as well as from other eminent men of science, with the result that, after another five years, he was persuaded, in 1809, to become editor of the *Edinburgh Encyclopedia*, a job that he held for fully twenty-two years, during the course of which, however, he began and long continued his work in science, having, as early as 1813, sent his first paper to the Royal Society of London,

at the theory of colors. Newton was being humble at the very time he was denying, and rightly so, that any before him, and particularly not Hooke, had come upon the theory he had himself evolved. The versatile character of the Aphorism could not have been displayed to better advantage.

What set off this great quarrel with Hooke (in the prolonged course of which Newton wrote his now famous letter with its even more famous sentence) was the first appearance of Newton's letter on light and color. This was in 1672, in the *Philosophical Transactions*. It was, as I. B. Cohen in his magisterial *Franklin and Newton* (1956, p. 51) reminds us, "the first time that a major scientific discovery was announced in print in a periodical." *

From the time of that publication and intermittently throughout the decade of the 1670s, the quarrel with Hooke grew alternately hot and cold, but, in spite of the

this paper, appropriately enough, in view of the subject now under discussion, being entitled "Some Properties of Light" and being soon followed by an entire series of papers, most of them on the polarization of light, with the result that these important contributions soon elicited the respect of colleagues and shortly afterwards the symbolic rewards of the Copley medal, then the Rumford medal and still later, one of the Royal medals, all this honor being supplemented, in 1816, by the French Institute's Award of half the prize then given for the two discoveries in physical science made *in Europe* – a restriction far from unjust, with the state of American science being what it was back in those days – that were adjudged to be the most important of the year.

* New evidence discovered by A. R. Hall in 1948, "Sir Isaac Newton's notebook, 1661–1665," *Cambridge Historical Journal*, 9, 239–50 proves that the theory of colors had been completed by the winter of 1666. Newton, you will remember, had a way of not putting things into print until he was good and ready – and sometimes, not even then.

best efforts of their joint friends, it was never really negotiated into a common understanding, satisfactory to both the great scientists. Though not of the same stature as Newton — who was? — Hooke can be grouped with him, without giving offense to his most devout admirers and without being guilty of a gaffe. Hooke's was a genius that is only now being recognized as it should have been, long since.

Had I the time and you the patience, I should review the known details of that decade of conflict and perhaps even carry the story right up to 1704, a year after Hooke's death, when Newton finally did publish his *Opticks,* which had been ready for at least ten years. But there is really no need for this. For it is not at all germane to the story of how it was that the Aphorism adapted by Newton came to be known as one newly-minted by him. The only really germane fact is, that for a long time now and for reasons that seem reasonably evident the saying *has* been popularly taken as Newton's coinage. Not that he claimed this, or even intimated it. Quite the contrary. He simply saw no need, even in a time when a Bartlett's *Familiar Quotations* was not on everybody's bookshelf, to advertise the ancient lineage of the saying. After all, if Bartlett was not on hand, Burton, that unsystematic predecessor of Bartlett, was. It was scarcely for Newton to insult Hooke by doubting this aspect of his knowledge, although he managed to do pretty well when it came to other, more damaging insults, as when he claimed Hooke to be alternately a fool and a charlatan, the first in not understanding some elementary matters of optics and the second in, so Newton charged, stealing some ideas from "Honoratus Faber, in his dialogue *De Lumine,* who had it from Grimaldi." There was just no point in irritating Hooke about small things by reminding him of the varied provenance of the Aphorism. Nor was there any point in Newton's turning pedant by citing, secondhand, the source in Didacus Stella that Burton had provided for him. As reasonably cultivated men (though some die-hards still doubt this of Hooke), both Hooke and Newton might be expected to remember that the metaphysical poet George Herbert, in his *Jacula Prudentum*, had declared that

A dwarfe on a gyant's shoulder sees further of the two,

this, back in 1640.*

Furthermore, although Hooke may not have been, in his origins, a gentleman beyond all dispute, he was, like the rest of his colleagues, capable of gentlemanly conduct.†

⫶ ℭ *iii*

UPON re-reading the casual innuendo in the preceding note, I must confess and try to rectify the injustice I have

* Bartlett, as was his wont, unconscionably modernized Herbert's version of the Aphorism. I am grateful to Stephen Cole for digging up the authentic original in the Columbia library as it is recorded in *The Complete Works of George Herbert*, edited by the Rev. Alexander B. Grosart and Printed for Private Circulation as part of The Fuller Worthies' Library; you will find it in Volume 3, p. 317.
† I should qualify this allusion to Hooke's birthright; that genial columnist and man-about-seventeenth-century-London-town, John Aubrey, reports that he was "of the Hookes of Hooke in Hants" and that "his father was Minister" at "Fresh-water in the Isle of Wight" where Hooke "was borne." But then, Aubrey is not always beyond suspicion.

done the author of the informative and delicious *Brief Lives*.* It does no good for me to argue that others, before me, have also treated Aubrey unkindly; for a notorious example, his good friend, Anthony à Wood, who described him as "roving and magotie-headed." (This is, just as you suppose, that churlish Wood who authored the priceless *Athenae Oxoniensis* and noted in his journal one day, after he had a run-in with his sister-in-law: "Cold meat, cold entertainment, cold reception, cold clownish woman." But from this chilling note, I happily return to the warm and benevolent Aubrey.)

This is the same Aubrey, of course, who as a child hit upon the idea of oral history (which some mistakenly take to be the twentieth-century invention of that imaginative historian, Allan Nevins). For, as Aubrey tells of himself in the incredulous third person, "when a Boy, he did ever love to converse with old men, as Living Histories." He is the same Aubrey, furthermore, who, alerted to the pleasures of serendipity, reports two great serendipitous moments in the history of science and technology. On the off chance that you may have momentarily forgotten his accounts of happy accidents in man's efforts at discovery and invention, I quote them here. (Incidentally, the first episode plainly shows how evil intent *can* generate benign consequences [as Goethe was later to remark in describing "Die Kraft, die stets das Böse will, und stets das Gute schafft."]) In his typically compact prose, Aubrey reports: "A woman (I thinke in Italy) endeavoured to poyson her Husband (who was a Dropsicall Man) by boyling a Toade in his Potage; which cured him: and this was the occasion of finding out the Medi-

* My own copy of Aubrey, now lying upon the table before me, happens to be the Andrew Clark edition published by Oxford at the Clarendon Press in 1898 rather than the fairly

cine." And that, it seems, is how a prodigious accumulation of serous fluid in the body first came to be neutralized.

The second episode (anticipating the methodological moral of Lamb's justly famous gem of serendipity, "Dissertation Upon Roast Pig") concerns the seventeenth-century invention of a technique for ventilating coal mines. This is how Aubrey reports that happy occasion:

> Sir Paul Neale sayd, that in the Bishoprick of Durham is a Coalery, which by reason of the dampes ther did so frequently kill the Workemen (sometimes three or four in a Moneth) that he could make little or nothing out of it. It happened one time, that the workemen being merry with drink fell to play with fire-brands, and to throwe live-coales at one another by the head of the Pitt, where they usually have fires. It fortuned that a fire-brand fell into the bottome of the Pitt: where at there proceeded such a noise as if it had been a Gun: they likeing the Sport, threw down more fire-brands and there followed the like noise, for severall times, and at length it ceased. They went to work after, and were free from Damps, so having by good chance found out this Experiment, they doe now every morning throwdown some Coales, and they work as securely as in any other Mines.

Indeed, the more I ponder the life of Aubrey, the more I would erase my unthinking slander that he was not really above suspicion. After all, this is the same perceptive man who, during his strenuous bout of field work in cemeteries designed to discover when little lives were *actually* rounded with a sleep, concluded that even

recent edition by Oliver Lawson Dick, published by Secker and Warburg (London) in 1950. But any edition will serve, should you want to search out further details for yourself.

epitaphs etched on tombstones might deceive the literal-minded; as, for example, the stone which asked passers-by to "Pray for the soul of Constantine Darrel Esq. who died Anno Domini 1400 and his wife, who died Anno Domini 1495." Ever since, tombstone-readers have learned to be wary.

When Aubrey says, then, that Robert Hooke was "of the Hookes of Hooke in Hants," he probably reports nothing but the truth. He was, of course, decidedly partial to Hooke, despite the grievous fact that Hooke was, by Aubrey's own observant account, "but of midling stature, something crooked, pale faced, and his face but little belowe, but his head is lardge; [and mark this well] his eie full and popping, and not quick; a grey eie." It was this friend with grey, full and popping eye who put the premises of the Royal Society to special and amiable use by sheltering Aubrey there while a bailiff hunted him far and wide for failure to pay his considerable debts, thus earning Aubrey's eternal gratitude. As a final token of his enduring affection for Hooke, Aubrey charged him, in his last will and testament, with the task of ensuring his posthumous fame by preparing his manuscripts for publication. All the more ironic, then, that Aubrey, fascinated by tombstones for so much of his genial and turbulent life, should have been laid to rest in an unmarked grave (although we now know, from a belatedly discovered entry in a church register, that in "1697, JOHN AUBERY a Stranger was Buryed June 7th" in the graveyard of the Church of St. Mary Magdalene).

One thing more about Aubrey: there never was another, before or after him, with so keen an ophthalmological eye. This claim is amply documented, as you can see for yourself in the anthology I have culled from his various brief lives:

Francis Bacon: He had a delicate, lively, hazel Eie; Dr. Harvey tolde me it was like the Eie of a viper.

Sir John Birkenhead: He was of midling stature, great goggli eies, not of sweet aspect.

James Bovey: . . . a dark hazell eie, of a midling size, but the most sprightly that I have beheld . . . Redhaired men never had any kindnesse for him. In all his Travills he was never robbed.

William Camden: 'Tis reported, that he had bad Eies (I guess Lippitude) which was a great inconvenience to an Antiquary.

Thomas Chaloner: sawe him dead: he was swoln so extremely that they could not see any eie he had, and no more of his nose than the tip of it, which shewed like a Wart, and his Coddes were swoln as big as one's head.

Elizabeth Danvers: Very Beautifull, but only shortsighted.

Sir John Denham: His Eie was a kind of light goosegray, not big; but it had a strange Piercingness, not as to shining and glory, but (like a Momus) when he conversed with you he look't into your very thoughts . . . He was much rooked by Gamesters, and fell acquainted

	with that unsanctified Crew, to his ruine.
Venetia Digby:	Her face, a short ovall; darke-browne eie-browe about which much sweetness, as also in the opening of her eie-lidds.
Thomas Goffe the Poet, his wife:	She [wearing the Breeches] look'd upon [his Oxford Friends] with an ill Eye, as if they had come to eat her out of her House and Home (as they say).
William Harvey:	little Eie, round, very black, full of spirit.
William Herbert:	He was strong sett, but bony, reddish-favoured, of a sharp eie, sterne looke.
Thomas Hobbes:	He had a good eie, and that of a hazell colour, which was full of Life and Spirit, even to the last. When he was earnest in discourse, there shone (as it were) a bright live-coale within it. He had two kinds of lookys: when he laught't, was witty, and in a merry humour, one could scarce see his Eies; by and by, when he was serious and positive, he open'd his eies round (i.e. his eie-lids.) He had midling eies, not very big, nor very little. . . . He was never idle; his thoughts were always working.
Robert Hooke:	his head is lardge; his eie full

	and popping, and not quick; a grey eie.
Ben Jonson:	Ben Johnson had one eie lower than t'other, and bigger, like Clun the Player; perhaps he begott Clun.
Ralph Kettell:	His gowne and surplice and hood being on, he had a terrible gigantique aspect with his sharp gray eies.
Sir Henry Lee['s gamekeeper's son]:	a one-eied young man, no kinne to him.
Andrew Marvell:	He was of middling stature, pretty strong sett, roundish faced, cherry cheek't, hazell eie, browne haire.
John Milton:	His sight began to faile him at first upon his writing against Salmasius, and before 'twas full compleated one eie absolutely faild. Upon the writing of other bookes, after that, his other eie decayed. His eie-sight was decaying about 20 yeares before his death. His father read without spectacles at 84. His mother had very weake eies, and used spectacles presently after she was thirty yeares old . . . His eie a darke gray. . . . He had a delicate tuneable Voice, and had good skill.
[Isaac Newton:	Because of his burning dislike for him, Aubrey evidently could

not bring himself to write a brief
life of this greatest among his
contemporaries. But Bernard le
Bovier de Fontenelle in his
Elogium of Sir Isaac Newton, the
very first biography of that great
man, notes, in the English translation of 1728, that "he had a
very lively and piercing eye."]

William Oughtred: He was a little man, had black
haire, and blacke eies (with a
great deal of spirit). His head
was always working.

John Overall['s wife, the greatest Beautie of her time in
England]: She had (they told
me) the loveliest Eies that were
ever seen, but wondrous wanton.

Sir William Petty: His eies are a kind of goose-gray,
but very short sighted, and, as to
aspect, beautifull, and promise
sweetnes of nature, and they doe
not deceive, for he is a marvel-
lous good-natured person. Eie-
browes thick, darke, and straight
(horizontall).

Francis Potter: He was pretty long visagd and
pale cleare skin, gray eie.

William Prynne: His manner of Studie was thus:
he wore a long quilt cap, which
came 2 or 3, at least, inches over
his eies, which served him as an
Umbrella to defend his Eies from
the light. About every three
houres his man was to bring him

a roll and a pott of Ale to re-
focillate his wasted spirits: so he
studied and dranke, and munched
some bread; and this maintained
him till night, and then, he made
a good Supper: now he did well
not to dine, which breakes of
one's fancy, which will not presently be regained; and 'tis with
Invention as a flux, when once it
is flowing, it runnes amaine: if it
is checked, flowes but *guttim:* and
the like for perspiration, check
it, and 'tis spoyled.

Sir Walter Raleigh: He had a most remarkeable
aspect, an exceeding high fore-
head, long-faced and sour eie-
lidded, a kind of pigge-eie. His
Beard turnd up naturally. . . .
He tooke a pipe of Tobacco a
little before he went to the scaffold, which some formall persons
were scandalised at, but I thinke
'twas well and properly donne, to
settle his spirits.

John Selden: He was very tall, I guesse about
6 foot high, sharp ovall face,
head not very big, long nose in-
clining to one side, full popping
Eie (gray). He was a Poet. . . .
Mr. J. Selden writt a 4to booke
called *Tabletalke;* which will not
endure the Test of the Presse.

Edmund Waller: He is of somewhat above a middle stature, thin body, not at all

robust; fine thin skin, his face
somewhat of an olivaster, his
hayre frizzd, of a brownish
colour; full eye, popping out and
working; ovall faced, his forehead high and full of wrinckles:
his head but small, braine very
hott, and apt to be cholerique.
He is something magisteriall,
and haz a great mastership of
the English Language.

❡ iv

THE PERCIPIENT and sensitive Aubrey, then, is
warrant enough for the claim that Hooke was indeed a
gentleman. Hooke's own behavior testifies as much. In the
thick of the quarrel with the younger Newton, for
example, just half way through the noisy decade of the
1670s, Hooke could still preserve the niceties in addressing the man he was accusing of maligning him and of
stealing from him in a letter that begins

These to my much esteemed friend, Mr Isaack Newton, at his chambers in Trinity College in Cambridge

and ends, after the polite fashion of the time, by express-
ing the hope that Newton would "pardon this plainness
of your very affectionate humble servt." * Hooke could
hardly have been more conciliatory.

* The original of Hooke's letter is in the Trinity College
Library at Cambridge; an authentic copy of it can more easily
be found on pages 412–3 of the first volume of the new and
authoritative edition of *The Correspondence of Isaac Newton,*

In his reasonably prompt answer (5 February 1675/6),* Newton addresses Hooke a little less warmly than Hooke had addressed Newton, writing only: "Sr." But he makes up for this aloofness at once, as he goes on to say:

At ye reading of your letter I was exceedingly well pleased & satisfied with your generous freedom, & think you have done what becomes a true Philosophical spirit. There is nothing wch I desire to avoyde in matters of Philosophy more than contention, nor any kind of contention more then one in print: & therefore I gladly embrace your proposal of a private correspondence.

Newton then makes a profoundly sociological observation about the behavior of men in general and by implication, the behavior of men of science in particular, that, until this moment, I had thought *I* was the first to have made. That anticipatory plagiarist, Newton, follows the sentences I have just quoted from his letter with this penetrating observation:

What's done before many witnesses is seldome without some further concern then that for truth: but what passes between friends in private usually deserves ye name of consultation rather than contest, & so I hope it will prove between you & me.

So much for the Newtonian version of the doctrine; now consider my own. I had put the matter a little less

edited by H. W. Turnbull and published for the Royal Society at the University Press in Cambridge, 1959.
* Thanks to the kindness of the Library of the Historical Society of Pennsylvania, located in Philadelphia, which happily possesses Newton's original letter, I can reproduce it as the frontispiece to this narrative.

aptly, I'm afraid, but the essential idea is there, all there! It was set out in my paper, delivered at the first plenary session of the Fourth World Congress of Sociology held in Milan and Stresa in the year 1959 from September 8 to 15. I read my paper on September 8th at about 16:30; there were many witnesses, about a thousand of them, and a canvass of their collective memory could easily pinpoint the exact time. The point is, Newton barely nosed me out.

In that paper, on page sixteen (about a third of the way through the entire thing),* I formulated, in complete independence of Newton,† the same sociological truth about the differing behavior of men, especially men of science (and in the more particular case, especially men of sociological science), in the public forum and in the private study. What I said was this, and please note the similarity of ideas to those of Newton but not, I regret to say, a similarity of language:

> I suggest that often these polemics have more to do with the allocation of intellectual resources among different kinds of sociological work than with a closely formulated opposition of sociological ideas.
> These controversies follow the classically identified course of social conflict. Attack is followed by counter-attack, with progressive alienation of each party to the conflict. [And *now*, we come to the sociological discovery made in full independence, I repeat, of

* This refers to the pages of my manuscript. The crucial passage appears on pages 29–30 of the paper as published by the International Sociological Association (under the prophetic and not merely retrospective title, "Social Conflict over Styles of Sociological Work") in the *Transactions of the Fourth World Congress of Sociology*, 1959, Vol. III.
† It's true I had read Brewster's life of Newton, as I had read More's, and Keynes's spirited essay on him, and Andrade's

what Newton recorded in his long unpublished letter to Hooke of some 283 years before.] Since the conflict is public, it becomes a battle for status more nearly than a search for truth. (How many sociologists [I am still quoting my paper here, not supplying an afterthought] how many sociologists have publicly admitted to error as a result of these polemics?)

Surely you will grant me that this passage states the doctrine most comprehensively. It is with no little pain, then, — and no little pride — that I acknowledge Newton's priority of conception.

❡ *v*

BUT THE biography of this sociological idea does not end there. For only now do I come to its crux. If Newton anticipated Merton, then — lese-majesty aside — *Hooke anticipated Newton!!!*

❡ *vi*

BE ASSURED that in announcing this startling claim, I have no intention of stirring up fresh quarrels among historians of science. After all, the controversies over

essay and before that, Augustus de Morgan's long essays on Newton, his friend and his niece, and his life and works. It is also true that I had studied Koyré's piece in *Isis* on the unpublished letter of Hooke to Newton. But I do not remember having fastened on Newton's sociological observation of 1675/6 in his letter to Hooke. At most, it might be a tenuous case of cryptomnesia. Priority I am willing to grant Newton, but not at the price of being tagged as a plagiarist. Mine was an essentially independent, though somewhat belated, discovery.

priority of discovery in which Hooke involved Newton
(and a good many others) are plentiful enough and irritating enough to have engaged the interest of historians
for a long, long time. I have no interest in once again
kindling the coals of these disputes, let alone adding fresh
fuel to the ensuing flames. Unlike Aubrey, I am not so
deeply committed to Hooke that I take his side against
all others — particularly Newton. (Perhaps that is because, unlike Aubrey, I never received a brusque note
from Newton which reads in its entirety:

> I understand you have a letter from Mr Lucas for me.
> Pray forebear to send me anything more of that
> nature.) *

Unlike Aubrey, then, I am not one to charge Newton
with plagiarizing Hooke. For I am persuaded that it
was Newton's brusque treatment of Aubrey,† far more
than the objective facts of the case, that led Aubrey to
write the passage, in his *Brief Lives,* where he coolly accuses Newton of having purloined his most enduring
scientific contribution from Hooke. Since, like me, you
may have repressed the Aubrey accusation from your
memory if only because it is so painful to recall, I repeat
it here:

> About 9 or 10 years ago, Mr. Hooke writt to Mr.
> Isaac Newton, of Trinity College, Cambridge, to make
> a Demonstration of this theory [An Attempt to prove
> the Motion of the Earth], not telling him, at first,
> the proportion of the gravity to the distance, nor what
> was the curv'd line that was thereby made. Mr. New-

---

* You have only to look into Turnbull's edition of Newton (II,
269) to find this curt note fully reproduced.
† Poor Aubrey! He had the misfortune to be the bringer of evil
tidings as the intermediary between Newton and Anthony Lucas,
that Jesuit professor of theology at Liége who repeatedly

ton, in his Answer to the letter, did expresse that he had not thought of it; and in his first attempt about it, he calculated the Curve by supposing the attraction to be the same at all distances: upon which, Mr. Hooke sent, in his next letter, the whole of his Hypothesis, *scil.* that the gravitation was reciprocall to the square of the distance: which is the whole coelastiall theory, concerning which Mr. Newton haz made a demonstration, not at all owning he receiv'd the first Intimation of it from Mr. Hooke. Likewise Mr. Newton has in the same Booke printed some other Theories and experiments of Mr. Hooke's, without acknowledgeing from whom he had them.

This is the greatest Discovery in Nature that ever was since the World's Creation. It never was so much as hinted by any man before. I wish he [Hooke] had writt plainer, and afforded a little more paper.

From this accusatory passage, you will easily infer that the attraction exerted by Hooke upon Aubrey was directly proportional to the square of Aubrey's (psychological) distance from Newton. As a doubly biassed witness, therefore, Aubrey cannot be taken seriously when he argues that Newton was indebted to Hooke for one of the principal laws of gravitation. But when it comes to Newton's sociological discovery about the distorting effects of public (as distinct from private) polemics among men of science — *my* discovery which I freely acknowledge Newton anticipated — then my testimony must be taken far more seriously than Aubrey's. For the demonstrable fact is that Hooke, in what I describe as his

plagued Newton by impertinent objections to one or another of his experiments and theories. The sometimes irascible Newton promptly channeled the overflow of his anger upon the messenger bringing bad news and so, understandably enough, evoked in Aubrey something less than deep affection.

"kindle Cole" letter,* was the Giant upon whose shoulders
Newton climbed to rob me of priority. Hooke says it all
in a now unforgettable passage which I take pleasure in
quoting at length:

> Your Designes and myne I suppose aim both at the
> same thing wch is the Discovery of truth and I sup-
> pose we can both endure to hear objections, so as they
> come not in a manner of open hostility, and have
> minds equally inclined to yield to the plainest deduc-
> tions of reason from experiment. If therefore you will
> please to correspond about such matters [and now
> note what follows] by private letter [again, I ask that
> you observe what Hooke says here: "by private
> letter"] I shall very gladly imbrace it and when I
> shall have the happiness to peruse your excellent dis-
> course (which I can as yet understand nothing more
> of by hearing it cursorily read) I shall if it be not
> ungrateful to you send you freely my objections, if I
> have any, or my concurrences, if I am convinced,
> which is the more likely. [And now comes the de-
> cisive formulation which plainly gave rise to Newton's
> anticipation of my sociological dictum.] This way of
> contending I believe to be the more philosophicall
> of the two, for though I confess the collision of two
> hard-to-yield contenders may produce light yet if they
> be put together by the ears of other's hands and incen-
> tives, *it will produce rather ill concomitant heat which
> serves for no other use but . . . kindle cole.* Sr I
> hope you will pardon this plainness of your very
> affectionate humble servt
>
> ROBERT HOOKE

You probably assume that I have italicized one small
portion of the letter only to alert you to Hooke's ingenious, metaphorical version of the sociological law

* You'll see why, in just a moment.

whose history we are examining. But I had yet another reason for underscoring the passage. Hooke's private code-name for this crucially important letter is also contained in the italicized passage as you will discover by looking into his *Diary* * under the date of 20 January 1675/6. There he enigmatically notes: "Wrot letter to Mr Newton about Oldenburg kindle Cole."

It is then the "kindle cole" letter of Hooke that fanned the flame of Newton's inspiration and led him, such a long time before me, to recognize that when scientists report their differences in public, they are often moved to engage in polemical discourse designed to save their hypotheses (and so their faces) rather than to strive, quite disinterestedly, for Discovery of the Truth. What we have before us, then, is virtually a self-exemplifying theory: in the very letter in which Newton is about to set down his immortal version of the shoulders-of-Giants Aphorism, he first exemplifies the Aphorism itself by building on Hooke's rationale for a private correspondence to arrive at what must hereafter be known as the Hooke-Newton-Merton principle of interaction among scientists. In fact, so great is my admiration for Hooke's indispensable role in the early evolution of this idea that I, for one, am prepared to scrap the tripartite eponymy and have the idea known simply as the "kindle cole" principle.

❡ *vii*

BUT WE cannot afford to pause any longer over this complex sociological matter if we are to pursue the story of the giant-and-dwarf Aphorism. In the letter to Hooke

* *The Diary of Robert Hooke* — first published in 1935!

where Newton tosses out his sociological remark, as
though it were a discovery of no great consequence, he
goes on to write as follows. (I must quote at length so
that his ideas are not wrenched out of context.)

> Your animadversions will be therefore very welcome
> to me: for though I was formerly tired with this sub-
> ject, & have not yet nor I beleive ever shall recover so
> much love for it as to delight in spending time about
> it; . . .

This, of course, is Newton in one of those recurrent
moods in which he sometimes threatened to abandon the
entire scientific enterprise, just as he was when he wrote
Leibniz that "I was so persecuted with discussions arising
out of my theory of light, that I blamed my own im-
prudence for parting with so substantial a blessing to run
after a shadow." This Newton wrote to the same man
with whom he was ironically enough to become entangled
in that notorious conflict over priority of inventing the
calculus, a conflict, moreover, which proved to be one of
the most violent in the entire history of science and one in
which, as I once wrote and as I know from your letter,
you once read, but which I nevertheless cannot resist
quoting here,

> when the Royal Society finally established a committee
> to adjudicate the rival claims, Newton, who was then
> president of the Society, packed the committee, helped
> direct its activities, anonymously wrote the preface
> for the second published report — the draft is in his
> handwriting — and included in that preface a disarm-
> ing reference to the old legal maxim that 'no one is a
> proper witness for himself [and that] he would be an
> iniquitous Judge, and would crush underfoot the laws
> of all people, who would admit anyone as a lawful
> witness in his own cause.' We can gauge, [you remem-

ber I went on to write] the immense pressures for self-vindication that must have operated for such a man as Newton to have adopted these means for defense of his valid claims. It was not because Newton was weak but because the institutionalized values [affirming the merit of originality] were strong that he was driven to such lengths.*

Newton continues with his letter of 5 February 1675/6 to Hooke:

> yet to have at once in short ye strongest or most pertinent Objections that may be made, I could really desire, & know no man better able to furnish me with them then your self. In this you will oblige me. And if there be any thing els in my papers in wch you apprehend I have assumed too much, or not done you right, if you please to reserve your sentiments of it for a private letter [rkm: *n.b.*] I hope you will find also that I am not so much in love with philosophical productions but yt I can make them yeild to equity & friendship. But, in ye meane time you defer too much to my ability for searching into this subject. What Des-Cartes did was a good step. You have added much several ways, & especially in taking ye colours of thin plates into philosophical consideration. [And now comes The Aphorism just as he set it down.] *If I have seen further it is by standing on ye sholders of Giants.*

The italics are just as they appear in Brewster's printing of the letter, but there are no italics at all in the actual letter. I cannot forbear, therefore, from reporting that my scholar's nose for a problem did not fail me. In the draft of this narrative written at the time I was wholly

---

* As you may remember, this passage is drawn from pages 653-4 of my paper, "Priorities in scientific discovery: a chapter in the sociology of science," published in the *American Sociological Review*, December 1957, vol. 22.

dependent upon Brewster (Turnbull and the holograph letter not yet being at hand), I remarked: "Whether the crucial sentence was underscored by Newton, I cannot at the moment say — no sources in my study permit me to say — but I doubt it. Remember that Newton was living in the seventeenth century, not the twentieth; that Burton was being reprinted, and presumably read, with great regularity; that George Herbert had set down the Aphorism in his tract. Why should Newton have singled out this sentence from all the other sentences in his letter and underscored it? Had he possessed a genuine prescience, he might have underscored that sentence stating a sociological truth, but then I am persuaded that he didn't really appreciate the value of what he said there and, in any event, it's abundantly evident that his biographer Brewster didn't. There's not a word in Brewster's text that takes note of this anticipation of Merton by Newton; of course, Brewster couldn't have known of the anticipation (though he might at least have observed that Hooke anticipated Newton in the kindle-cole letter). Nevertheless, had he possessed a genuinely sociological eye, Brewster could have seen for himself that Newton had here hit upon a singularly illuminating sociological 'insight,' as the ugly cant has it."

⊂ viii

— BUT TO return to the shoulders of giants.

We have discovered Newton making truncated, idiosyncratic use of what we must still assume to be the Aphorism initially found in Didacus Stella. As I've tried to suggest, the Aphorism thereafter became Newton's own, not because he deliberately made it so but because admirers of Newton made it so. Once the letter was published (and the date and occasion of its first *publication* is something else I should one day track down),* it was only natural that this unsententious sentence should be eagerly read, remembered and, by those who could not readily know better, be attributed to him. Perhaps this began to happen even before the letter saw print. In these matters, and in spite of his quest for privacy, Newton was not exactly a silent man, although he kept his counsel on almost everything else. He may have shown the letter to his friends † or to that member of his kitchen-

---

* I first came upon it in David Brewster's once-magisterial *Memoirs of the Life, Writings, and Discoveries of Sir Isaac Newton*, published in 1855 by Thomas Constable and Co. in Edinburgh and by Hamilton, Adams, and Co. in London. It appears on pp. 141–43 of volume one.

Now that I have examined Newton's letter for myself, I find that Brewster was not so magisterial as I once supposed. For all his having been "One of the Eight Associates of The Imperial Institute of France, Honorary or Corresponding Member of the Academies of St. Petersburgh, Vienna, Berlin, Copenhagen, Stockholm, Munich, Göttingen, Brussels, Haerlem, Erlangen, Canton de Vaud, Modena, Washington, New York, Boston, Quebec, Cape Town, etc. etc." (as we learn from the travelogue of honors on the title page of his biography), he failed to transcribe the Newton letter with complete fidelity. He systematically bowdlerized — one might now say, brewsterized — the text of the letter to delete every one of Newton's intimations that he might not have done right by Hooke.

† However this might be, it is possible that the shoulders-of-giants letter never reached Hooke! As Turnbull observes: "No reply to this letter has been found. POSSIBLY HOOKE NEVER RECEIVED IT [emphasis mine], for he does not mention its receipt in his *Diary* (London, 1935). Yet the cover of the letter is endorsed in what certainly appears to be Hooke's handwriting: 'Mr Newtons letter & catalogue of Loadstones.'" In short, Hooke might have received it — or again, he might not have. This is not a matter easily settled.

cabinet, Edmond Halley. (I vaguely remember something of the sort, but now I've grown fatigued, and won't even search my own library to get the story on this. It's not of tremendous importance, in any case. I'm not even sure that it's pertinent to the story I'm tracing.)

In short, I just don't know the details of how word about the Aphorism got around, but this I do know: at least by the nineteenth century, and I suspect even before, it was commonly attributed to Newton as his original saying. After all, the idolatry of Newton, some of us think the largely justifiable idolatry of Newton, was in full course in the eighteenth century: remember Voltaire's "splendid vulgarization," *Elémens de la Philosophie de Neuton?* (Why did Voltaire apparently publish this in "Londres"? Oh yes, he was an exile in England, but that was in the 1720s, wasn't it, and this book, at least the *"Nouvelle édition"* cited by I. B. Cohen, bears the date 1737.* Surely, Voltaire was by then back in France. Or perhaps Voltaire's Anglomania was regarded as insufferable and he had to publish it in the land that would better appreciate this particular mania. Well, someday I'll straighten this out.)

As it turns out, not "someday" but just the next day. I've located my copy of Brandes' *Voltaire*, put out by Albert & Charles Boni in 1930, which has the entire story in volume one. I find that my guess was thoroughly right in principle though wrong in every detail. Voltaire was, once again, fleeing from the wrath of the authorities,

---

* At least, that is the date cited in I.B.C.'s bibliography. But that meticulous scholar throws me off a bit by reporting on p. 210 of his text that "Voltaire's *Elements,* printed in French *in 1738,* was published *in the same year* in an English translation . . . [the italics are mine]." Now, if it was first (?) published in French in 1738, how could a "nouvelle édition" have appeared the year before? Is this still another case of Voltaire

outraged by his poem, *Le Mondain,* which mocked all those who praised the truly olden days, not those of mere antiquity but the golden age of Adam, Eve and their immediate progeny who went around naked and ate acorns. He moved on to the safety of Amsterdam and Leyden where *Neuton's Elémens* was set in print. You will remember, though I had forgotten, that this greatly disturbed Voltaire's lovely, talented and devoted companion of some fifteen years, Gabrielle Émilie le Tonnelier de Breteuil, Marquise du Châtelet-Lomont, whose role in the making of the book was described by a contemporary prior in the Sorbonne in an unforgettable sustained metaphor —

> Newton's system is a maze, through which Monsieur de Voltaire has found his way by the aid of a thread which was put into his hands by the modern Ariadne. The Theseus and Ariadne of our own time are the more deserving of praise, for those in the Greek legend burned for each other in a sensual love only, while these feel for each other an intellectual love only.

The Marquise wrote, urging Voltaire "to be cautious about having *Neuton* printed in France," and he delayed the printing in Holland, still hoping to gain permission to have it done back home. But, as always, he was doomed to trouble. Although he had withheld the end of his manuscript to keep the book from being prematurely published, his greedy Dutch publisher not only hired a plaguing later scholars by his notorious practice of mis-dating books, ascribing them to pseudonymous or other authors and mis-stating the place of publication, all this merely to escape the persecution to which he was periodically subjected for his enraging opinions and judgments? At any rate, we do know that the book appeared in the late '30s.

35

mathematician to finish the manuscript but appended to
the modest and scholarly title, *Elémens de la Philosophie
de Neuton,* a catchy subtitle that claimed Newton's complex work to have been made understandable for everyone
(the exact words being *mis à la portée de tout le
monde*). [In all justice, the avaricious book-publisher
didn't exaggerate much.] Evidently, then, there really
was something of a story behind the seemingly innocent
fact of the *Elémens* having first been printed outside
of France (even though it happened to have been in
Holland and not, as I ignorantly supposed, in England).
You will note, I trust, how indirectly Voltaire enters our
narrative of the Aphorism, — and, of course, it would
have to be indirect, for can you imagine *him* likening
himself to a dwarf perched high on a giant's shoulders?
Yet, if Voltaire did not avail himself of the Aphorism, we
know that his idol did.

Anyway, Newton was a popular and revered idol of
the time much as Einstein is in our time. This we know
from Voltaire's eulogy. We can surmise it also, for some
circles, from the dedication of Voltaire's book to his
dearly beloved Marquise. (But now, my memory fails me.
How *does* that dedication read?)

Having at hand Catherine Drinker Bowen's superb
account of the life of a biographer, I can unexpectedly
turn for help to her — unexpectedly, because I had never
known, before reading her book, that she had once con-
templated doing a biography of Newton. I'm sorry, in a
way, that she didn't take it on. Is she unquestionably right
in thinking that her vast ignorance of science would have
made impossible, or indescribably inept, any kind of
biography of Newton? I have more confidence in
Catherine Drinker Bowen than she evidently had in herself; but again, if I really mean that, perhaps I'd better

accept her judgment on this matter. But if she didn't succeed in making Newton her subject for a biography, and wrote her great book of the life and times of Sir Edward Coke instead, she does succeed in giving me what I need at the moment, the exact words of Voltaire's dedication to his Marquise, in his book on the elements of Newton's philosophy. It reads so (and I rely enough on Mrs. Bowen to refuse a further search): "Minerve de la France, immortelle Émilie, Disciple de Neuton et de la Vérité."

❡ *ix*

SINCE it is clear that I won't be able to trace out the entire history of the Aphorism in this one letter, I break into the strict continuity of my exposition, and refer to the note of inquiry that George Sarton published in *Isis* (1935, 24, 107–9). In that note, Sarton characteristically detects the importance of the Aphorism, as it turned up in Bernard of Chartres though we know this only through the writings of his devoted pupil John of Salisbury. Bernard died in 1126.* His presumably voluminous works have been lost and so we are indebted to the scholarly filiopiety of John of Salisbury for what remains the first authenticated appearance in writing of the idea of pigmies on the shoulders of giants.

To get a line on John, I turned to the index of volume II of Sarton's monumental *Introduction* in search of Sarton's account of him. The index itemizes some three columns of "Johns" of one variety or another, be-

* *Cf.* Sarton, *Introduction to the History of Science* (Vol. II, Pt. I, 195–6) for more.

37

ginning with "John, St." and ending with a cross-refer-
ence that reads: "John, see also Yaḥyā and Yūḥanna."
More precisely, there are 143 Johns, of one sort or
another catalogued at this point in the index, these referring only to the Johns of the twelfth and thirteenth
centuries that are now worthy of note. In the first volume
of Sarton's *Introduction*, covering the period from Homer
to Omar Khayyam, or roughly the period from about
the ninth century B.C. to the end of the eleventh century
A.D., the Johns are few and far between. There are
only eight of them all told. To these should probably be
added, however, four Joanneses, since Sarton advises
readers looking up John to "see Joannes" just as he advises those of us searching for Joannes to "see John." But
the Joanneses, too, are scarce, numbering four altogether.
We might dub in one Joannitus, to give us a grand total
of thirteen Johns or variants thereof for the approximately
two millennia covered by Sarton's first volume, scarcely
any competition for the 143 Johns, *without* variants, to be
found in the two centuries covered by Sarton's second
volume. There are also, I find, eleven "Yaḥyās" in this
latter period, so evidently the Arab-speaking world was
not entirely ill-disposed toward the Christian name of
John, or had we better say, the praenomen, John, as
translated into the Arab name, Yaḥyā. Add to this, on
Sarton's suggestion, the citation of Yūḥanna, of which
there is only one during the twelfth and thirteenth centuries, this solitary being listed as "Yūḥanna, b. al-'Ibrī-
al-Malatī." He turns out to be a Syriac historian, grammarian, philosopher, theologian, physician, astronomer,
man of letters and translator from Arabic into Syriac who
was originally named Abū-l-Faraj Yūḥanna ibn al-'Ibrī-
al-Malatī, and can be described as Bar Hebraeus or, if
you will, as Bar 'Ebhrāyā. All things considered, this lone

Yūhanna had best be scratched, leaving us a maximum total of Johns, inclusive of Arabic variants, of fully 154 for the two centuries between 1100 and 1300.*

In the pantheon which Sarton has erected for the giants of science and learning as well as for the indispensable dwarfs who climb upon their shoulders are found medieval Johns of every variety. There is John Argyropulos, known only (and then to only a few) for his translation of Aristotle's categories into Latin; the 13th-century John Basingstoke who studied not only in Oxford and Paris, but, extraordinarily, at Athens, too, thus becoming, Sarton tells us, "one of the earliest Englishmen having a real knowledge of Greek." To pick up just one other as we continue the search for our John, there is John of Montecorvino, known in his homeland as Giovanni di Montecorvino among those who preferred the vernacular and as Joannes de Monte Corvino among the rest. Although he was born near Salerno, he died, from all accounts, at Peiping. For, during his approximately eighty years of life, he travelled as a missionary to the East, and, by 1305, was thoroughly established

---

* Of course, all this is as nothing compared to the 14th century, which was chock-full of scientific Johns. Sarton lists 426 of them in Volume III, to say nothing — and I really won't — of those bearing the cross-referenced names of Johanan, Johann, Johannes, Johannitius, Gian, Ion, Yaḥyā, Yūḥanna and, of course, Jack. I say "of course" only because Sarton's index advises us, when we look for John, to "see also . . . . Jack." But I urge you not to heed that advice for if you do, you are bound to be disappointed. The only entry is Jack Straw, no scientist at all, but the fellow who collaborated with Wat Tyler and John Ball in heading up the English revolt of 1381. Ion also turns out to be a lone entry, a certain Mayster Ion Gardener who is cited as having written a poem of 196 English lines entitled, understandably enough for this particular John, "The feate of gardeninge."

in Khānbaliq (Peiping, of course) where he was "in high favor with the Great Khān." This John moves us, at last, to our John, John of Salisbury, who saved for posterity his master's, Bernard of Chartres's, aphorism about the ways in which knowledge advances.

Only it is not quite fair to imply that Bernard, as he comes to us through John, tossed off an aphorism. True, one can discern in what he is reported to have said the possibility of an Englished version that does state a truth pithily. This can be very roughly put, as indeed Sarton puts it, so:

> In comparison with the ancients, we stand like dwarfs on the shoulders of giants.

But as John (of Salisbury) himself reports it in his *Metalogicon,** it goes like this:

> Dicebat Bernardus Carnotensis nos esse quasi nanos gigantium humeris insidentes, ut possimus plura eis et remotiora videre, non utique proprii visus acumine, aut eminentia corporis, sed quia in altum subvehimur et extollimur magnitudine gigantea.

You will notice that when the sententious saying was quarried from the rocklike solidity of what Bernard

---

* This is how it appears, at least, in the edition of the *Meta-logicon* by C. C. J. Webb, published in 1939; you'll find it on p. 136, says Sarton. You had better make note of that page number if you want to locate the passage, which seems to have shown peripatetic tendencies — peripatetic, that is, in the itinerant sense, not the philosophically-tinged one. For in his *Introduction to the History of Science* (II, 196), Sarton, who for the moment remains my chief authority on Bernard, locates the key passage in book 3, chap. 4 of the *Metalogicon*, but in *The History of Science and the New Humanism*, his little book of Colver Lectures published in 1931, the same year as the

(is reputed to have) said, something is gained but something is also lost. The gain is in terseness: the compact Aphorism enlists the interest of the reader or hearer and he is the more apt to carry it off with him and pass it on to others. This is net gain (provided it is not repeated with such frequency that it loses both interest and meaning and ends up as a tired cliché). But there is loss also. For Bernard made explicit the singularly important idea that the successors need be no brighter than their predecessors — not even *as* bright — and yet, the accumulation of knowledge being what it is, they can know far more and thus come to see farther. This is caught up by implication in the aphoristic version. But as we have come to see, the implications do not always move along with the explicit statement as it enters upon its travels. What is completely lost from the Aphorism is the respect in which Bernard's perhaps vague but detectable understanding of how science cumulates helped set the stage for the great "Battle of the Books" which debated the comparative intellectual (and other) merits of the Ancients and the Moderns, a battle that raged intermittently throughout the seventeenth century and into the eighteenth. But that is quite another story and one into which I cannot go except insofar as it bears upon our composite figure of giants-and-dwarfs.

second volume of the *Introduction,* Sarton reverses the location of the passage and now makes it book 4, chap. 3. Since he insisted on proofreading everything he wrote, it's impossible for me to judge (while I am still here in my study) which one of the two has it straight. But you can presumably find it on p. 136 of Webb's edition of *Metalogicon* (which, you must remember is by Bernard's student John, not by Bernard himself).

[Book III, chap. 4 it is, as you will find by glancing at the *Metalogicus* in the *Patrologiae Latinae,* ed. J. P. Migne, Paris: 1853.]

❡ *x*

I CAN pick up this thread of the story by turning once again to the seventeenth century. This time, I'll ignore (or try to ignore) Burton, Newton and all the rest we have encountered before, and move in the more nearly subterranean regions of that century's small talk, tracts and quarrelsome books.

Take the case of Godfrey Goodman, to whose sermons Richard Foster Jones tells us,* John Donne was manifestly indebted for ideas and metaphors adopted in his, Donne's, *An Anatomie of the World: The First Anniversary,* published in 1611. Beginning his curvilinear career by holding the sinecure rectory of Llandyssil, Goodman moved on to the better one of Ysceifiog (near Holywell) and eventually reached his peak as Bishop of Gloucester. Then, almost as though he were driven to exemplify metaphorically the title of his major book, *The Fall of Man,* he accentuated his Romish tendencies until he was cast down by Cromwell and ended, in the words of Carlyle, as "a miserable impoverished old piece of confusion." This Goodman — he was for a time chaplain to the Queen (not Elizabeth, of course, for Goodman was an unordained stripling of 20 in the year of her death, but James the First's Queen Anne) — gloomily expressed his

* In his *Ancients and Moderns,* 1936, p. 26. Locked up in my study, I must for a time adopt Jones, the onetime Professor of English at Washington University, as my guide to the tractarians of seventeenth-century England (who of course have nothing whatsoever to do with the Tractarians of nineteenth-century England).

feelings about the whole controversy between the Ancients (their cause being eloquently argued by their seventeenth-century advocates and not by the prescient Ancients themselves) and the Moderns (their cause being just as eloquently defended by other seventeenth-century men). All this was set out in his aptly entitled *The Fall of Man,** which appeared in 1616, that year in which one of the Moderns, Will Shakspere, died.

The chaplain Goodman alerts us to the double-edged character of the giant-and-dwarf figure. It now appears that it can be used just as effectively to extol the dwarfs who are raised high on the giants' shoulders as to extol the giants without whom there would be no eminence from which the little men could see far and wide. The gloomy cleric Goodman detects chicanery deeply implicit in the figure:

> But this great learned age hath found out a compari-
> son, wherein we might seeme to magnifie the Ancients,
> but indeed very cunningly do depresse them down,
> making them our footestooles [Goodman does have a

* Actually, I mislead you a bit here and do thorough injustice to Goodman's capacity for creating a title that really describes the content of the book. The short title, *The Fall of Man*, is of course intended only for quick allusion. But to get a fuller sense of what Goodman was really writing about, we must attend to the expanded title, which reads in its entirety as follows: *The Fall of Man, or the Corruption of Nature Proued by the light of our naturall Reason, Which being the First Ground and Occasion of our Christian Faith and Religion, may likewise serue for the first step and degree of the natural mans conuersion. First Preached in a Sermon, since enlarged, reduced to the forme of a treatise, and dedicated to the Queenes most excellent Maiestie.* By Godfrey Goodman, her Maiesties Chaplaine, Bachelour in Divinity, sometimes a member both of Trinitie Colledge in Cambridge, and of Saint Peters Colledge in Westminster.

43

point here, and one that practically every one else
we've encountered so far managed to miss]; preferring
our selves before them, extolling and exalting our
selves above measure [Goodman is ingeniously cheat-
ing a bit here; to be sure the dwarfs *are* "exalted"
in the prime sense of being "set up on high" but a
midget remains an unprepossessing and necessarily
modest fellow at best]; for thus it is said, that we are
like dwarfes set upon the shoulders of Gyants, discerning little of our selves but supposing the learning and
ground-worke of the Ancients, we see much further
than they, (which in effect is as much, as that we
prefer our own judgements, before theirs): in truth,
in truth, a very wittie comparison, certainly it is either
a dwarfe or a Gyant, for it will admit no mediocrity.
But I pray let us examine it. . .*

This is how Goodman proceeds with his sharply
penetrating examination. It is all very well, he writes, to
assume that the dwarfs are raised up high, but should we
not first ask how they manage to get there at all? Or, to
put it in Goodman's own words, we must consider

first how these dwarfes should be exhaled and drawne
up to the shoulders of the gyants; here is a point of
great difficulty as yet not thought upon.

You will grant that the ingenious Goodman has
scored again. Not one of his predecessors or successors —
not even such a successor as Newton who would adapt
the Aphorism only some sixty years later — has thought to
ask how the dwarfs manage to mount upon the eminence
of the giants. The Aphorism simply *assumes* that it is
an easy task to clamber onto the shoulders of the Ancients.
Yet once the assumption is put in question, it becomes

* This, and all that follows, you will find in Part III, pp. 361–3
of Goodman's *Fall.*

questionable indeed. Consider only, by way of analogy, says Goodman, that "in digging the earth some mettals are found, and some are undiscovered, so is it in reading and perusing the works of the fathers; we may continually learne, and daily finde out new mynes in their writings . . ."

To my dismay, I find this a thoroughly congenial observation. Even worse, it forces me to recognize that once again I have been anticipated. For, like some others among my contemporaries, I have long argued that the writings of classical authors in every field of learning can be read with profit time and time again, additional ideas and intimations coming freshly into view with each re-reading. What is to be found in writings of the past is anything but fixed, once and for all. It changes as our own intellectual sensitivities change; the more we learn on our own account the more we can learn by re-reading from our freshly gained perspective. As you can see, Goodman has come dangerously close to anticipating this sound idea (although you will surely notice also that he has not actually hit upon the *core* of my idea). Now, it is one thing to find belatedly that one has been scooped by such a giant as Newton; it is, in fact, a rather edifying experience. But it is quite another thing to find that a dwarf, such as Goodman, might have come, more than three centuries ago, within an ace of an idea which one has labored mightily to evolve for oneself. It is almost enough to create a motivated hostility toward a forerunner.

But harsh words have no place in my narrative and so I return to the second of Goodman's attacks on the concealed implications of our simile. Suppose, he says, that the dwarfs unaccountably do make their way onto the giants' shoulders. Then, a fresh problem arises: how are they to *maintain* their position? At such a lofty altitude, they are apt to become light-headed. Or, as the gloomy cleric puts it, "it is to bee feared, lest seeing so steepe a descent, they will rather fall to a giddines than be able rightly to judge of the objects, lest they should be confounded with the multiplicity of learning in the fathers, not able to fathome the depth of their grounds; for wil you suppose, that these Gyants should so infinitely exceed the dwarfes in length and in strength, and yet will you equall them for goodness and quickness of sight? [Then he concludes, modestly but tendentiously in a dwarfy mood] I cannot stay long upon the shoulders of Gyants, for heere is but slippery hold . . ."

Give the good Goodman his due. He is the first to see that the Aphorism cunningly makes foote-stooles of the Ancients. He is the first to see that the Aphorism adroitly evades the issue of how we dwarfs are elevated onto the lofty shoulders of the Ancients. He is the first to ask the embarrassing question of how the dwarfs, once mounted on high, maintain their precarious position. And, as though all these subtleties were not enough, he is the first (at least among the new conservatives of 17th-century England) to picture the grievous consequences should "these gyants stumble or fall."

Consider the full import of this most daring of all Goodman's vivid dissections of our Aphorism. Here he is, the staunch conservative battling its usual progressivist implications and yet prepared to concede that the giants may sometimes have erred or even come a cropper. But save your plaudits for this seeming evidence of intellectual integrity driving a scholar to ineluctable conclusions, however repugnant they may be to him personally. Before you credit Goodman with a genial and lambent wit, for his oxymoronic imagery of an occasional giant stumbling or even falling flat on his face, note how he uses this temporary concession to flail the modern dwarfs for their arrogancy, pride and spleen. Suppose, writes Goodman,

> that these gyants should stumble or fall, take heede of the dwarfe, take heede of the dwarfe. Nay, rather cries out the dwarfe, I will guide and direct them, and keep them from falling; if they will not uphold me, then I will uphold them. Here is presumption indeed . . .

So you see that when the giant falls into error, the dwarf promptly falls into sin. I suppose that Goodman's point is this: the Ancients may occasionally be fallable, but the Moderns are always morally and intellectually fallible.

❪ *xi*

NOW this kind of interpretation of the simile, ascribing wily purposes to men who thought themselves eminently modest in using it, could scarcely have been expected to go unchallenged. Goodman's partisan reading of the simile was soon countered by George Hakewill's reading. Hakewill first published his book in 1627 and it, too, achieved a third and enlarged edition — by 1635. (Incidentally, it was in this edition that Hakewill clearly anticipated the "equal time" provision for political disputants appearing on today's television. He provided Goodman ample space for candid criticisms of the arguments Hakewill set forth in previous editions and then provided himself roughly equivalent space for respectful rebuttals.)

In accord with the intelligent practice of the time, Hakewill's book also had a short working title, cryptically condensed to *An Apologie,* and a longer descriptive title, giving more of the details.*

In the "Epistle Dedicatory" to his *Apologie,* Hakewill wastes no time. He gets to the epigrammatic simile at once and denies the strange interpretation put upon it by such suspicious worthies as Goodman. This is how Hakewill sees the significance of the figure:

> But if we conceive them [these being the Ancients] to be Gyants, and ourselves Dwarfes, if we imagine all sciences allready to have received their utmost perfection, so as we need not but to translate and comment upon that which they have done, if we so admire and dote upon Antiquity as we emulate and envy, nay scorne and trample underfoot whatsoever the present age affords, if we spend our best time and thoughts in clyming to honour, in gathering riches, in following

* In the thought that you might want these details, I append the fuller title: *An Apologie of the Power and Providence of God in the Government of the World. Or an Examination and Censure of the Common Errour Touching Natures Perpetuall and Universall Decay, Divided into Foure Bookes: Whereof the first treates of this pretended decay in generall, together with some preparatives thereunto. The second of the pretended decay of the Heavens and Elements, together with that of the elementary bodies, man only excepted. The third of the pretended decay of mankinde in regard of age and duration, of strength and stature, of arts and wits. The fourth of this pretended decay in matters of manners, together with a large proofe of the future consummation of the World from the testimony of the Gentiles, and the uses which we are to draw from the consideration thereof.* The modest signature on the title-page reads simply: "By G. H., D. D." But scholars have not had the least trouble in ferreting out the identity of "the Authour," as he impersonally describes himself in the third and last edition of 1635, to which he added "two entire bookes not formerly published," the two books amounting to 378 pages, these of folio dimensions, and devoted to counter-criticisms of those contemporary wits who had disagreed with one or another of his ideas.

our pleasures, and in turning the edge of our wits against another, surely there is little hope that we should ever come near them, much less match them.

I have quoted Hakewill here just as Richard Jones quotes him, since the books I happen to have in my library at home do not include any of the editions of Hakewill's *Apologie*. But Jones was a serious scholar and I do not doubt that this is just as Hakewill set it down.* Of course, Hakewill may have had much more to say that is pertinent for my purpose though it was not for Jones's, and so I'm probably missing out on what is there for the having. Nevertheless, this must wait for another time, since I want to get this letter off to you and don't want to take time for a serious search.

---

* Not quite. Now that I have searched out the third edition of Hakewill's *Apology,* I must report, to my deepest regret, that my confidence in Jones's strict scholarship was badly misplaced. His extract from Hakewill, as I naively quoted it above, is checkered with literal errors. On two occasions, in this one short passage, Jones mis-spells Hakewill's "wee" as "we" just as he mis-spells his "neere" as "near." (Almost, I was tempted to interpolate several ironic *sics* [encased in brackets] to signal you of these errors of commission. But I leave the passage, just as I initially and innocently took it from Jones [p. 32].) There is more of this same kind of lapse in scholarship. Jones omits the word "of" in the quoted phrase, "In gathering [of] riches" and omits "one" in the phrase, "wits [one] against another." And to cap all this, he takes Hakewill's two distinct words, "an other," and fuses them into one. Although I do not for a moment doubt Jones's integrity, I must say that this is the sort of thing that tries one's faith in fellow scholars. It only goes to. show that there is no satisfactory substitute for going directly to the sources.

ℂ *xii*

[IT IS just as I supposed. Now that I have actually
looked into Hakewill, I must report that my ambivalence
toward Jones deepens. True, his gentle help has led me
to many a seventeenth-century expositor of the Aphorism.
Yet what kind of help is this that also misleads? Or, to
put it less brutally, that obscures from me the provenance
of the Aphorism as it moves into that century of genius?
Perhaps it *is* ungrateful of me to grow bitter about what
you may describe as a mere sin of omission. But restraint
is not easy, for rancor will out.

Here, in a nutshell, is the whole sad story. In good
faith, I had quoted Jones's quotation from Hakewill, with
just a tincture of suspicion that Jones might not have
told all. But, in all candor, I did not really suspect the
full extent of his omissions. See for yourself; here is how
Hakewill actually introduces the passage I have quoted
from Jones, this on pages 2–3 of his Epistle Dedicatory:

> I do not beleeve that all Regions of the World, or all
> ages in the same Region affoord wits alwayes alike:
> but I thinke, [and now, note well] neither is it my
> opinion alone, but of *Scaliger, Vives, Budaeus,
> Bodine,* and other great *Clearks,* that the wits of these
> latter ages being manured by industry, directed by
> precepts, regulated by method, tempered by diet, re-
> freshed by exercise, and incouraged by rewards, may
> be as capable of deepe speculations; and produce as
> *masculine,* and lasting birthes, as any of the ancienter
> times have done. [Only now follows the passage
> quoted by Jones:] But if we conceive them to be

Gyants, and ourselves Dwarfes; if we imagine [and
so on] . . .

You will have noted Jones's unforgivable omission for
yourself. Here is Hakewill emphatically italicizing his
great debt to *"Scaliger, Vives, Budaeus, Bodine,* and other
great *Clearks,"* and there is Jones blithely passing this
by, thus attributing to Hakewill what Hakewill attributes
to these others. And what others! — GIANTS, every one of
them.

The Scaliger in question is of course Joseph Justus,
known in his own day (1540–1609) as "the bottomless
pit of erudition" and later proclaimed (by such as his
biographers Jacob Bernays and Tamizey de Larroque) as
holding first place among the scholars of all times. It is
this immensely learned Scaliger of whom it was commonly said, as Aubrey reminds us, "that where he erres,
he erres so ingeniosely, that one had rather erre with him
than hitt the marke with Clavius."

Or as George W. Robinson, onetime Secretary of your
own Harvard Graduate School of Arts and Sciences, put
it in his preface to the *Autobiography of Joseph Scaliger,
With Autobiographical Selections from His Letters, His
Testament, and the Funeral Orations by Daniel Heinsius
and Dominicus Baudius,* this being, after an unaccount-
able — and disgraceful — lapse of more than three
centuries, the *first* translation into English of these extraordinary documents: "Whether Joseph Scaliger should
be reckoned the greatest scholar of all time, or should
share that palm with Aristotle, is, perhaps, an open question; of his primacy beyond all rivalry among the scholars
of modern times there can be no doubt." And a man of
this stature is only one of the quadrivirate of giants
effaced by Jones from Hakewill's forthright acknowledgement of scholarly indebtedness.

But then, the greatest of Scaligers in all the twelve-hundred-year history of that princely and scholarly family had the wretched fortune of being mistreated in one way or another by his contemporaries and by generations to come. As Heinsius said of him in his funeral oration, with an oblique, unwitting, and partial allusion to our Aphorism: "Nor does there seem a better way for heroes to rise to heaven than on the shoulders of scoundrels."

Hakewill's allusion is definitely to this Scaliger, Joseph Justus, *not* to his father Julius Caesar Scaliger who, according to Sarton, was merely one of the greatest classical scholars of France (and who, as a botanist of the first rank, once caustically remarked that "the local herbalists should better be called verbalists").

ℂ xiii⃛

HAVE you, like me, long wondered about the identity of Clavius (in the apophthegm quoted by Aubrey four paragraphs back)? Have you taken his name as only the Latinized appellation for the man who created that key-noted instrument with strings which was later developed into the piano(forte)? * If so, you are badly mistaken: Clavius had nothing at all to do with the clavichord (although he did much work in mathematics which, at

* It comes hard to follow the mob and refer to this glorious instrument to which the player can with facility give a soft or strong expression by the amputated word — piano. Pianoforte was the apt term for Samuel Johnson and it should remain the apt term for us. For you will instantly recognize in this vulgar truncation, in this apocope, just another example of that cor-

least since Pythagoras, all of us know to be the key to the structure of music). In actual fact, he was a German Jesuit, Father Christopher Clavius, born in Bamberg (!) — site of that twelfth-century cathedral which enshrines our Aphorism in unprecedented style. (But of that, more later.) It was the good Father who actually engineered the reform of the calendar which, since the pontiff naturally overshadowed the astronomical technician, we still persist in describing as the Gregorian reform. Our Scaliger got into quite an argument with Clavius over the merits of the calendrical change which he disliked almost as much as Protestant mathematicians did. Clavius, by the way, never could get to understand decimal fractions.

ruption of the language which Jonathan Swift anonymously deplored in *The Tatler* N°230 (Dateline: September 28, 1710):

> . . . the *Refinement*, which consists in pronouncing the first syllable in a word that has many, and dismissing the rest, such as *Phizz, Hipps, Mobb, Pozz, Rep*, and many more, when we are already overloaded with monosyllables, which are the disgrace of our language. [How good it is to find at last a man who has had his fill of short words and speaks out for long ones.] Thus we cram one syllable, and cut off the rest, as the owl fattened her mice after she had bit off their legs to prevent them from running away; and if ours be the same reason for maiming our words, it will certainly answer the end; for I am sure no other nation will desire to borrow them. Some words are hitherto but fairly split, and therefore only in their way to perfection, as *Incog.* and *Plenipo:* but in a short time, it is to be hoped, they will be further docked to *Inc.* and *Plen.* This reflection has made me of late years very impatient for a peace, which I believe would save the lives of many brave words, as well as men. The war has introduced abundance of polysyllables, which will never be able to live many more campaigns, *Speculations, Operations, Preliminaries, Ambassadors, Pallisadoes, Communication, Circumvallation, Battalions:* as numerous as they are, if they attack us too frequently in our coffee-houses, we shall certainly put them to flight, and cut off the rear.

Piano!!!

ℭ *xiv*

OF VIVES, I shall presently have more to tell you since
it turns out that he holds a singular place in our narrative (although you would never suppose so from the
silence about him that Jones unaccountably imposed upon
Hakewill).

ℭ *xv*

BUDAEUS you will recognize at once as the Latinized
name of Guillaume Budé, that leader of the French
Renaissance who gave Francis I the idea of founding the
Collège de France and who befriended the young Rabelais
years before he conceived his romance of the giant Gargantua and his son Pantagruel.

ℭ *xvi*

AND FINALLY, "Bodine" is of course Jean Bodin
about whom we are surely agreed. Or do you have some
other candidate, writing before this sixteenth-century
giant, for the signal honor of having first tried to develop
a comprehensive philosophy of history?

⟨ *xvii*

SO YOU see that by taking no notice of Hakewill's announced debt to this quartet of giants, Jones for a time succeeded in obliterating every trace of their contribution to the diffusing Aphorism. I am at a loss to account for Jones's behavior. Can he have been an unwitting Francophobe (this possibly being the obverse side of his having been an admitted Anglophile)? * After all, three of the four "great *Clearks*" actually mentioned by Hakewill were French through and through, and the fourth, Vives, although a Spaniard (the first to enter this narrative!), studied long at Paris. In any event, we now know, in spite of Jones's diversionary tactics, that the Englishman Hakewill took the giant-and-dwarf imagery from the leading lights of the French Renaissance.†

Now that I have turned to Hakewill's original text, I can report that he took much more — from at least one of them. But rather than run ahead of the strict chronology of my story, I had better return to my account of how it all seemed to me when, immured in my study, I was wholly dependent upon Jones for my knowledge of Hakewill.]

* Yet surely Jones must have heard that they order this matter better in France.
† Yet we must not assume that the Aphorism was highly contagious; mere exposure to it did not invariably lead to its spread. Pepys was exposed but evidently remained immune. Under the dateline, 4 Feb. 1666/7, he records:

> Fell to read a little in Hakewill's Apology, and did satisfy myself mighty fair in the truth of the saying that the world does not grow old at all, but is in as good condition in all respects as ever it was as to nature.

Consult any edition of the *Diary;* in all, 'tis the same.

ℭ *xviii*

JONES reports a conception of Hakewill's, without quoting his exact language, that is even more ingenious than Goodman's. [I realize that, after my long complaint about Jones's misdeeds, you may have almost forgotten Godfrey Goodman: he is the gloomy cleric who wrought so many conservative changes in the Aphorism.] I happen to believe, incidentally, that the first part of what Jones has Hakewill say is right in principle and if you grant me this, then Hakewill's observation is not only ingenious but true — true today, as it was three hundred years ago. Hakewill says, in Jones's paraphase (*Ancients and Moderns*, page 32):

> Men of all times are of one stature, neither giants nor dwarfs [this being the part with which I agree in principle] with the difference, however, that if the moderns possessed the studiousness, watchfulness, and love of truth which characterized the ancients, they would be lifted up higher by means of the latter. He who claims to be a dwarf sitting on a giant's shoulders is nothing but a man of competent stature grovelling on the earth.

So Hakewill cuts the giants down to medium size and rearranges the simile in the process. For of course at least some of the fellows who, in what the 17th-century John Parkinson * called "the middle times," invented and transmitted this figure intended the giants to refer to the ac-

---

* Not to be confused with the discoverer of Parkinson's Law: he came later.

cumulation of knowledge in the past and not to the intellectual size of the individual men who together created this knowledge. But since Hakewill is caught up in a polemic, — and I hope you remember what Hooke, Newton and I have had to say about the distorting effect of these public controversies in science and scholarship — he adapts the lingering simile to his own polemical purposes and, strangely enough, manages to emerge with a new truth in the process. For there really is no evidence that the quality of mind has greatly improved or greatly deteriorated in the course of the last two or three millennia.* In this sense, Hakewill's overdetermined distortion of the earlier meaning of the figure has led him to a valid idea. I cannot say, not having his book around, whether he recognizes that this does not imply the placing of all minds on a par but only that the statistical distribution of minds of each grade of quality is, in his opinion and now mine, pretty much the same in each cultural epoch.† Of course, the statistical distribution — *i.e.* the percentage of all minds found in each grade at a particular time — is not the whole story, when it comes to affecting *rates* of cultural development. Here, the absolute number of minds, not their relative distribution, matters much. The point is evident — and easily overlooked. The more than three billions of human beings who threaten to inhabit our earth are appreciably more than the half-billion estimated for the mid-seventeenth

* I should confess, however, that the careful and imaginative work of S. L. Washburn and J. N. Spuhler which examines the old dogma that "the human organism has been essentially static since the development of culture," goes on to ask whether this is really so and concludes by finding that it is not. But in the span of time Hakewill must have had in mind, there cannot have been much change in man as organism.
† Now that I have looked into his book: he does.

century (to go no further back into highly supposititious estimates for much earlier centuries). If the same percentage of talented minds obtains in all these periods, this would mean a vastly greater number of these minds around now than long before. And, of course, it is the absolute number of minds able, willing and allowed to work that determines the rate of intellectual advance. (Some day, when I'm taking an excursion from my study, I'll dig up Hakewill's book to see if he has plagiarized me on this just as blatantly as Newton plagiarized me on that other idea.)

❡ xix

NOW that I have read Hakewill, I find that he did plagiarize me — unmercifully. But this is of little consequence, compared with what else I found. It is not that Jones's paraphrase, upon which I relied so heavily, fails to match the felicitous language of the original; I do not hold Jones to this impossible standard, for what present-day academician can be expected to achieve such stately prose? But surely I can hold him to the standard of seeing to it that his paraphrase faithfully records the genealogy of ideas as this was set forth in the original text. Instead, by a singular omission, Jones once again credits to Hakewill what Hakewill quietly credits to another. Note what is omitted from the Jones version as, turning back to page 56 of my text and then going on to read what follows, you make a studied comparison of the two. Here is Hakewill, honest, plainspoken and perceptive, all in one:

Beside the infinite and bitter controversies among *Christians* in matters of *Religion* since the infancie thereof even to those present times, hath doubtless not a little hindered the advancement and progresse of other Sciences, together with a vaine opinion, that all *Arts* were already fully perfected, so as nothing could bee added thereunto and that the Founders of them were *Gyants,* more than men for their wits in regard of us, and we very *dwarfes,** sunke below our *species* in regard of them. *Sed non est ita,* saith *Ludovicus Vives, nec nos sumus nani, nec illi homines Gigantes, sed omnes ejusdem staturae, quidem nos altius erecti eorum beneficio, maneat modo in nobis quod in illis, studium, attentio animi, vigilanti et amor veri, quae si absint, jam non sumus nani, sed homines justae Magnitudinis humi prostrati.* It is not so, neither are wee Dwarfes,† nor they Gyants, but all of equal stature, or rather wee somewhat higher, being lifted by their meanes, conditionally there be in us an equal intention of spirit, watchfulnesse of minde, and love of truth: for if these bee wanting, then are we not so much dwarfes, as men of a perfect growth lying on the ground.‡

Where shall I begin to plumb the depths of what is here contained? I turn from all peripheral questions, though each of these has its excellent demand for our attention, and move at once to the heart of the matter. As he himself makes plain, Hakewill took directly from

---

* You will surely not miss Hakewill's nuance of the capitalized "G" in "Gyants" and the diminished "d" in "dwarfes."
† Here, my preceding footnoted hypothesis of the subtle lower-case "d" in "dwarfes" temporarily breaks down.
‡ For this passage, I suggest that you turn directly to Book III, ch. 6, Section 1, pp. 257–8 of Hakewill's *Apologie* rather than rely upon the helpful but not altogether reliable Jones.

Vives the major idea that companies of men are equal in all ages: he quotes (and sometimes misquotes, but let's not go into that) Vives' original Latin and thereafter assists those of us with little Latin by immediately translating it into English. Yet not the slightest hint of all this appears in Jones's paraphrase. Had we continued to rely on it, we could only have supposed, as I did in fact suppose, that this powerful idea was originated by Hakewill. Yet as he himself forthrightly announces, he had it from the giant, Vives.

ℂ *XX*

I HAVE reluctantly restrained myself from attending much to Hakewill's ancestors, Scaliger, Budé and Bodin, in order not to be diverted from the main course of this inquiry into the complex history of the Aphorism, but I must pause, if only for a moment, to renew and enlarge our acquaintance with Johannes Ludovicus Vives (or, in the vernacular which he loved so well, Juan Luis Vives). For in passing silently over Vives in his paraphrase of Hakewill, Jones was only perpetuating the studied neglect of Vives by generations of otherwise discerning scholars. Your own George Ticknor, who, before he was succeeded in his professorship of modern languages and belles-lettres by Longfellow, managed to indict Harvard as "neither a university – which we call ourselves – nor a respectable high school – which we ought to be" and managed, also, to inaugurate that departmental system which was only later fully developed by his wife's nephew, President Eliot, never so much as mentions Vives in his *History of Spanish Literature,* although this was surely the most comprehensive scholarly survey of the entire range of Spanish letters to his time, being incomparably superior to the works of Bouterwek and Sismondi. Nor is there a word about Vives in J. B. Bury's magisterial *Idea of Progress,* although Vives was, as others long before me have doubtless noted, the antecedent Spanish equivalent of Francis Bacon (who is, of course, and rightly so, accorded much attention by Bury).

What was good enough for Ticknor, Bury and Jones is not good enough for me. I cannot ignore Vives. I could not ignore him even had he not been a crucial link in transmitting the Aphorism to Hakewill (and an untold number of others). He has a far greater claim to our notice — and to immortal fame. To make no bones about it: * Vives anticipated the Hooke-Newton-Merton hypothesis (or what we have come to know as the "kindle cole principle")! What is more, he epitomizes the hypothesis in the same work that includes the Aphorism, the *de Causis Corruptarum Artium* (*i.e.* the Causes of the Corruption of the Liberal Arts),† formulating the hypothesis in the same kind of wrangling invective that he deplores (thus presenting us with another case of a self-exemplifying doctrine):

> When a boy has been brought to the school, at once he is required to dispute; on the very first day, he is immediately taught to wrangle, though as yet unable to talk . . . These beginners are accustomed never to

* In adopting this strange culinary figure, I ask you only to act like a prudent cook careful to avoid leaving bones in the soup that would serve as an obstacle to its being easily swallowed.
† I have not been able to put my hands on the first, the 1531, edition of *De Causis* but have had to content myself with the version that appears in Ludovicus Vivis [just so], *Opera Omnia,* Basil [just so], 1555.

61

be silent, to asseverate confidently whatever is in
their mouths, lest at any time they should seem to have
ceased speaking. Nor does one disputation a day
suffice, or two, as with eating. At breakfast they
wrangle; after breakfast they wrangle; at supper they
wrangle, after supper they wrangle. In the house they
wrangle; out of doors they wrangle. At meals, at the
bath, in the sweating-room, in the temple, in the city,
in the country, in public, in private, in every place,
at every time, they are wrangling.*

This monomanic devotion to wrangling among ignorant boys is just prelude to that love of public disputation
among learned men which results in such base and odious
practices as these:

There is a pandering to the audience, as it were to
the public in the theatre, who are pleased not with the
best man, but with the best actor. For the hearers
cannot pass an opinion on what they are ignorant of.
Hence strife is received by the audience with great
applause,† for the spectacle of a fight is most pleasing
to them.

* Though others might, you, of course, will not mistake these
contentious fellows as wranglers, in the Cantabrigian sense of
those who have been placed in the first class in the mathematical tripos, or as wranglers, in the sense current in the western
United States of those who are in charge of a string of horses
or ponies on the range. No, you will recognize in Vives' reit-
erations an unspoken admonition by the pre-Socratic Prodicus
reported in Plato's *Protagoras*, 337a, as he begs both "Protagoras and Socrates to grant our request, which is, that you will
argue with one another and not wrangle; for friends argue with
friends out of good-will [as you and I do], but only adver-
saries and enemies wrangle."
† You are probably aching to remind me that Bacon had, in the
Aphorism LXXVII of his *Novum Organum*, picked up and

As you can see, this sort of thing was going on for quite some time before it was instituted anew by producers of panel discussion programs on TV.

Vives innovated all over the lot. He was practically the (fore)father of experimental psychology and developed methods for judging boys' characters and intellectual powers in what he described as the "trial of wits," this giving rise, in 1557, to Juan Huarte's *Examination of Men's Wits* * or what we would now describe as Educational Tests and Measurements.

The versatile Vives would of course put his own idiosyncratic stamp upon the Aphorism. He squeezes out of it every excess of humility *and* of egotism, remarking that "it is a false and fond similitude, which some writers adopt [this cuing us to the fact that even by 1531, the simile had been widely diffused], thinking it witty and apt, that we are, compared with our ancestors, as dwarfs upon the shoulders of giants." It is not so, as Vives and

adapted the same thought about catching the common herd with an *ad captandum* argument from that fourth-century Athenian general immortalized by Plutarch: "We may very well transfer therefore from moral to intellectual matters, the saying of Phocion, that if the multitude assent and applaud, men ought immediately to examine themselves as to what blunder or fault they may have committed." From which jointly Græco-Anglo wisdom I infer, in most personal vein, that both you and I should devoutly hope never to suffer the symptomatic indignity of having one of our works on the list of best-sellers.
* Since you might want to consult Huarte's work directly, I should tell you that its original title was *Examen de Ingenios para las Ciencias*. As a matter of fact, in view of the trauma Jones has inflicted upon me through his version of Hakewill, you better had return to Huarte's original, for the English translation by Richard Carew, which I cite in the body of this letter, was not even taken directly from Huarte but from an Italian translation by Camillo Camilli in 1582. This suggests a double hazard: *traduttore, traditore.*

the derivative Hakewill remind us, because we are all of one stature — except that latecomers benefit by the legacy of their predecessors. So you see that it was the twentieth-century Jones who, in effect, imposed a seeming plagiarism upon the seventeenth-century Hakewill from the sixteenth-century Vives.

ℂ *xxi*

SPEAKING of plagiary, real or imaginary, and returning to the seventeenth century and in particular, to Hakewill, he evidently had his troubles in coping with the publication by others of ideas much like his own. Or, at least, so he was convinced. When he got around to writing another edition of his *Apologie* — not the one to which he appended 378 folio pages of print — he had a good deal to say about a certain Perugian named Secondo Lancellotti. (I have no idea of the whereabouts of Primo Lancellotti, but no doubt he was in the offing, too.) This second Lancellotti published in 1627, the same year in which Hakewill's *Apologie* appeared, a book going by the reasonably short title, *L'Hoggidi Overo Il Mondo Non Peggiore ne piu Calamitoso del passato.** In the book

---

* At least, that is the way Jones has it; no aphæresis here. The initial "h" in "Hoggidi" was probably aspirated then just as it is now, in and around Perugia, although I don't know whether it was subjected to a kind of Cockney ambivalence in which it is dropped when it should be prominently breathed or improperly inserted when it should be ignored. In any case, that is how my authority Jones records it, and so I follow suit. As for the Cockney dialect. when it began and how it came to flourish, I know only from Partridge that there's a pretty good account of it in his *Slang To-day and Tomorrow: a Study and a History*. But that too is mysteriously missing from my library at home, so I'll have to put the matter to one side.

with this fairly restrained title, Lancellotti, in Hakewill's opinion, managed to say just about everything Hakewill himself had said in his strictly contemporaneous *Apologie.* To prove the point, Hakewill adopts the age-old practice — no one knows when *it* actually began — of drawing a close parallel between his text and Lancellotti's. He translates the titles of every one of Lancellotti's chapters in order "that it may appeare in how many pointes hee accords with mee." As far as I can make out, the Englishman is deriving comfort from this multiple coincidence of points in his work and in the Italian's; he is not grousing at having been scooped, or nearly so. Having been up against some heavy fire from critics during the eight years between the first and third editions of the *Apologie,* Hakewill seeks moral support for his opinions, finds it in their agreement with the opinions of Lancellotti and cheerfully pays the price of abandoning any claims to decisive and unique originality for them.* Evidently, even scholars (at least of the 17th

* The essentials of the Hakewill-Lancellotti story I had picked up from Jones while I was still ensconced in my study, and so unable to pore through Hakewill for myself. Now that I have scrupulously read and re-read every page of that wordy book, I am thrown into a state of acute bewilderment. The volume, including the two books added to the third edition, contains not the least scintilla of the story told by Jones which I have faithfully reported to you! At most, there are two miserable allusions of remote pertinence: one to "Lancellot" and the other to "secundo Lancellotti." Yet so circumstantial is Jones's account that I cannot bring myself to expunge it. After all, *se non è vero, è molto ben trovato* (or, as Hakewill might say, if it is not true, it is very well invented). In the spirit of atonement for my vicarious sin of innovation, I give you the title page of Secondo Lancellotti's book, which *does* exist.§

§ But had I looked into the *second* edition of Hakewill rather than the third and studied the 64 pages of Advertisements

L'HOGGIDI'
OVERO
IL MONDO NON PEGGIORE
ne più calamitoso del paſſato.

DEL P. D. SECONDO LANCELLOTI
Da Perugia Abate Oliuetano.

Accademico Infenfato, Affidato, & Humoriſta.

ALLA SANTITA' DI N. S.

APA VRBANO VIII.
Quarta Impreſſione.

CON LICENZA DE' SVP. ET PRIVILEGIO.

IN VENETIA, MDCXXXVII.
Appreſſo gli Guerigli.

century) can be scared into putting other things ahead of
public recognition of their originality of thought.

❦ xxii

BUT NOT altogether so. Deeply hurt by a wholesale
pilfering of the method and substance of his treatise,
Hakewill cries out his protest in "An Advertisement to
the Reader occasioned by this third impression." Evidently, Hakewill could take just so much of a bad thing
before striking back. At least, that seems to be the sense
of his announcing in the Advertisement that since the
second edition of his book, "some occurents have falne
out which I could not well passe over in silence." He
breaks the silence with a bang, identifying the thief with
withering scorn and describing the theft with deadly
precision:

> About two yeares since there came to mine hands a
> little booke, intituled De Naturae constantia . . .*
> The author of it calles himselfe Iohannes Ionstonus a

at the close, I should not have falsely indicted Jones for my
faux pas. I repeat: mea culpa.

* As a scholar, you will of course not be content with this short
title of the book in which Johnstone engages in literary larceny
on the grand scale. Here, then, is the title in full: De Naturae
constantia, seu Diatribe in qua posteriorum temporum cum
prioribus collationem, mundum nec ratione suipsius, nec ratione
partium, universaliter et Perpetuo in pejus ruere ostenditur.
Should you not want to plow through Johnstone's tortuous
Latin, you might turn to the English translation by J. Rowland,
published in 1657: An history of the constancy of nature,
single copies of which can be found in your own incomparable
library at Harvard, in the libraries of the University of California at Berkeley and at Los Angeles, in the library of the
University of Pennsylvania and — wonderful to tell — in the
Detroit Public Library.

Polonian. This booke after the receit therof I soone perused, and found it to be upon the matter little else but a translation of mine contracted into a narrower compasse, the methode is mine, the arguments are mine, the authorities mine, the instances mine, but by mangling and gelding of it, hee hath neither retained the force of my reasons, nor the face of my discourse . . .

I care not to pursue the question whether the man who "calls himself John Johnstone a Pole" actually stole and compressed the prolix, sententious and insufferably dull substance of Hakewill's noble Elizabethan prose. Whatever the truth of the indictment, it is quite in keeping with the practice of the time to charge, and be charged with, plagiarism. Can you think of any one of consequence in that energetic age * who escaped unscathed, either as victim or alleged perpetrator of literary or scientific theft, and typically, as both filcher and filchee? I cannot.

In that day, practically no one was safe from the charges and countercharges of pillage in the public prints. Even that saintly tinker's son, John Bunyan, did

---

* Not only contemporaries were subjected to the charge. See how Joseph Glanvill, that 17th-century divine to whom we are forever indebted for the unforgettable meteorological metaphor, "the climate of opinion," riddles the character of The Philosopher: ". . . in the *absence* of this *Art* [of printing], 'twas easie enough for one *Aristotle* to *destroy* the most considerable *Remains* of the *Ancients,* that the power of his *great* Scholarship put into his hands; which, 'tis credibly reported of him, that he did, to procure more *fame* for his *own* Performances: as also to *conceal* his *thefts,* and injurious dealings with those *venerable* Sages, whom he seems to take a great delight to *contradict* and *expose,* as I have elsewhere proved." You will find this composite indictment of theft and forgery in Glanvill's *Essays on Several Important Subjects in Philosophy and Relig-*

not escape (and so was driven to this kind of defensive versifying in the preface to his *Holy War*):

Some say Pilgrim's Progress is not mine,
Insinuating as if I would shine
In name and fame by the worth of another,
Like some made rich by robbing of their brother.

Or that so fond I am of being sire,
I'll father bastards, or, if need require,
I'll tell a lie in print to get applause.
I scorn it; John such dirt-heap never was
Since God converted him. Let this suffice
To show why I my Pilgrim patronize.

It came from my own heart, so to my head,
And thence into my fingers trickled;
Then to my pen, from whence immediately
On paper I did dripple it daintily.

Manner and matter too was all mine own;
Nor was it unto any mortal known,
Till I had done it. Nor did any then,
By books, by wit, by tongue, or hand, or pen,
Add five words to it, or wrote half a line
Thereof; the whole and every whit is mine.*

ion. London: Printed by *J. D.* for *John Baker*, at the Three Pidgeons, and *Henry Mortlock*, at the Phoenix in St. *Pauls* Church-Yard, 1676, pp. 31–2.
* Surely, the protesting John convicts himself in the last three lines of this versified defense as he echoes Omar Khayyam's manner and even a little of his matter. Recall only Stanza 71 of Fitzgerald's immortal paraphrased translation of the *Rubaiyat:*

The Moving Finger writes, and having writ,
Moves on: nor all your Piety nor Wit
    Shall lure it back to cancel half a Line,
Nor all your Tears wash out a Word of it.

Now note the tell-tale signs: "having writ" in the one and "wrote" in the other; "wit" in both; and, most tellingly of all,

69

Now it is not my business to take sides in a controversy that I stumble upon only in search for the
antecedents of Newton's Aphorism. Yet I must say that a
charge of plagiary levelled against a great and good man
with grace abounding is, on its own face, incredible. Can
we conceive of this man, grave and sedate of countenance,
"his forehead something high and his habit always
modest," prolifically stealing another's parable, this man
who with prelapsarian innocence masochistically confessed that the four chief sins of his youth were dancing,
playing tipcat,* ringing the bells of the parish church and
— reading the history of Bevis of Southampton, a
work of *fiction?* The very accusation is an absurdity self-
revealed.

As with John Bunyan, so with many, many of his
contemporaries: they were the targets and often the
entirely innocent targets for calumnious charges of
plagiarism. The calendar of such indictments is far too
full for me to list it here in its entirety and the charges
too unsavory for me to rake them up anew, yet, as an
historian committed to recording even the most squalid
truths, I cannot pass over them entirely. So I report that

---

the identical "half a line" that ends the penultimate lines in
both. Was proof ever more positive?

Or does the matter stand quite the other way? Clearly, John
could scarcely have borrowed from Omar since the *Rubaiyat*
did not become known to the West until the magic year of
1859, when Edward Fitzgerald published his lovely and
imaginative translation. Must we not therefore leap to John's
defense against this newest charge of plagiary and suppose
rather that his verse lingered, in cryptomnesic fashion, in Fitzgerald's subconscious memory? Or do we have here still another
case of multiple independent invention in poetry?

* As a boy playing tipcat in the narrow streets of Philadelphia,
I never once supposed that I was indulging in a rural pastime
well known for centuries in the English kingdom, let alone

Arago maintains of Descartes' observation, "the earth [does] not differ from the sun in any other respect than in being smaller," that "Leibniz conferred upon this hypothesis the honour of appropriating it to himself." John Wallis, in turn, accuses "this Descartes [who] has received in geometry very great light from our Oughtred and our Harriot, and has followed their track though he carefully suppressed their names." In still another turn, John Aubrey writes of the indignant accuser Wallis:

> he is extremely greedy of glorie, that he steales feathers from others to adorne his owne cap; *e.g.* he lies at watch at Sir Christopher Wren's discourse, Mr. Robert Hooke's, Dr William Holder, &c; putts downe their notions in his Note booke, and then prints it, without owneing the Authors. This frequently, of which they complain. [And then comes the one extenuating circumstance:] But though he does an injury to the Inventors, he does good to Learning, in publishing such curious notions, which the author (especially Sir Christopher Wren) might never have the leisure to write of himselfe.

indulging myself in sin. Whenever I struck the cat [§] (or tip-cat) with a stick in such manner as to cause it to spring up preparatory to its being knocked a far distance, I thought I was only having some innocent fun while testing my athletic prowess. Even now, when I know better, I am inclined to defend my boyish self; unlike the sinful Bunyan, I never went so far, in those youthful days, as to read the history of Bevis.

[§] In my youth I was not a confirmed ailurophile; that was to come much later. Even so, I was a reasonably humane child not apt to strike that carnivorous quadruped, *Felis domesticus*. No, the cat I struck was a wooden cat, a small piece of wood tapered at each end which, when competently hit by the cat-stick, would spring from the ground to be driven far off by a hefty side stroke.

Descartes, Leibniz and Wallis, Wren, Hooke and
Holder (and I might as well add Flamsteed, Newton and
Halley, Pascal, Cassini and Fabri) are only a few of the
many who both charged plagiary and were charged with
it. Things got so bad that Robert Boyle published a long
Advertisement, back in 1688, announcing his intended
course of defense against this epidemic kleptomania. He
writes of himself in the discouraged third person, that
several writers have been emboldened,

> both formerly and of late, to usurp from him a great
> many things whereof they were not the authors;
> sometimes transcribing this or that particular out of
> his book into theirs, and sometimes transferring whole
> sets of experiments, if not reasonings too, perhaps
> somewhat abridged or otherwise disguised. And this
> hath been done by some of them, without so much as
> naming the true author, and sometimes naming him
> indeed as it were incidentally, and peradventure
> reflectingly, for some inconsiderable part of what they
> took from him. Of these several sorts of plagiaries, it
> would not be difficult to give particular instances: it
> will be done, if it be thought fit and desired.

And so Boyle resolves, as a simple act of self defense, "to
write in single sheets, and other loose papers, that the
ignorance of the coherence might keep men from thinking
them worth stealing." * From all this, you plainly see
that Hakewill was not alone in advertising his complaints
against larcenous wits of the time.

* Should you want to read the whole of Boyle's extensive indictment, you need only turn to the first of those six lovely folio
volumes, *The Works of the Honourable Robert Boyle,* to
which is prefixed *The Life of the Author,* by J. Birch, London,
1772, pp. cxxv–cxxviii, cxxii–cxxiv.

⟪ *xxiii*

SO MUCH for Hakewill and plagiary; back, once again, to the giant-dwarf simile. You may possibly remember my conjecture that Newton got on to this figure from Burton and I think I ought to tell you that I'm beginning to waver on this guess. I'm not made any more confident about it even when I now discover that the incomparable scholar George Sarton had made the same guess long before I got around to it. You will remember that back in December 1935, in *Isis,* the journal of the history of science he founded and then edited for thirty-five years or so, Sarton had introduced a query, in the section devoted to "notes and correspondence," about the history of the saying: "standing on the shoulders of giants." * In this query, Sarton remarks that "Newton probably obtained it from Burton, whose *Anatomy* was already appearing in its eighth edition in the year of (1676) Newton's letter to Hooke" (in which, you'll remember, Newton uses his version of the saying for the first and,

---

* The more precise citation is *Isis,* December 1935, xxiv, 107–9. This, you will find, is one of the two citations I mentioned at the beginning of this letter. Not having my file of *Isis* here in my study at home, I sent for the two numbers that were in my office at Columbia, together with a third number which has more on the subject. Now, I had evidently read Sarton's query a long time ago; at least, I better had, since I cite it in print. Yet in arriving at my guess of how Newton may have come by the saying, I had no idea that I was walking in Sarton's spacious footsteps. Evidently, one can't remember everything one has read. This is the more interesting since I now consider this guess of Sarton's (and secondarily and temporarily, mine) as questionable at best and thoroughly mistaken at worst. If you'll return to the text of this letter, you'll soon see why.

so far as we know, the only time). Sarton was right in being cautious, because it now seems that the Aphorism, in one form or another, was being repeated on all sides by men who were rushing into print to help win the battle of the books during the seventeenth century.

By this time, we might describe the Aphorism, in a fit of alliterative paronomasia, as a mnemonic gnome about gnomes on the shoulders of giants. And that, I suppose, makes me a gnomologist—twice over.

ℭ *xxiv*

WE'VE already come on Goodman and Hakewill as disseminators of the saying, but there were plenty of others.

Turn for a moment to France for a case in point. It was perhaps inevitable that, as a friar of the Minim mendicant order, Père Marin Mersenne should pick up the dwarf-on-giant simile for, naturally, he would be sensitive to the usually neglected merits of minimism and minimists.* I wish there were time and space enough to sing the praises of the good Father whose many-sided role in providing a great clearinghouse for early seventeenth-century science is now too often forgotten. (Rather than "clearinghouse," I would do better to say that he was one of the great "philosophical merchants," as Robert Boyle

---

* As you see, I am sceptical of the alleged wisdom incorporated in the old maxim that the law does not concern itself with exceedingly small matters: *de minimis non curat lex.* The maxim may be good enough for the famed "young man whose name was X, who had a very small - - - - - of - - -, ... ," but, nonsense-verse notwithstanding, it is not good enough for me.

described the scientific intelligencers of the time or, even better, in the words of Carlo Dati, "Gran trafficante fù il Mersenno tenendo commercio con tutti i Litterati d'Europa.") * But I cannot begin to recount Mersenne's many achievements as a transmitter of scientific knowledge and an evoker of scientific excellence. It may be enough to say that he conveyed many of Galileo's observations to France (often before Galileo got around to publishing them); that he needled Descartes into putting some of his salient ideas into print; that he wrote brilliantly perceptive accounts of the necessity for *both* specialization and collaboration in science; and that he created a small informal circle to discuss contemporary arts and sciences (a circle whose meetings were assiduously attended by the elder Pascal, often accompanied by the boy-genius, Blaise).†

But this is about as much attention as we can afford to give to Mersenne the man and his circle of intimates, though you might possibly glimpse the cross-pressures to

* Dati wrote this opinion that Mersenne was a great trafficker in scientific intelligence, holding commerce with all the learned men of Europe, in his Italian (but here gallicized) *Lettre à Philatète*, published under the pseudonym of Timauro Anziate, in Florence, 1663. I preserve the French version of the title because my source for this piece of information – Robert Lenoble, *Mersenne ou La Naissance du Mécanisme*, Paris: J. Vrin, 1943 – does so, as does *his* source, Adrien Baillet, *La Vie de Monsieur Des-Cartes*, Paris, 1691.
† Mersenne soon recognized the young Pascal's genius. And the elder Pascal, Étienne, soon recognized the intellectual pleasures gained by being in the vicinity of Mersenne. Pascal Sr. even gave up his rented house in the Rue de Tisseranderie (a street delightfully intersected by the Street of the Two Doors, the Street of the Bad Boys, Cock Street and the Street of the Devilish Wind), moved for a time to the Left Bank and then took up residence close to the Friary of Père Mersenne where he remained until 1648, the year of Mersenne's death.

which this thoroughly congenial man was subjected when
I report the letter in which Descartes implored Mersenne
to preserve his, Descartes', intellectual property intact:

> I also beg you to tell Hobbes as little as possible
> about what you know of my unpublished opinions, for
> if I'm not greatly mistaken, he is a man who is
> seeking to acquire a reputation at my expense, — and
> through shady practices.*

Despite the difficulties he confronted in trying to keep
the peace among his many scientist-friends, Mersenne
managed to come upon the giant-dwarf Aphorism a good
forty years before Newton. Naturally, he *minimizes*
the Aphorism. He excludes all reference to both the giants
and dwarfs but retains intact the imagery of the enlarged
vision that comes to us as we stand on the shoulders of
our predecessors:

> . . . car, comme l'on dit, il est bien facile et mesme
> nécessaire de voir plus loin que nos devanciers, lors
> que nous sommes montez sur leurs espaules: ce qui
> n'empesche pas que nous leur soyons redevables.†

"*Comme l'on dit* . . ." Again, the figure figures as a
virtual commonplace — in 1634 and in France! Although,

* Should you want more specimens of this kind of mistrust
among the intellectual élite of the time, you have only to look
into René Descartes, *Oeuvres* (edited by Charles Adam and
Paul Tannery), *Correspondance*, Paris, 1899, Vol. III–V. The
particular slur on Hobbes appears in Vol. III, p. 320.
† This beautifully compact and generous version of the Aphorism appears in Mersenne's *Questions Harmoniques, dans
lesquelles sont contenuës plusieurs choses remarquables pour
la Physique, pour la Morale, et pour les autres sciences* [in-
cluding, I might happily add, some observations on what was
to become known as "Sociology"]. A Paris, chez Jacques
Villery, 1634. Avec Privilège du Roy. I have it on the authority
of Lenoble (for the reference, see the third note before
this one) that it appears on page 262 of that 276-page book.

considering Mersenne's intricate network of communication, this inference from the French idiom does not necessarily follow. With his farflung and relatively prompt sources of information, Mersenne might have come to believe that even the very newest idea was well-known and much bruited. Still, *"comme l'on dit"* speaks volumes about the currency of the Aphorism, years before Newton was born.

And quietly contrasting with the noisy quarrels between the advocates of Ancients and of Moderns is Mersenne's gentle reminder that although we Moderns can easily and even necessarily see farther than our predecessors (if only because we are mounted upon their shoulders), this does not keep us from being beholden to them. In short: to each his due. Or, as I have had occasion to write elsewhere, "the community of scientists extends both in time and space."

Here, as throughout his adult life, Father Mersenne remains a statesman of science. So much for France.

* * *

We return to England and now visit the poet and pamphleteer, John Hall.* At age 22, he was publishing

---

* This is the John Hall who died in 1656 at the early age of 29. Since he was something of a youthful prodigy — his first essays, published at nineteen, created a considerable stir — he managed to do a good bit before his premature death. In the light of current medical doctrine about the relation of obesity to longevity, it's of some interest that Hall greatly objected to any form of exercise, and " 'being inclined to pursinesse & fatnesse, rather than he would use any great motion, he thought fitter to prevent it by frequent swallowing down of pebble-stones, which proved effectuall.' " He was also a great friend of Hobbes. At any rate, don't confuse this John Hall with the John Hall who was Shakspere's son-in-law; that one had nothing at all to do

a tract against the current decline of standards in English universities, urging, in a manner that makes him seem almost twentieth-century in outlook, that they have more endowed professorships. He called his tract of 1649 *An Humble Motion to the Parliament of England concerning the Advancement of Learning: And Reformation of the Universities*, thus achieving a middle-sized title that, with true contemporary insight and historiographical prescience, couples phrases reminiscent of both Bacon and Nonconformism, thus simultaneously endearing himself to the reigning Cromwellians and to later scholars such as Max Weber, Dorothy Stimson, James B. Conant, Richard Foster Jones and, I must add, myself, who have variously identified intimate connections between Puritanism and the efflorescence of science in England.

Hall has barely begun his *Humble Motion* — he is only on page six — when he is ready to draw upon the now abundantly familiar simile. In true obstetrical style, he delivers himself of the opinion that

we seem insensible of that great Genius which animates and conducts this present Age, and therefore sleight the discovery of that in particular persons, who

---

with the giant-dwarf simile. Nor should he be confused with the John Hall who, as a divine, occupied himself instead with such writings as this: "Grace leading unto Glory: or a Glimpse of the Glorie, Excellencie, and Eternity of Heaven . . ." *Our* John Hall was something of a rake; in fact, Anthony à Wood, that well-born and rich biographer of his contemporaries, went so far as to say in the classic *Athenæ Oxonienses* that "his debauchery and intemperance diverted him from the more serious studies." It's the talented alcoholic, not his more sober and pedestrian namesakes, who interests us here.

being many times big with Heroick designes, perish
for want of assistance in the delivery; or in case they
be delivered, are found to have wasted themselves in
the production of a weak or abortive infant, which
otherwise might have been strong and goodly; whereas
men if they would but set themselves to awaite and
receive every glimpse and dawning of knowledge (or
at least cherish those that would doe so) would finde
it easie to bring into a just and beautifull body,
and make an happy inversion of that common
saying, that our Ancients were Gyants, and we are
Dwarfs.

I need hardly point out the two features of the concluding observation by Hall that stare us in the face, —
but I shall. First, he refers to the Aphorism as "that
common saying," this, mind you, in 1649, a full quarter-
century before Newton adapted it to his purposes. And
that it was a common saying we may safely infer from
the fact that Hall evidently expected the allusion to be
understood by the *Rump*, those fifty Independent members of the Long Parliament that were then holding firm,
at least in theory, to the legislative power. Second, the
simile is well on the way to being entirely inverted;
indeed, Hall is proposing that it should be. In this inversion, the moderns, presumably because they are puffed up
with knowledge, become giant-like in contrast to the
ancients who lived at an earlier age before knowledge had
greatly accumulated and so were condemned to remain
puny and dwarflike.

You will better understand why Hall considered the
saying familiar enough to qualify as commonplace when
I tell you that a generation before, in 1621, Nathanael
Carpenter, a philosopher of sorts, had already published
his first book, *Philosophia libera triplici exercitationum*

decade proposita,* in which, as you're beginning to
suspect, he had found the saying familiar enough to justify
his ringing in some changes on it. I don't have the exact
wording of his paraphrase at hand. But the gist of it is
(as I understand from Jones) that "if in the decrepit age
of the world, the moderns are but boys sitting on the
shoulders of the gigantic ancients," then the boys, with
the help given them by their predecessors, can ferret out
those secrets of nature that the ancients only guessed at.
What seems to be happening, in this scrambled version
of Carpenter's, is a kind of halfway merger between the
giant-dwarf simile and Francis Bacon's ingenious paradox, *Antiquitas saeculi, juventus mundi.* What Bacon
meant by this, of course, is that when you start to
think about the matter, it turns out that the moderns
are the true ancients, and the ancients, so-fallaciously-
called, the youth of the human race. The longer that
mankind has been around — and in Bacon's time, it's the
moderns who have been around the longest (just as

* For reasons not entirely clear to me, Carpenter published this
book in Frankfort, under the anything but provincial pseudonym, N. C. Cosmopolitanus. Why he should have thought that
his anti-Aristotelianism was dangerous enough to warrant this
double caution, I don't know. Anyway, it wasn't and when later
editions — there were three more of them — were issued (to be
sure, after his death), they appeared under his name. There's
really nothing else of particular interest about Carpenter, unless
I stretch a point. How about this? Archbishop Ussher thought
well of him and it's said, "tempted him into Ireland," where a
short while later he died. As for Archbishop Ussher, I don't
have to tell you who *he* was. But why does everybody remember
only that he worked out a chronology that firmly fixed the
creation in the year 4004 B.C.? Is it simply because this official
date was for so long a time fixed in the margins of the Author-
ized Version of the Bible? After all, he was a good man and
a great scholar; it's a pity to have all his merits obscured by his
one dramatic misadventure into religio-scientific chronology.

in our time, it's us, and after us, who knows?) — then the older and so the more ancient it is. There's a rhetorical switch in the argument, all right, but Bacon emerges with the right answer, even though he fudges a bit to have it come out as he wants.

Anyway, Carpenter was writing his *Philosophia Libera* in the very year that Bacon was in headlines, Coke having just succeeded in getting Commons to send to the House of Lords charges that Bacon had engaged in bribery on the grand scale. Now Bacon may or may not have published his paradox by then; I don't have my set of Bacon's writing at home so that I must wait to check this point.* But whatever the actual historical filiation be-

* Of course, he had — more than once (and I take no pride in having forgotten that he had first published the paradox as far back as 1605 when, in *The Advancement of Learning,* he put it so: "And to speak truly, 'Antiquitas saeculi juventus mundi.' These times are the ancient times, when the world is ancient, and not those which we account ancient 'ordine retrogrado,' by a computation backward from ourselves."). And only now do I rediscover, what I must of course have known only to forget, that Bacon loved the idea enough to embellish it analogically in his *Novum Organum* (Aphorism LXXXIV, I believe it is, where he puts it somewhat as follows:

> For the old age of the world is to be accounted the true antiquity; and this is the attribute of our own times, not of that earlier age in which the ancients lived; and which, though in respect of us it was the elder, yet in respect of the world it was the younger. And truly as we look for greater knowledge of human things and a riper judgment in the old man than in the young, because of his experience and of the number and variety of the things which he has seen and heard and thought of; so in like manner from our age, if it but knew its own strength and chose to essay and exert it, much more might fairly be expected than from the ancient times, inasmuch as it is a more advanced age of the world, and stored and stocked with experiments and observations.)

Let us continue to refer to this thought as the *Baconian Paradox,* just as was the practice here and there in the seven-

tween Bacon and Carpenter — Jones seems to think there
was a close one — it is evident that Carpenter has taken
the giant-dwarf simile and the equivalent of the Baconian
paradox, mixed them up, and emerged with modern boys
who are really more informed than the people of an
earlier time, for these boys actually represent the old age
of the world. It's quite a scrambled figure, this historical
omelet of similes, but knowing as we do that only good
things went into it, we need not find it indigestible.

❡ XXV

NOT MUCH later, in 1642 — the year of Newton's
birth and so far removed from *his* version of the Aphorism — the renowned Thomas Fuller served up the same
dish of Bacon's Paradox, seasoned with just a dash of the
Aphorism.* He is presenting a series of maxims that
characterize "The True Church Antiquary" when, in
Maxim viii, he amalgamates Aphorism and Paradox, so:

> He doth not so adore the Ancients as to despise the
> Moderns. Grant them but dwarfs, yet stand they on

---

teenth century, even though, as Ellis and Spedding bear witness,
the essentials of the paradox appear, before Bacon, in Galileo,
in Campanella, in Casmann's *Problemata Marina* of 1546, and
most of all, in Giordano Bruno's *Cena di Cenere*. As a matter of
fact, you have only to look into the second book of *Esdras*,
those books of the Old Testament and Pseudepigrapha, to detect the germ of the paradox about the ancient youth of the
world, thus: "Seculum perdidit juventutem suam, et tempora
appropinquant senescere" (this at 2 *Esdras*, xiv, 10).
* Fuller sets it down in *The Holy State and the Profane State;*
I have had to use the third edition where it can be found in
chapter 6, pp. 63–5.

giants' shoulders, and may see the further. Sure, as stout champions * of Truth follow in the rere, as ever marched in the front. Besides, as † one excellently observes, Antiquitas seculi, juventus mundi. These times are the ancient times, when the world is ancient . . .

Fuller you will remember as that cleric much beloved by many worthies, from Aubrey to his posthumous admirer Coleridge ("God bless thee, dear old man!"). One can understand why this "pregnant wit" was loved and esteemed, as he is pictured running around London with his big book under one arm and his little wife under the other. Nor is there any great mystery about the ease with which he wrote so many books, big and small, for he had hit upon an admirable device which more of us could put to the same ingenious use: he would simply write the first word on every line on a sheet and then fill up all the remaining space, a most infectious method for rapid composition.

Fuller thus provides us with a quick remedy for periodically soothing the *itch to publish*. Physicians of the soul will at once see beneath this plain English phrase and recognize the malignant disease known, since the days of Juvenal, as the *insanabile scribendi cacoëthes*. Its etiology is obscure but epidemiological evidence affords some clues. There are indications that its frequency increases steadily in those educational or research

---

* Mark this well for, soon in this narrative, we shall come upon Alexander Ross, an ingenious reactionary who works wonders with his phrase "the ancient Champions of learning" unlike the moderate Fuller who here makes a place for the champions of truth in both the new and the old times.
† *This* note is Fuller's, not mine: Sr. Fran. Bacon, *Advance. of Learn.*, p. 46.

institutions which lavish rewards upon the prolific author of scientific papers or scholarly books. Age seems to be an important predisposing factor, largely as the result of a basic social process: with the passing of years, scientists and scholars who have published in abundance are actively solicited by editors, bookmen, and publishers for still more wordage to be put into print. Nevertheless, the general liability to the disease seems less widespread than the nothing-to-report syndrome (although, on many an occasion, the two have a way of coinciding). Sucklings are rarely attacked. A few scientists and scholars escape in their early professional years; others escape until full maturity; a good many never take it. But with the vast growth in the number of periodicals and with the urgent needs of publishers to keep their presses busy, the disease threatens to become endemic. Attacks are recurrent, never conferring immunity. Susceptibility may be determined by intrapsychic injection of the toxin — what might hereafter be most appropriately called *the Merton test*. With a positive reaction, signs appear in ten minutes (or less) after seeing one's name in print, reaching toward an asymptotic maximum with each successive injection. The local reaction subsides temporarily but swiftly returns. The source of infection often remains undiscovered in particular cases, especially when insufficient attention is devoted to the social ecology of the patient. *Carriers* are important, especially those who have been abundantly rewarded for effusions of print. Onset is as a rule sudden. preceded by a slight, scarcely noticeable publication. The fever to publish is intense; rising rapidly, it may within a few years reach the degree of 15 or 20 publications annually. The articles or books are unusually dry and to the reader's eye may give a sensation of acute boredom. Complications and sequelae are too numerous to be considered here.* It is a pity, therefore, that Fuller never made widely known his easy means for satisfying the itch to publish. He might have spared many generations of sufferers the acute discomforts of that irritating need to get things into print. But now that I have rediscovered his plain and inexpensive remedy, the itch can be relieved just as soon as it begins — simply by scratching some initiating words down on paper. You may have your own favorite description of this "shrewd, sound-hearted and sensible" physician to the literati, but give me the incomparable Aubrey's:

> Thomas Fuller was of a middle stature [*i.e.* situate 'twixt giant and dwarf]; strong sett; curled haire; a very working head, in so much that, walking and meditating before dinner, he would eate-up a penny loafe, not knowing that he did it. His naturall memorie was very great, to which he added the Art of Memorie: he would repeat to you forwards and backwards all the signs from Ludgate to Charing-crosse.

> According to Pepys's testimony, Dr. Fuller could also deliver a "poor dry sermon."

❡ xxvi

THERE is no need to acquaint you with the fact — which I mention only to demonstrate to you that I too know

---

* The newest researches into this ailment do not require me to change more than a word here and there in this nearly definitive account of the *insanabile scribendi cacoëthes* since I first published it in "The Ambivalence of Scientists," *Bulletin of the Johns Hopkins Hospital*, February 1963, Vol. 112, No. 2, 77–97, at 89n.

it to be fact — that the Baconian Paradox and the Aphorism are untiringly amalgamated throughout the seventeenth century. In 1665, not long after Fuller, — and so still a good ten years before Newton got around to the Aphorism in his letter — one Marchamount Nedham (or, should you prefer, Marchamont Needham) marries the Paradox-and-Aphorism in an indissoluble union, this event taking place in his *Medela Medicinae: a Plea for the Free Profession and a Renovation of the Art of Physick.* He quotes the Great Instaurator in the now familiar maxim:

> *Indeed, to speak truly,* Antiquitas Seculi, Juventus Mundi; *Antiquity of Time is the Youth of the World. Certainly our Times are the ancient Times, when the World is now ancient; and not those which we count ancient,* ordine retrogrado, *by a computation backward from our own Times.* [This you will find early on in the book: pages 6–7.]

Having transmitted the Baconian arithmetic of generations, Nedham could have gone on to transmit the Aphorism as well. After all, he had been exposed to it more than once. This we know from his fond allusions to "Dr Hackwel, in the Preface to his Apology" and, before him, to the "famous Quercetan." But Nedham was a constitutionally perverse fellow who simply would not behave as he ought. As a result, he cannot bring himself to cite the Aphorism straight from the shoulder, but skirts it in such an allusive way that only a committed scholarship can detect his peripheral allusions. See how he plays with the imagery of the Aphorism, as he writes of "Heathen Logick and Philosophy":

> . . . they are fallen now so low, that the most excellent Sr. *Kenelm Digby,* and that noble Philosopher

Mr *Boyle,* [here it comes] and others not so tall as they, do not only look over but far beyond them; for, to say no more at present [and, as it turns out, to say no more of this later as well], the Lord *Bacon* hath shewn of how little use that Logick is, and *that the Physicks were corrupted by their being accomodated thereto;* which makes that searching Wit and learned Head Dr *Henry More* of *Cambridge . . .* in a Latine Epistolary Discourse of his newly published, concerning the *Cartesian* Philosophy, vouchsafe *Aristotle* no greater title than this, *Argutus ille Graeculus* [note the diminutive well] in comparison of the Philosophers of latter Times; yet he rode a long while upon the shoulders [!] of the blind World, while others have walked afoot . . . or have been laid by the heels . . . [all these figures on pages 11–12]

Just consider the wretchedly wayward behavior of the man. He fragments the Aphorism and distributes the pieces at random. He has Digby and Boyle peering far beyond the non-ancient Ancients, partly owing to their great intellectual stature but not entirely so, since some of their smaller contemporaries can also gaze at vistas closed to philosophers of the past. Nedham pauses for a moment and then begrudgingly provides us, thanks to Henry More, with another snippet: Aristotle is a Graeculus, a decidedly *small* Greek. And where does he finally locate this little man? On the *shoulders* of the unseeing world. Surely no other author we have met has gone to such great pains to avail himself extensively of the Aphorism while firmly refusing to quote it in so many words.

But then, what else can we expect of such a one as Nedham? This unprincipled journalist, this paid assassin of character, this columnist, this calumnist would of course behave just so. (So quick was his reaction-time that he was always ready for second thoughts.) Only re-

call his mutable and turbulent career. We discover him
first in his green years — he is only 25 — when in that
scurrilous sheet, *Mercurius Britannicus,* he raises a "Hue
and Cry after a Wilful King," said King then being
Charles I. Two years later, Nedham is at his "Majesty's
royal feet" kissing his Majesty's royal hand.* Cromwell
takes over and our adroit friend turns his coat again,
writing with expedient passion his "Discourse of the Ex-
cellency of a Free State above a Kingly Government."
Properly appreciated by the newmade powers that be,
Nedham becomes the proud recipient of an annual pen-
sion of £100 "whereby he may be enabled to subsist while
he endeavours the service of the Commonwealth." When
Cromwell dies and Charles II ascends into power, can
Nedham be far behind? The question answers itself. He
resharpens his quill and assails the parliamentary opposition to the divinely ordained King. For this royal service,
he graciously accepts the mundane sum of £500. Understandably, then, this master of improvisation treats our
Aphorism as he treated all else: in a self-serving fashion
that sacrifices integrity (of quotation) to an expedient
fragmentation, in which the several pieces of the dismem-
bered Aphorism must wait three centuries to be laboriously fitted together.

ℂ *xxvii*

IT IS A relief to turn from the rascally Nedham to the
virtuous Thomas Sprat who, in euphonious sequence, was

* The quoted phrase, as you will instantly recognize, is from
Robert Hooke's dedication of his classic *Micrographia* (1665)
to Charles II.

born at Beaminster, was installed as dean at Westminster
and was elevated as Bishop at Rochester. In the year
1667 — which approaches still more closely to the year
of Newton's Aphorism — "fat Tom Sprat" (he loved good
living) published his beautiful *History of the Royal-
Society of London,* a book much admired and often
reprinted, in which, among a vast variety of other accomplishments, he censured with an admirable diligence the
prevalent abject "slavery to dead Mens names" and employed the Aphorism to good purpose as, with a keen
EIE for the power of the rhetorical question, he asked
about those who advocated the cause of the Ancients:

> What kind of behavior do they exact from us . . . ?
> That we should reverence the Footsteps of *Antiquity?*
> We do it most unanimously. That we should sub-
> scribe to their sense, before our own? We are willing,
> in probabilitics; but we cannot, in matters of Fact: for
> in them we follow the most antient Author of all
> others, even *Nature* it self. Would they have us make
> our eies behold things, at no farther distance than
> they saw? That is impossible; seeing we have the ad-
> vantage of standing upon their shoulders.

When the matter is put so plainly — and crisply — it is
not for me to add a long and tedious gloss.

ℂ *xxviii*

TOWARD the end of the century — we are now located
some sixteen years *after* Newton's distinctly private use
of the Aphorism in his letter to Hooke — Sir Thomas

89

Pope Blount beats Nedham all hollow and even surpasses Sprat. In his *Essays on several subjects,** he comes straight out with it, stating both the Paradox and the Aphorism in their entirety, as you can see for yourself:

> Let not Men deceive themselves, and think that we live in the Dregs of Time [a phrasing, you will grant, that demands our instant appreciation], and what mighty advantages the Ancients (as they call them) had over us; . . . For Antiquity consists in the old age of the world, not in the youth of it. 'T is we who are the Fathers, and of more Authority than former Ages; because we have the advantage of more time than they had, and Truth (we say) [*i.e.* Francis Bacon says] is the Daughter of Time. And besides, our Minds are so far from being impaired, that they improve more and more in acuteness; and being of the same Nature with those of the Ancients, have such an advantage beyond them, as a Pygmy hath upon the

---

* Published in London in 1692; the extract, I should tell you, is from the fifth Essay, pp. 94–5.

And I should confess that in moving on to Blount, I have leaped over a near-miss allusion to the Aphorism that turns up in 1659 in Francis Osborne's *A Miscellany of Sundry Essays, Paradoxes, and Problematical Discourses, Letters and Characters; Together with Political Deductions from the History of the Earl of Essex, Executed under Q. Elizabeth,* the allusion appearing in the essay entitled "Conjectural Queries, or Problematical Paradoxes Concerning Reason, Speech, Learning, Experiments, and other Philosophical Matters," on p. 584 of the only edition available to me, the seventeenth, which was not published until 1673 (but still three years before Newton's private usage of the Aphorism). To be frank about it, I've omitted this allusion out of a growing impatience with those prolific essayists of the day who signal us, by a knowing cue or two, that they are thoroughly familiar with the Aphorism but, flirtatiously, will go no further toward an outright commitment. Should you think that I do Osborne an injustice, let me tell you, first, that this man clearly knew the work of Hakewill (he

shoulders of a Gyant; from whence he beholds not
only so much, but more than his Supporter
doth.

Do not cavil. True, Blount announces in one phrase
that we moderns are more acute than the ancients and in
the next that we are on a par with them, until we clamber
upon them to gain greater vision. But there is a sagacity
in this seeming contradiction that is apparent enough not
to require my elucidation. Yet to measure our tribute to
Sir Thomas with all possible exactness and precision –
neither heaping up an excess nor denying him his due –
you and I should not be too quick to shower kudos on
him; for this scholar, who was himself the beneficiary of
the world's learning (since, in his time, he drew upon
the works of some six hundred learned men), was capable
of saying "There is not a simpler animal and a more
superfluous member of the state than a mere scholar." *

admits as much – for example, on p. 557 of the ninth edition)
and so was almost bound to know the Aphorism and second,
that he guiltily hints at this knowledge in the kind of oblique
language which neither of us can abide:

> And this *inspection into things* at the beginning dim and
> modest, became by handing from one generation to another,
> *so huge a Mountain* in their estimation who presumed to
> have made a full and exact *Survey* of the Land of *Knowledge;*
> that the Giants of Old [there is more than an echo here!],
> they did not only rant it over mens *Persons* and *Consciences,*
> by proportioning what extent of worship befitted the gods,
> but erected their *Pillars* upon the borders of *Philosophy*
> under such an *imperious injunction,* as none, till of late have
> ventured to discover anything beyond them . . .

Need we put up with this sort of thing?

* But, yet again, let us not be too hasty in condemning this
Blount talk. There is an air about his statement that is more
than a little reminiscent of a statement in our own day made by
that profound, enigmatic, and purest of mathematicians, G. H.

ℂ *xxix*

LIKE most of the other writers we have met who in the seventeenth century took up the giant-dwarf simile, Carpenter, Fuller, Nedham, Blount, and Sprat were on the side of the moderns. The one exception, you will remember, was the cleric named, ironically enough, Godfrey Goodman. Now another pessimist joins the gloomy and suspicious Goodman who saw in his present and in that future which is now our present and even beyond that only the prospect of continuing decay: in nature, which grows more barren as it withers in old age and in man, whose loathsome corruption, begun in The Fall, continues to fester until, in the end, it will utterly decay. Goodman's brother-in-gloom was his near-contemporary, that irascible writer of many small books on miscellaneous subjects, Alexander Ross.

ℂ *xxx*

ROSS has not a few claims to enduring fame, it seems. He is, for example, the same Ross who was immortalized

---

Hardy (who happened also to be a passionate fan of his native cricket, international tennis and alien baseball):

> I have never done anything 'useful.' No discovery of mine has made, or is likely to make, directly or indirectly, for good or ill, the least difference to the amenity of the world . . .
> Judged by all practical standards, the value of my mathematical life is nil; and outside mathematics it is trivial anyhow. I have just one chance of escaping a verdict of complete triviality, that I may be judged to have created something

in Butler's couplet (*Hudibras*, pt. i. canto ii.):

> There was an ancient sage philosopher
> That had read Alexander Ross over.

(You will notice that Ogden Nash didn't really invent this sort of thing.)

Almost as though he were revenging himself for this parenthetical remark, Ogden Nash has exacted an eye for an eye. As Butler anticipated him, he has anticipated me. Since he has done so, at least in the public prints, it will do no good to gnaw my lips and gnash my teeth as I dispute my independence, if not my priority, of perception. The sad story, simply told, is this: I had faithfully collected my anthology of Aubrey's eies and even arranged it under the heading that at once imposed itself upon me, only to find, to my horror, that Ogden Nash had, to considerably better effect, been there before me. Here is how it all appears to that master of the rimester's art:

BRIEF LIVES IN NOT SO BRIEF – II *

John Aubrey had a nose for news,
In many a closet did he pry,
And on each side of his nose for news
John Aubrey had an eye for an eie.
See now his note on Francis Bacon,

---

worth creating. And that I have created something is undeniable; the question is about its value.

Blount may have been making A Scholar's Apology in precisely the same ironic sense that Hardy was to make *A Mathematician's Apology*. I am not one to contest the point.

* Copyright © 1962 by Ogden Nash. From *Everyone But Thee and Me* by Ogden Nash, by permission of Little, Brown and Co.; J. M. Dent & Sons Ltd.

93

Who died dishonored and forsaken:
"He had a delicate, lively, hazel Eie; Dr. Harvey tolde
me it was like the Eie of a viper."

When Aubrey drank with Edmund Wyld
At the Blackmores Head in Bloomsbury,
The talk inevitably turned
To aspects of the human eie.
The satirist, Sir John Birkenhead,
Whose poems I have never read,
"Was of midling stature, great goggli eies, not of
sweet aspect."

John Aubrey was a genial man;
I fancy that as he imbibed
A host of eies rolled through his brain,
All clamoring to be described.
Wouldst know the true philosopher's look?
Pause and consider Robert Hooke:
"His head is lardge; his eie full and popping, and not
quick; a grey eie."

He garnered eies in town and shire
And on the winding roads between 'em,
And eies he hadn't seen himself
He snatched from people who had seen 'em.
He gives a glimpse of Sir Walter Raleigh
Not to be found in Lord Macaulay:
"Long-faced and sour eie-lidded, a kind of pigge-eie."

The strictest pedant can but praise
His brisk and lively observation,
And yet it tempted him at times
To publish idle speculation.
How will the schoolgirl in Wisconsin
Shudder to learn that rare Ben Jonson
"Had one eie lower than t'other, and bigger like Clun
the Player; perhaps he begott Clun."

I heard one tell who heard one tell
Who heard one tell of old John Aubrey
That when he emerged from the Blackmores Head
His eie was rather like a strawberry.
— Ogden Nash

❡ *xxxi*

NOW THERE is nothing in this world I detest more than to hear someone say to another who has anticipated his thoughts — or his anthology — *tu quoque:* but you have *also* been anticipated! Not that this defensively offensive maneuver lacks the authority of great men who have executed it with rare skill, the incomparably greatest of these being Sir Isaac Newton himself.* Yet in spite of

---

* Back on page 13, we already witnessed one case in which Newton deployed this tactic of *tu-quoque-ism* against Hooke; here is another. In his letter of 20 June 1686 to Halley, Newton mounts his new counterattack thus:

> I am told by one who had it from another lately present at one of your meetings [of the Royal Society, naturally], how that Mr. Hooke should there make a great stir, pretending that I had it all from him, and desiring they would see that he had justice done him. This carriage toward me is very strange and undeserved; so that I cannot forbear in stating the point of justice, to tell you further, that he has published Borell[i]'s hypothesis in his own name; and the asserting of this to himself and completing it as his own, seems to me the ground of all the stir he makes. (Brewster, *op. cit.*, I, p. 442.)

Should you mistakenly assume that Newton preempted the tactic of *tu-quoque-ism*, I give you just one other among many instances of its effective use. Adam Ferguson replies to the charge of having plagiarized the lectures of his dear friend, Adam Smith, by admitting that "he had derived many notions

95

such glorious precedent, I cannot easily bring myself to practice *tu-quoque-ism*. But here it is not *my* priority or *my* pride I seek to protect in the conflicting claims of Nash and myself to having been first to see the aesthetic merit of bringing together an anthology of eyes (which, as it happens, lay hidden in the copious pages of John Aubrey). I have no need to gasconade. It is a far, far greater name whose inspired priority in the collation of eyes I defend — the name of our master Tristram who comprehensively brought the entire subject within our field of vision by devoting to it, as you will at once see, the whole of

Book VIII, Chapter 25.

An eye is for all the world exactly like a cannon, in this respect; That it is not so much the eye or the cannon, in themselves, as it is the carriage of the eye — and the carriage of the cannon, by which both the one and the other are enabled to do so much execution. I don't think the comparison a bad one; However, as 'tis made and placed at the head of the chapter, as much for use as ornament, all I desire in return, is, that whenever I speak of Mrs. Wadman's eyes (except once in the next period), that you keep it in your fancy.

I protest, Madam, said my uncle Toby, I can see nothing whatever in your eye.

It is not in the white; said Mrs. Wadman: my uncle Toby looked with might and main into the pupil —

---

from a French author, and that Smith had been there before him." At least, that is how the battle for priority is reported by William Robert Scott in his extraordinarily illuminating monograph, *Adam Smith as Student and Professor*, published in Glasgow by Jackson, Son & Co., in 1937. The account appears on p. 119.

Now of all the eyes which ever were created — from your own, Madam, up to those of Venus herself, which certainly were as venereal a pair of eyes as ever stood in a head — there never was an eye of them all, so fitted to rob my uncle Toby of his repose, as the very eye, at which he was looking — it was not, Madam, a rolling eye — a romping or a wanton one — nor was it an eye sparkling — petulant or imperious — of high claims and terrifying exactions, which would have curdled at once that milk of human nature, of which my uncle Toby was made up — but 'twas an eye full of gentle salutations — and soft responses — speaking — not like the trumpet stop of some ill-made organ, in which many an eye I talk to, holds coarse converse — but whispering soft — like the last low accents of an expiring saint — 'How can you live comfortless, Captain Shandy, and alone, without a bosom to lean your head on — or trust your cares to?'

It was an eye —

But I shall be in love with it myself, if I say another word about it.

— It did my uncle Toby's business.

∗   ∗   ∗

And there you have it, the whole of that ophthalmic chapter which fully anticipates both Nash's and my backward glance at Aubrey's "host of eyes." *

We would both do well to step down.

* Unaccountably, Tristram does not cite that admirable Egyptian ophthalmologist of the fourteenth century, Ṣadaqa ibn Ibrāhīm al-Misri al-Ḥanafī al-Shādhilī, who in part I, faṣl 6 of his treatise *Kitāb al-'umda al-kuhlīya fī-l-amrād al-baṣarīya* compares the eyes of Turks, Bedouins, and city people. The reason for the ingenious Tristram's silence could scarcely be the minor detail that the text of the *'Umda* remains unpublished to this day.

What is even more remarkable, Tristram does not even men-

97

⟨ *xxxii*

AND NOW back to our story of the Aphorism and Alexander Ross. He is, I should tell you, the same Ross whose *Virgilius Evangelizans* (*i.e.*, Christ's history in Virgil's words) was, according to that excessively suspicious man, Lauder, plagiarized by Milton. And to close out this short inventory of his claims to historical distinction, he is the Ross who, "Echard says . . . died very rich." Whether this is so or not, we do know that his will provided legacies, some of sizable amounts (up to £700) to the town of Southampton, to the poor householders of All Saints' Parish in Southampton and of the parish of Carisbrooke (wherever that may be),* to the senate of Aberdeen University for the maintenance of two poor

---

tion the Persian littérateur, Sharaf al-dīn al-Ḥasan ibn Muhammad al-Rāmī, whose work we can judge from the evidence internal to the chapter on Mrs. Wadman's eye he must have known — intimately. Al-Rāmī's *Anīs al-'ushshāq* (*The Lover's Companion*, dedicated to Abū-l-Fath Uwais Bahādur [īlkhanī sultān of Ādharbāijān, 1356–73]) was designed to help poets find fitting similes when describing their beloved. Its 19 chapters are nothing if not thorough, dealing not only with eyes but most comprehensively, from head to foot (*a capite ad calcem*) with the hair, forehead, eyebrows, eyelashes, face, down (on lips and cheeks only), mole or beauty spot, lips, teeth, mouth, chin (singles only), neck, bosom (by present-day standards, in surprisingly cursory fashion), arms, fingers, figure, waist, and legs. Lovers are lunatics (moonstruck; *amantes amentes*).
* It turns out to be on the Isle of Wight; Ross had been vicar there for a time.

scholars and "for two poor men in the hospital," to the university libraries at Oxford and Cambridge and, naturally, to his four nieces and one nephew. What is more, and this would seem to clinch the matter of his having been well-heeled, that redoubtable reporter, Anthony à Wood, says that the executor of his estate (a man named Henley, who doubled as guardian to Ross's nephew) found in Ross's library at Bramshill £1000 in gold, most of it between the pages of books. (There is no known record of the books which served in the capacity of an informal treasury. But it is good thus to stumble, serendipitously, upon the historical origins of Golden Books and Treasuries of Verse and Prose.)

This undoubtedly rich Ross was not really as pessimistic a fellow as Goodman, but he did evidently partake of his conservatism. ("Conservatism" is here used loosely, as it usually is by most people most of the time. Ross didn't exactly believe in the possibility of conserving anything.) Ross was conservative in the sense that, even after Bacon (or, who knows, perhaps because of him and his works), he believed that Aristotle had had all the answers. He also believed that the Copernican theory was "false, absurd, and dangerous . . . having neither truth, reason, sense, antiquity, or universality to countenance it."

Having thus disposed of Copernicus and many other moderns, Ross turns to the most modern of them all and goes to work on Bacon's equivalent of the giant-dwarf theme, the expressive paradox, *Antiquitas saeculi, juventus mundi.* Ross doesn't think there's anything to it, and he says so in so many words [the italics are all his, too]:

> You are *the fathers (you say)* in such learning as *may be increased by experiments and discoveries, and of more authority than former ages.* Why doe you not tell us plainly, that you are fathers of learning, as well

99

as in learning? but indeed you are not the fathers of learning, you are only fathers of your new discoveries and fresh experiments; that is, of new, fond, and savourless phansies: and why you must be of more authority than former ages, I see no reason.*

As you can see from this passage, Ross was nobody's fool. Like so many new conservatives in every age, he has a point, although he's so irritated by the willful activity of the liberals, like Bacon, that he's moved to garble the point he does have. There is, after all, a distinct difference between being a "father *of* learning" and being "a father *in* learning." The ancients, comparatively speaking, — I mean only our intellectual ancestors — are bound to be, for everything except that which is being originated here and now, the "fathers *of* learning." The moderns can't rightly claim that title, although some of the more arrogant ones, again in every age, have a way of doing so. What Ross is doing here, and then discarding as he rides off on his hobby-horse to announce that intellectual authority is properly supplied only by ancient lineage, — what Ross is doing here, holus-bolus, is converting Bacon's figure of youth-and-old-age into its kinship equivalent and concluding, what is only the plain truth, that there are fathers of particular parts of learning in every time.

⟮ *xxxiii*

WHICH brings me, unavoidably, to that minor disquisition on fatherhood in science I wrote some time ago.†

* This, Jones reports, is in Ross's *The New Planet,* published in 1646.
† This in my paper, "Priorities in Scientific Discovery," (which I tire of citing anew and so record here only as *op. cit.*).

This kind of paternity is of course less a biological phenomenon than a sociological one. It is merely a concentrated form of eponymy, the practice of affixing the name of the scientist to all or part of what he has found, as with the Copernican system, Halley's comet or — the Hooke-Newton-Merton hypothesis. Entered in the highest ranks of eponymy are the peerless scientists credited with having fathered a new science or a new branch of science (at times, according to the heroic theory of creativity, through a kind of parthenogenesis for which they apparently needed no collaborators). Of the illustrious Fathers of this or that science (or of this or that special division of a science), there is an end but an end not easily reached. I submit to you only these few (culled from a list many times the length of any available to that comparative ancient, Alexander Ross):

Morgagni, the Father of Pathology
Cuvier, the Father of Palaeontology
Faraday, the Father of Electrotechnics
Daniel Bernoulli, the Father of Mathematical
    Physics
Bichat, the Father of Histology
van Leeuwenhoek, the Father of Protozoology and
    Bacteriology
Jenner, the Father of Preventive Medicine
Chladni, the Father of Modern Acoustics
Herbart, the Father of Scientific Pedagogy
Wundt, the Father of Experimental Psychology
Pearson, the Father of Biometry
            and, of course,
Comte, the Father of Sociology

(I say "of course" with some misgivings. For, as we know, sociology was officially born only after a long period of abnormally severe labor. Nor was the post-partum any more tranquil. It was disturbed by noisy controversies between the followers of Saint-Simon and Comte as they quarreled over the delicate question of which of the two was really the Father of Sociology and which merely the obstetrician.)

In a science as farflung and differentiated as chemistry, there is room for several paternities. If Robert Boyle is the undisputed Father of Chemistry (and, as his Irish epitaph has it, also the Uncle of the Earl of Cork), then Priestley is the Father of Pneumatic Chemistry, Lavoisier the Father of Modern Chemistry, and the greatest of American scientists, Willard Gibbs, the Father of Physical Chemistry.

On occasion, the presumed father of a science is called upon to prove his paternity, as with Johannes Müller and Albrecht von Haller, who are severally claimed to be the Father of Experimental Physiology.

Once established, this eponymous pattern of fatherhood is stepped up to engaging extremes. Each new specialty has its own parthenogenetic parent, whose identity is often known only to the happy few at work in the specialty. Thus, Manuel Garcia emerges as the Father of Laryngoscopy, Adolphe Brongiart as the Father of Modern Palæobotany, Timothy Bright as the Father of Modern Shorthand and Father Johann Dzierson (whose important work may have influenced Mendel) as the Father of Modern Rational Beekeeping.

Sometimes, a particular form of a discipline bears eponymous witness to the man who first gave it shape, as with Hippocratic medicine, Aristotelian logic, Euclidean geometry, Boolean algebra, and Keynesian economics. On rare occasions, the same individual acquires a double immortality, both for what he achieved and for what he failed to achieve, as in the cases of Euclidean and non-Euclidean geometries, and Aristotelian and non-Aristotelian logics. Most rarely of all, there are eponymies within eponymies as when Ernest Jones bestows on the Father of Psychoanalysis the title of "the Darwin of the Mind."

And, then, most finally, there is the eponymy that promises to dispose of Fatherhood altogether — E----d T----r, the Father of the Hydrogen Bomb.

ℂ xxxiv

AFTER this swift review, we are ready to return to that defender of the ancient fathers of learning, Alexander Ross.

You remember that Ross had disposed of the modern, Bacon, just as he had disposed of the modern, Copernicus. This enables him to proceed to the issue which is at the continuing focus of your ravening curiosity and mine. He turns to the giants and the dwarfs. As you might suppose, he pulls out all the stops:

> in this age, the Dictates and Opinions of the ancient Champions of Learning, are sleighted [a pretty unintentional pun] and misconstrued by some modern Innovators [for a conservative, this is a rather nasty epithet]; whereas we are but children in understanding, and ought to be directed by those Fathers of Knowledge: We are but Dwarfs and Pigmies compared to those Giants of Wisdom, on whose shoulders we stand, yet we cannot see so far as they without them. I deny not but we may and ought to strive for further knowledge [and this, no mistake about it, is quite a concession for Ross to make; one can almost hear him groan as he makes it], which we shall hardly

reach without their supportation. I disswade no man from inventing new; but I would not have him therefore to forget the old, nor lose the substance whilst he catches the shadow.*

How can I do justice to the richness of this passage? I obviously can't, but I can try. Let's pass swiftly over the talented hint and drift of "the ancient *Champions* of Learning." In the seventeenth century, "champion" had not yet taken on the meaning of "one who holds the first place in prize-fighting, rowing, walking, or other trial of strength or skill; [of] one who has defeated all opponents, and is open to contend with any new competitor." *This* meaning had to wait for the nineteenth century. It meant only, as with Shakspere's "A stouter Champion neuer handled Sword," a fighting man or combatant; or, as in the King James version, one who fights on behalf of another, so in 1. Sam. xvii. 51, "when the Philistines sawe

---

* This, Jones says, is from Ross's *Arcana Microcosmi*, 1652. By now, you're prepared to guess in just what part of the *Arcana* this passage has for so long lain buried — and you're entirely right. It's in the Epistle Dedicatory. In giving us only the succinct title, Jones does less than justice to Ross's knack for contriving a title that is as fully controversious as it is descriptive; thus: *Arcana Microcosmi: or, the hid secrets of mans body disclosed: first in an anatomical duel between Aristotle and Galen, about the parts thereof; secondly by a discovery of the . . . diseases, symptomes, and accidents of mans body. With a refutation of Doctor Browns Vulgar Errors, and* [as we finally come to *our* subject] *the ancient opinions vindicated*, London: 1651. (Evidently, Jones referred to the second edition.)

Incidentally, larcenous scholars with highly developed instincts for the jugular have seen to it that I must continue to rely on Jones for extracts from Ross, for the one copy of the *Arcana* immediately available to me — the one in the library of the American Institute of Electrical Engineers — has been robbed of just those pages on which the pertinent passages are reputed to occur.

their champion was dead, they fled"; or, again as in Shakspere's, "'To heauen,* the widdowes Champion," "'one who in any kind of contest or conflict acts as the acknowledged defender of a person, cause, or side; one who stoutly maintains any cause." All this and more, Ross ingeniously smuggles into his phrase, "the ancient Champions of Learning."

As for his use of "sleighted," it's not at all clear that Ross deserves credit for a shattering pun. It's true that at the time he was writing these words, "'sleight" was used variously to denote the act of dealing guilefully just as it was used as a variant spelling for "slight" in the now obsolete sense of "a very small amount or weight; a small matter, a trifle." (In his *Poems*, for example, Henry More could argue that "'The same sleights, By turns do urge them both in their descents and heights.") But this secondary meaning had not yet flowered into today's meaning of a "display of contemptuous indifference or disregard"; that didn't come along, it seems, until just after the turn of the next century when William Penn, properly enough, used it in this wise: "'Pray don't hurt him by an appearance of neglect, less of slight." If Ross actually intended the multifaceted pun, he was in advance of his time (and *he* wouldn't have liked *that* charge). Let's then simply scratch "sleighted," and not give Ross credit for something he would have probably disowned in any case.

But now, as you'll see by looking back to the quoted passage, Ross is at his ingenious best. And luckily, he reaches his peak just as he comes to that part of his remarks which is dead center on the subject we are exclusively concerned with. He goes on to write: "'whereas

---

* Or do you prefer the variant reading? "'To God, the widow's champion."

we are but children in understanding, and ought to be directed by those Fathers of Knowledge." Here, he has hoist Bacon with his own petar[d], as Shakspere might say (if indeed, it was not the Lord Chancellor himself who said it for him).* For having adapted Bacon's kinship-terminology, Ross proceeds to make the moderns "children *in* understanding," not, mind you, "children *of* understanding," and once having achieved this, the rest is easy sailing. The ancients appear as the "Fathers *of* Knowledge" (and we've been through *that* one) and the modern juveniles have no alternative but to follow the line set down by their dads. It begins to look as though few could match Ross in his tactical — one might almost say, strategic — use of the insinuative preposition. Certainly, I've run across no others who can do so much with such little words.†

❡ *XXXV*

ROSS now moves into high gear. He writes, you remember, "We are but Dwarfs and Pigmies compared to those

* Do give me credit here for refusing to perpetuate a widespread illusion. I did not write "as Shakspere was *wont* to say." For the plain fact is, and the record is indubitably clear on this, that once he had planted the phrase in Hamlet, he never used it again. The general belief that he was given to this originally vivid figure stems entirely from its millions of repetitions by those of us who insist on converting the language of giants into the clichés of dwarfs.
† I refuse to enter into a debate with you, if, by some ill fate, you belong to that crowd that doesn't consider prepositions to be *words* actually, but a kind of formal, contentless connective that should be sharply distinguished from words that have referents of quite another kind.

Giants of Wisdom, on whose shoulders we stand, yet we cannot see so far as they without them." The moderns are made out not only to be dwarfs, but pigmies too. Ross might have gone on to compound his description had he Roget's *Thesaurus* before him, adding to dwarf and pigmy (with which Roget too almost but not quite begins), dwarfling, midget, midge, manikin, chit, fingerling [rare], pidwidgeon [now rare], Pigwiggen, urchin, elf, mite [coll.], atomy, dandiprat [arch.], micromorph [Zool.], homunculus, dapperling, Tom Thumb,* hopo'-my thumb, runt, shrimp, small fry [chiefly coll.], and

* Tom Thumb was not, as some people think, the creation of Barnum, even though the London *Daily Chronicle* of February 6, 1907, might lead you to think so. The *Chronicle* is thoroughly misleading when it says that " 'Tom Thumb' is a name generally given by showmen to lilliputians [and that] the first holder of this 'title' was Charles Stratton, who was brought to London by Barnum." True enough, but the *Chronicle* might have done better to supply more of the historical antecedents of Barnum's coup. The English Tom was actually of Scandinavian descent, as can be inferred from his close connection with the mystic Little Thumb, or Tom-a-lyn, Thaumlin, Tamlane and, not least, Tommelfinger. As early as 1621, R. Johnson was writing *The History of Tom Thumbe*, followed less than a decade later by an anonymous piece entitled *Tom Thumbe, his Life and Death*. Sometime between 1630 and the present, Tom dropped the final "e" in Thumbe: it's not clear just when. At times, the amputation was even more drastic. Needham, for example, writing in 1661, went so far as to make reference to "Tom Thums." And the anonymous *An exact Survey of the affaires of the United Netherlands* rang in another change in its allusion to "Tom Thombs." But by 1700, B. E., who can be no further identified, pretty well settled the whole matter in his *A New Dictionary of the Terms ancient and modern of the Canting Crew*, saying straight-out, and with a certainty that was persuasive enough to carry force right down to our own day, "Tom-thumb, a Dwarf." (The hyphen fell of its own weight in a few years.)

wart [slang].* Had Ross not been biassed in favor of his
ancient "Giants of Wisdom" and had he been in a position to consult Roget, he might have found quite a
few alternate words for them too; for example, in addition to giant (or gyant or gyante), giantess [*fem.*], gigant
[obs.], colossus, titan, Antaeus, Goliath, Polythemus,
Titan, and, of course, Titaness, Briareus, Norn, Hercules,
Cyclops, Aegir, Hler, Gymir, Ran, Fafnir, Fenrir, [those
Old Norse, or Icelandic, Eddas and the Volsunga Saga,
too, were quite prolific of giants, although I must say that
Bishop Brynjólf Sveinsson, who discovered the Eddas
back in 1643, was mistaken in attributing the *Elder,* or
Poetic, Edda, to the historian Saemund Sigfusson (1056–
1133), with the unfortunate result that it is still known
to some who do not track down their sources as the *Edda
of Saemund the Wise;* the whole thing, apparently, getting
all bogged down simply because the *Younger,* or *Prose,
Edda was,* beyond all reasonable question, edited by the
historian and poet Snorri Sturluson (1178–1241) and
therefore is *rightly* known alternatively as the *Edda of
Snorri Sturluson,* and should you doubt me here, then you
too can go to Webster's *International Dictionary of the
English Language,*† at least to the Second Unabridged
Edition – I'm not prepared to speak for the Third – and
find it all there in black and white, as you might suspect,
inasmuch as this edition utilizes "all the experience and
resources of more than one hundred years of genuine
Webster dictionaries," as it says, right there on the title
page]. Repeating a little, then, to preserve some sense of

* As a confirmed gnomologist, I have only this to ask of Roget:
why, sir, does this list of diminutives not so much as mention
— — gnomes?
† Webster is of course only the most convenient reference on
the Eddas; scarcely the most authoritative. Should you want to

continuity: Fafnir, Fenrir, Gerth, Grendel, Hymir, Loki, Mimir, Wade, Ymir, Jotumn, Gog and Magog, monster [this *is* stretching connotations a bit], leviathan, and the like.

ℭ *xxxvi*

BEFORE you indict me for committing a contingent anachronism when, at the beginning of the last paragraph, I pictured the results of the seventeenth-century Ross having access to Roget's *Thesaurus,* I hasten to plead guilty knowledge. Ross couldn't really have turned to Peter Mark Roget. That physician, savant and onetime secretary of the Royal Society was of course a nineteenth-century man (though he lived out his entire youth in the eighteenth). I realize too that only five years before he began in 1805 to jot down a catalogue of words for his private use, he had spent six weeks being consulted by that incomparable polymath, Jeremy Bentham, — himself no mean word-coiner, word-slinger and, in a very *special* sense, word-catcher — in their joint effort to devise an utilitarian scheme for turning to account the sewage of the metropolis. I know all this. I know too that in composing his masterly work, "Roget always used Feinaigle's system of mnemonics" (as his biographer Surgeon-Captain W. W. Webb reminds us).

pursue this thorny question to a conclusion, you would do far better to turn to that comprehensive *Bibliography of the Eddas* published by Halldór Hermannsson in *Islandica,* vol. 13, Ithaca (New York), 1920, or better still, read the brand-new translation of Snorri Sturluson's *Prose Edda* by Jean I. Young, published by the University of California Press.

Contrary to what you may be tempted to assume, the cognomen Feinaigle is *not* the source of that truly expressive verb, "to finagle," or its derivative noun, "finagler" — though, judging from the checkered career of Gregor von Feinaigle, it might well have been. Feinaigle spent much of his adult life delivering highly profitable lectures on his "new system of mnemonics and methodics," and he was regularly denounced as an impostor in the press and ridiculed as a cheat on the stage (the latter, for example, in Dieulafoy's farce, "Les filles de Mémoire, ou le Mnémoniste"), only because he refused to explain the details of his method for ensuring extraordinary feats of memory. In a sense, then, Feinaigle was being accused of being a finagler, of resorting to underhanded methods, of engaging in intrigue. (Since Count Metternich,* together with his many secretaries, followed Feinaigle's entire course of lectures, this alone might seem to support the hypothesis of the word's origin.) Yet, it simply is not true that Feinaigle was the root source of the seemingly mimetic word. It has quite a different genealogy, as you will discover if you turn to any truly *unabridged* dictionary of the French language. There you will find "fainaigue" defined as "to revoke at cards; hence, to cheat or resort to devious methods." It is the French word for trickery at cards, not the Austrian count from Baden, which has given us that gem of English dialect, to finagle. And now that its etymology has been cleared up, once and for all, I belatedly note *prima facie* evidence that

---

* I write *Count* Metternich, not because I willfully aim to downgrade this effective man, but only to be historically accurate. At the time he was wilefully following von Feinaigle's course of lectures on mnemonics, he had not yet ascended to the eminence of being Prince Clemens Wenzel Lothar Metternich-Winneburg, upwardly mobile son of Count Franz Georg Karl

finagle could not possibly have derived from Feinaigle.
Had this been the actual derivation, Roget, who was long
wedded to Feinaigle's system of Mnemonics, would surely
have included "finagle" in one or another of the many
editions of the *Thesaurus* published during his lifetime.

I know also that Roget himself was anything but a
finagler. Like Newton in his fashion, Roget waited a good
long time before he ever got around to publishing his
Thesaurus — that is, if you're willing to concede that 47
years is quite some time for gestation. And finally, I know
that he lived to be ninety, long enough to see twenty-eight
editions of the *Thesaurus,* which was then handed over
to his son, John, for still more editions (which have
since multiplied beyond easy count). Nevertheless, it is
intriguing to contemplate what our man Ross *might* have
accomplished in the way of a multiplicative vocabulary
for giants and dwarfs had he come along later or Roget
earlier.

⟦ xxxvii

BUT THERE is no profit in musing about might-have-
beens and so we had best not depart from the main line
of our story. Yet, against my will, I must devote some
space — if only a few words — to that great man who, a

von Metternich-Winneburg zu Beilstein and Countess Maria
Beatrix Aloisia von Kagenegg. Nor had he yet written in his
Memoirs that unforgettable perception: "Napoleon seemed to me
small." To judge from this judgment, the then complacent
diplomatic genius Metternich had not the wit to recognize that
this ostensibly *small* man was, after his fashion, a giant.

few sentences back, forced himself into our history. Roget's six weeks of consultation with Bentham, you might argue, are scarcely reason enough for us to admit that jurisprudent, philosopher, deontologist, educator, penologist, sanitarian, philanthropist and codifier into the midst of this narrative. Were his brief association with Roget on matters of sewage disposal Jeremy Bentham's sole ticket of entry, it would not be honored here. But he has, of course, many more claims on our attention. For one thing, Bentham apparently rediscovered the Baconian paradox for himself: "What is the wisdom of the times called old? Is it the wisdom of gray hairs? No. — It is the wisdom of the cradle." * For another thing, although Bentham was robust both in manhood and his long old age, he was, in his tender years, as his biographer John Macdonell emphatically describes him, "sensitive, delicate, [and] of dwarfish stature . . ." Bentham, then, is the second man in this circumstantial account of whom it can be said that he began as a dwarf and ended as a giant. (Newton was the other.) Regarded metaphorically, he therefore contains in his own person the extraordinarily inverted figure of a giant mounted upon a dwarf; a vivid figure which, you will surely grant, should give us pause for thought.

It can also give us occasion to redress an historical wrong. For too many generations, now, too many of us have allowed the well-advertised precocity of John Stuart Mill to overshadow the more thorough-going precocity of Jeremy Bentham. Mill celebrated his difficult years as a prodigy in his classic *Autobiography* and so we are bound

* *The Book of Fallacies* from Unfinished Papers of Jeremy Bentham. By a Friend. London: John and H. L. Hunt, 1824, Part the First, Chap. II, The Wisdom of our Ancestors, or Chinese Argument, — (*ad verecundiam*), p. 71.

to know all about his disciplinarian of a father who saw
to it that he learned the Greek alphabet by the age of
three and that he read, by the age of eight, Aesop's
Fables, Isocrates, Xenophon's *Anabasis*, six dialogues of
Plato, the whole of Herodotus, much of Lucian and some
of Diogenes Laërtius (that invaluable Cilician biographer
of the third century whose ten volumes you and I probably know only through their most famous quotations,
cited by all of us with nauseating frequency). Nevertheless, Mill's complaint about the regimen his father imposed upon him has detectable undertones of amazement
about his own prodigious accomplishments in learning.
Let it be noted also that we know of all this through Mill
himself (supplemented, of course, by Bain's even more
thorough account of Mill's curriculum as a child).

It is altogether otherwise with Bentham. Much research is required to discover the exact lineaments of his
childborne learning. It appears that he managed to learn
more than the rudiments of Latin at four and of Greek
at five, even though he had to wait until he was seven
before acquiring that idiomatic command of French
which made it his second native language. Evidently he
soon slowed the pace of his learning, for he did not enter
Queens College, Oxford, until he was twelve, with the
result that he had to reach the ripe age of sixteen before
achieving his B.A. and the advanced age of eighteen before
he could claim his master's degree. The plain fact is
that Bentham was hard on himself. How else shall we
account for his later judgment on the Latin ode he composed on the death of George II and the accession of
George III when he, young Jeremy, was thirteen? It was
this ode which the reigning Dr. Johnson described as "a
very pretty performance of a young man." And it was this
same ode of which Bentham himself said later on that "it

was a mediocre performance on a trumpery subject, written by a miserable child." *

Bentham belongs in this account for still another reason, albeit an anticipatory one. Later on in this narrative, I shall have much to say — and rightly so — of Macaulay's vicious attack on the complex sentence structure of Sir William Temple. You will see that, as an author intent upon following the complicated history of the giant-and-dwarf Aphorism, I encounter some difficulties in placing that attack in its chronologically ordained spot. If I decide to place it according to the years assigned the victim of the attack (1628–99), it belongs beyond all doubt in the portion of this narrative devoted to the seventeenth century; if I decide to place it according to the years assigned the man who mounted the attack (1800–59), it belongs, with equal certainty, to the first half of the nineteenth century. Bentham provides us with a reasonable, though, chronologically considered, a far from perfect compromise. Bestride the narrow last half of the eighteenth century and the widening first third of the nineteenth, this colossus of the intellect (if, as one of the petty men who walk under his huge legs and peep about, I might describe him so) provides me with a provisional solution. In this early chapter of the narrative, I shall report only a few lines about the judgments passed on Bentham's propensity for convoluted sentences, reserving for later extended treatment the same charge levelled against Temple by Macaulay. In this way, I shall insinuate this proleptic theme and only later develop it

* Still, it must be acknowledged that Bentham lagged far behind such "prodigies of childhood [as] Grotius, Scioppius, Heinsius, Politian, Pascal, Joseph Scaliger, Ferdinand de Cordouè . . ." And all these in turn, some of whom wrote tragedies at eight and mastered fourteen languages by ten, are far outdistanced,

in the considerable length which, in this day of proper
concern with the rapidly changing structure of our language, it amply deserves.

❡ xxxviii

(I AM aware, more than you might suppose, that in thus
revealing the complexities of this narrative, I rob it of
that first prerequisite of dramatic discourse: the composite sense of surprise-and-inevitability that is supplied
by the finished product after all the scaffolding that
enabled the structure to be built in the first place has
been removed. I know, in a word, that one should tell
the story, not tell how the story came to be told in one
fashion rather than another. But as Maria observed in *A
Sentimental Journey*, "God [or, *any creator*] tempers the
wind to the shorn lamb." Not that I consider you, my
lone reader, to be lamblike and clipped to boot, but only
that I recognize you have not the ample leisure to work
out for yourself the intricate structure of this tale. In
violating one rule, that of concealing my art, I abide by
another rule, that of maintaining a friendly regard for
your most valuable asset, — time. That is why I tell you,
in advance of the occasion itself, that what appears here,
in skimpy fashion, about Bentham is only prologue to
what you shall presently read about Macaulay's attack on
the complex sentence structure of Temple.)

in the words of Tristram's Yorick, by "the great Lipsius . . .
who composed a work the day he was born." The list of
prodigies and the compelling evidence for this last assertion
are set forth in Book VI, chap. 3.

ℂ *xxxix*

NOTE, then, how Bentham is treated by his young and ingenious friend, John Stuart Mill, who, like a small army of others, had undertaken to prepare some of Bentham's vast collection of manuscripts for publication. In that same *Autobiography* (to which I have made ambivalent allusion), Mill writes in so many words (at p. 113 of the 4th edition):

> Mr. Bentham had begun this treatise [on judicial evidence] three times at considerable intervals, each time in a different manner, and each time without reference to the preceding: two of the three times he had given over nearly the whole subject. These three masses of manuscript it was my duty to condense into a single treatise; adopting the last one written as the groundwork, and incorporating with it as much of the two others as it had not completely superseded. [And now we read the cavilsome judgment, which a less honest and more charitable editor might have left unsaid:] I had also to unroll such of Mr. Bentham's involved and parenthetical sentences as seemed to overpass by their complexity the measure of what readers were likely to take the pains to understand.

Not that Mill was unjust in his judgment; only that he preferred truth to charity. We, in turn, must be charitable with Mill. For he had the bad fortune to come upon Bentham's manuscripts which were written *after 1810,* that is to say, after that initial phase of composition in which Bentham's prose was sparse, lucid and shining only to give way, for reasons that remain inexplicable, to prose that was turgid, dull and hopelessly prolix (after a fashion that neither you nor I can in truth condone).

As John Macdonell, his well-wishing biographer, noted the contrast between Bentham's early and later periods:

> Originally simple and pure, his sentences became complex; *parenthetical matter was inserted anyhow* [this most unforgivable of stylistic sins we shall encounter in its most extravagant shape when Macaulay proceeds to wreck Temple]; and he who had satirised so keenly the laboured, technical style of lawyers and legislators, as kept up for purposes of corruption, lived to exemplify the very same faults.

As Mill, so Macdonell. Yet, in rebuttal, I submit that the grave charge far outruns the occasion, and I leave it to your judicial temperament to decide between the accusers and the accused. Here, for an example, is a sentence by Bentham — faithfully drawn from the period *after* 1810 — and representative, I believe, of the kind of careful writing which his self-anointed critics insist on describing as excessively complex — and *parenthetical.*

> How much enjoyment may grow from the collection of antiquities, with a view to illustrate the past, to assist the investigation of historical facts, and especially to throw light upon any topics which might be made instructive to the future; — from the collection of objects of natural history, in the animal, mineral, and vegetable field, but particularly in the two latter, since their collection inflicts no pain, and implies no destruction of life, or of happiness or enjoyment; and most of all in the last, the vegetable or botanical, which frequently gives the opportunity of diffusing pleasure to others by the multiplication of specimens; — and, as connected with such studies, the breeding of domestic animals, with a view to the observance of

their peculiar instincts, habits, and propensities; the power of education upon them; their aptitude for services to which they have not been before applied; — the culture of beautiful flowers, such as tulips, auriculas, or anemones, or of choice and useful plants for purposes culinary or medicinal.*

— The defense rests.

Others of Bentham's friends insist on perpetuating the myths about his unusual prose. Sir Samuel Romilly, as one instance, describes the mode of composition pursued by Bentham in his stately mansion Ford Abbey, near Chard (once occupied by Prideaux):

We found him passing his time, as he has always been passing it since I have known him, which is now more than thirty years, closely applying himself for six or eight hours a day in writing upon laws and legislation, and in composing his civil and criminal codes, and spending the remaining hours of every day in reading or taking exercise by way of fitting himself for his labours, or [and now we are treated to another piece of irremissible causticity], to use his own strangely invented phraseology, taking his ante-jentacular and post-prandial walks to prepare himself for his task of codification.

What is one to do with so wretched a critique of inventive phraseology? Must we abide this sort of egregious anti-sesquipedalianism? Would Sir Samuel have had Bentham be wordy and vague rather than compact and precise? Would he have had him abandon the expressive

* I draw this sentence from that deliberately simplified handbook of morals intended for popular consumption: *Deontology; or, The Science of Morality: in which the Harmony and Co-incidence of Duty and Self-Interest, Virtue and Felicity, Prudence and Benevolence, are Explained, Exemplified, and*

"ante-jentacular" and substitute the bland and wordy
"taken some time before breakfast"? Or perhaps he would
have had him bastardize the language by referring to a
post-dinner walk. Romilly's critique — and he was not
alone in this sort of thing — can no longer be regarded
as serious criticism; it is merely a frivolous and cruelly
ignorant expression of sentiment.

Once we ignore Romilly's pitiable efforts at literary
criticism, we can acknowledge his distinct service in
documenting the fact that Bentham was, like the philosopher of old, truly peripatetic. Actually, Bentham was
somewhat better than that; he was not merely given to
walking about but, as we learn from one of the many
obituaries, he "wended round the walks of his garden at a
pace somewhat faster than a walk, but not so quick as a
trot."

☾ xl

BUT ENOUGH of this inventory of the injustices done
Bentham; we had better not depart any longer from our
story of the Aphorism. I suppose you noticed a few pages
back some conspicuous omissions from the lists of synonyms and near-synonyms for dwarfs and for giants that
Alexander Ross might have used, but did not. The omissions are deliberate. It would have been impossible, of
course, for Ross to refer to Lilliputians, though how he
would have loved the opportunity, for it was just the

Applied to the Business of Life, arranged and edited by John
Bowring and published in 1834 by Longman, Rees, Orme,
Browne, Green, and Longman in London and, more parsimoni-
ously, by William Tait in Edinburgh. The interminable sentence appears just on page 129 of the second volume.

word he really needed to refer to the moderns. But it
would be about another half-century — Ross, you'll recall,
was writing around the 1650s — before the proposed
Travels of Martinus Scriblerus would even begin to sketch
out the satirical romance about Martin's voyages, first to
"the remains of the ancient Pygmaean empire," and
then, to the "land of the Giants, now the most humane
people in the world." In the last chapter of the *Memoirs
of Scriblerus,* Alexander Pope has not neglected to intimate these beginnings. Only for a short time could Pope
think it well enough to have people regard his *Martinus
Scriblerus: ΠΕΡΙ ΒΑΘΟΥΣ or the Art of Sinking in
Poetry* as practically the collective product of those wags,
like Arbuthnot, Swift, Gay, Parnell, Congreve, Lord
Oxford, Atterbury and Pope himself who met evenings
at Arbuthnot's rooms in St. James's palace and had a gay
old time.

I say POPE's *Martinus Scriblerus,* simply because I
don't want to get involved in old quarrels about the allo-
cation of authorship for a work that is the outcome of
the continued give-and-take between the men comprising
a team of collaborators. (Of course, the celebrated members of the celebrated Scriblerus club — Pope, Swift, Gay,
Parnell and all the rest — didn't describe themselves as
a team; keen individualists, all of them, they would have
resisted the tag, even had it been proposed to them; but
the fact remains that, so far as we can now tell, they much
resembled a research-team. They spent much time together, parried each thrust by a colleague with a counter
thrust, argued, debated, occasionally became fed up with
one another and, in the end, couldn't really straighten
out the question of who had contributed what to the book
published by any one of them.)

If you go along with Edward Bensly, M.S. Trinity

College, one-time professor of Latin at the University College of Wales, Aberystwyth, and a good enough papal expert to be selected by Ward and Waller, in their *Cambridge History of English Literature*, to do the all-too-short and not entirely satisfactory chapter on Pope, then, you call it Pope's *Martinus Scriblerus, etc. etc.* If you go along with George Atherton Aitken, M.V.O., who did the chapter following on Swift for Ward-and-Waller, then you speak of the *Memoirs of Scriblerus* as being by Arbuthnot, when it was finally published in 1741. And if, in the chapter after that, you go along with Aitken-truncated, that is, with G. A. Aitken, M.V.O., when he writes about "Arbuthnot and lesser prose writers" — these lesser folk evidently not being judged worthy of full titular designation by the literary commentator who, I suggest, is really the same George Atherton Aitken who smuggled a claim for Arbuthnot into the chapter ostensibly on Swift — if you do all that, you clean up the whole mess by noting that "The *Memoirs of Scriblerus* were printed in the second volume of Pope's prose works (1741), with a note from the booksellers to the reader which stated that the *Memoirs,* and all the tracts in the same name, were written by Pope *and* Arbuthnot [the italicized *and* is my insertion], 'except,' [these are evidently the words of the anonymous booksellers, not G. A. Aitken's or mine], 'except the *Essay on the Origin of Sciences* in which Parnell had some hand, as had Gay in the *Memoirs of a Parish Clerk,* while the rest were Pope's.' " Yet in spite of what the booksellers said, Aitken hangs in there and goes on to amend the understanding you only think has been reached. He says, with the kind of artless assurance that commonly attends a wishful thought: "There cannot, however, be any doubt that the *Memoirs* are wholly [and here Aitken prepares his line

of retreat], or almost wholly, by Arbuthnot, though sug-
gestions were probably made by his friends; Pope's earlier
editors admitted that the knowledge of medicine and
philosophy displayed marked many of the chapters as the
work of 'the Doctor.' "

I don't know about the earlier editors of Pope, but I
do know that when Sir Walter Scott, Bart. got around
to preparing the second edition (it may also be in the
first, but the second is the only edition I have here at
home) of *The Works of Jonathan Swift*, D.D., Dean of
St. Patrick's, Dublin, Sir Walter, in his preface to volume
XI, which is the volume containing *Gulliver's Travels*,
sidesteps the whole issue and says only that "the first
sketch of *Gulliver's Travels* occurs in the proposed
Travels of Martinus Scriblerus," adding in a footnote,
that "Pope has not forgotten to intimate this in the concluding chapter of *Memoirs of Scriblerus*." Perhaps we
should follow in Sir Walter's sidesteps and forget the
whole thing. It's beginning to get complicated.

By 1726, when *Gulliver's Travels* was first published,
Pope — not Arbuthnot, who was by then quite seriously
sick — might well have regretted his decision not to follow
through on the prospectus for a satire plotted around
some imaginary travels of a reasonably decent chap to
strange and far-off places. I judge this from the fact,
noted by both George Atherton Aitken (that indecisive
literary historian we have just met) and Sir Walter Scott
(him, too), that Pope said, I gather in 1741, that Swift
had his first hints for the *Travels* from the *Memoirs of
Scriblerus* (put together by Arbuthnot, surely; Pope, probably; and in some measure, possibly by the rest of the
club). I don't know why I go into all this, because
Aitken, who has been defending Arbuthnot's rights all
along, changes his tune in a way, denies the full force of

Pope's remark and says: "The connection of the *Travels*
with the original scheme [in the *Memoirs of Scriblerus*],
however, is very slight, and appears chiefly in the third
part of the work."

What may be going on here is that Aitken, having
undertaken to write a chapter on Swift and another on
Arbuthnot for the *Cambridge History of English Literature,* is under severe cross-pressures. Things are not made
any easier for him by having these chapters in strict
contiguity. So, like any Solomon confronted with trouble
of this kind, he proposes to cut things up: he assigns
full or substantial credit for the *Memoirs* to Arbuthnot
(who, I suspect, is his favorite) and grants, as you've just
seen, as much credit to Swift as Swift could ever have
wished for the *Travels,* and leaves Pope, who, anyway, has
had his innings in other places, holding the bag (or
whatever one does after one has finished having one's
innings).

ℂ *xli*

ALL THIS (by "all this," I mean the mixup between
Pope, Arbuthnot, Swift and the rest of the Scriblerians)
is not as remote from our subject of the giants-and-dwarfs
as you might think. For one thing, Swift was the onetime
secretary, dependent and eventual disparager of Sir
William Temple, whom I haven't yet gotten around to
discussing at all. Temple was one of those supporters of
antiquity who made use of the giant-dwarf figure, and
then promptly did everything he could to take away from
the moderns the solace and support it seemed to give
them. (If I find the occasion, I'll go into Temple's
maneuvers in more detail; you'll find them, if you look,

in his essay *Upon Ancient and Modern Learning*, 1690).
Temple at once found an adversary, of medium size, in
William Wotton and, in 1697, a defender of giant size in
Swift (who, inexplicably, didn't publish his *Battle of
the Books* until 1704, five years after Temple's death. Incidentally, Temple left Swift £100 as well as any profit,
and there was bound to be some, resulting from the publication of his posthumous works. As usual, Swift couldn't
cope with his good fortune and soon got into a prolonged
hassle with Temple's widowed sister, Lady Giffard, who
was somehow involved in the matter. These legal niceties
are beyond me, so I'll just leave them alone; anyway,
I'm not sure how the Swift-Giffard quarrel bears on the
quarrel between advocates of the ancients and the moderns or, in particular, between the dead Temple and the
very much alive Wotton about the relative merits of
the Ancients and the Moderns).

*The Battle of the Books,** Swift's contribution to the
controversy, was published, as I've said, in 1704. It was
not published by itself, I believe, but together with Swift's
A Tale of a Tub. The latter is the book about which
Swift, when he was rich in years and when his powers of
criticism were distinctly failing, was overheard to say:
"Good God, what a genius I had when I wrote that
book." † He didn't do too badly in *The Battle of the
Books*, either.‡

* That, of course, is only the short title; the complete title is
*Full and True Account of the Battle fought last Friday between
the Ancient and the Modern Books in Saint James's Library.*
   There are those who claim that the last part of the full title
eventually suggested a modern classic of jazz, but the evidence
is clear that Swift wrote, and meant, "library."
† Still, Swift may have had something there. For *A Tale of a
Tub* describes, with transcending genius, the masterly use of
that most essential tool of the writer's craft — the digression. I

do not refer to the outspoken Sect. VII, entitled "A Digression in Praise of Digressions" for this, it might be said, may qualify only as the rationalization of a defect. But consider how Swift pictures the quandary facing the writer possessed of a multitudinous confusion of thoughts, this in an aside to the reader while he is lampooning Bentley, Wotton and the rest of that lot, who were busily advancing the cause of the Moderns; thus: "But not to digress farther in the midst of a digression, as I have known some authors to enclose digressions in one another, like a nest of boxes. . ."

Quite evidently, two of our chief authorities stand opposed on the issue of the worth of digressions. Contrast Swift's ambivalence toward them, as I have just recorded it, with Tristram Shandy's univalence: "Digressions, incontestably, are the sunshine; — they are the life, the soul of reading! — take them out of this book, for instance, — you might as well take the book along with them; — one cold eternal winter would reign in every page of it; restore them to the writer; — he steps forth like a bridegroom, — bids All-hail; brings in variety, and forbids the appetite to fail.

[And then he draws the signal guidelines for the writer trapped by the digressionary dilemma.] All the dexterity is in the good cookery and management of them, so as to be not only for the advantage of the reader, but also of the author, whose distress, in this matter, is truly pitiable: For, if he begins a digression, — from that moment, I observe, his whole work stands stock still; — and if he goes on with his main work, — then there is an end of his digression. — This is vile work. — For which reason, from the beginning of this, you see, I have constructed the main work and the adventitious parts of it with such intersections, and have so complicated and involved the digressive and progressive movements, one wheel within another, that the whole machine, in general, has been kept a-going; — and, what's more, it shall be kept a-going these forty years, if it pleases the fountain of health to bless me so long with life and good spirits."

In Book I, chap. 23, — *ipse dixit*.

‡ I persist in this judgment even though you will want to remind me that the idea for *The Battle of the Books* was boldly taken from Coutray's lively poem, in eleven books, "Histoire Poétique de la Guerre nouvellement déclarée entre les anciens et les modernes." Swift stands here to Coutray as Shakspere stands to Holinshed.

The battle described by Swift takes place, as the full title of his account makes plain, in St. James's library. In setting the scene, Swift reminds us that it is with libraries as with other cemeteries: books, like dead bodies, are subjected to corruption, victimized by worms and destined to turn to dust. But apparently, this takes a longer time with books than with corpses. In the prolonged interim before they go the way of all flesh, the books can, and, in St. James's library, do engage in quite lively controversies. But it is only one battle, fought, it seems on a Friday, that attracts Swift's attention; the battle, of course, between the Ancients and the Moderns. Thoroughly saturated with the culture of his time, Swift begins, naturally enough, with the Baconian Paradox, not thinking it necessary to mention a source known to everyone who is anyone. (He appends a footnote to alert, though not to instruct, the occasional philistine among his readers, saying only of the passage I am about to quote that this is "according to the modern paradox.") After some preliminary skirmishes, the battle begins in earnest:

> While things were in this ferment, discord grew extremely high; hot words passed on both sides, and ill blood was plentifully bred.* Here a solitary ancient, squeezed up among a whole shelf of moderns, offered fairly to dispute the case, and to prove by manifest reason, that the priority was due to them,

* "Bred" it is in my copy of the work, this being page 233 in volume X of the Scott edition of Swift's *Works*, dated 1824. I believe and trust that it should indeed read "bred" rather than "shed," which has been so regularly coupled with blood, since at least the *Ancren riwle à 1225*. Swift was not a man for the cliché, except with satirical intent.

from long possession; and in regard of their prudence, antiquity, and, above all, their great merits toward the moderns. But these denied the premises, and seemed very much to wonder, how the ancients could pretend to insist upon their antiquity, when it was so plain, (if they went to that,) that the moderns were much the more ancient * of the two.

Though Swift gives us here the Baconian Paradox of modern mankind being old in years and ancient mankind young, there is still no sign of the giant-dwarf simile. Yet if Swift hasn't got around to repeating what we are beginning to suspect is an old saw (rather than a new saying to be ascribed to the incomparable Newton), he does manage, in *The Battle of the Books,* to create a simile of his own. Swift's figure includes a phrase that has its own subsequent history. It is picked up by a grateful posterity who find it apt and so much to their liking that they put it to work on millions of occasions until the shining freshness that once made it so attractive is grown thoroughly stale. The phrase is "sweetness and light," which comes to us from the following passage (as it came to Matthew Arnold when, in 1869, he made "culture" †

---

* It is here that he sets down his footnote: "According to the modern paradox."
† For a detailed history of the word "culture" and an inventory of 164 definitions of the word, look up the scholarly monograph by A. L. Kroeber and Clyde Kluckhohn, *Culture: A Critical Review of Concepts and Definitions,* Cambridge. Massachusetts, U.S.A.: Papers of the Peabody Museum of American Archaeology and Ethnology, Harvard University, Vol. XLVII, No. 1, 1952. Arnold's image of culture as "sweetness and light" can now be extended by further resort to Swift's original passage, to make "*material* culture" (as the sociologists and anthropologists have designated the artifactual parts of culture) essentially a compound of honey and wax.

a literary by-word and saw its main characters as those of "sweetness and light"):

> As for us the ancients, we are content, with the bee, to pretend to nothing of our own, beyond our wings and our voice: that is to say, our flights and our language. For the rest, whatever we have got, has been by infinite labour and search, and ranging through every corner of nature; the difference is, that, instead of dirt and poison [of the spider who, like the moderns, boasts of being obliged to none since he spins everything out of his own innards], we have chosen to fill our hives with honey and wax; thus furnishing mankind with the two noblest of things, which are sweetness and light.

Yet there is little either of sweetness or of light in the continuing battle between the ancients and moderns waged in St. James's library. Instead, there is much stercoraceous wit (as in many another of Swift's writings). What is worse, the essay ends with nary an allusion to the giant-dwarf Aphorism and so, despite the promise contained in its (full) title, there is really nothing in it for us.*

---

* Swift's essay did give rise, however, to some pretty miserable versifying. Listen for a viscous example to this rhymed synopsis of the essay:

"Verses on the Battle of the Books
  by Mr James Sterling, of the County of Meath.

WHILE the Dean with more wit than man ever wanted,
Or than Heaven to any man else ever granted,
Endeavours to prove, how the ancients in knowledge
Have excell'd our adepts of each modern college:
How by heroes of old our chiefs are surpass'd
In each useful science, true learning, and taste:
While thus he behaves, with more courage than manners,
And fights for the foe, deserting our banners;

❡ *xlii*

WE SHALL fare no better, I'm afraid, when we turn
to *Gulliver's Travels*. True, as we know, we shall find
much there about pigmies and giants or, more idiomat-
ically, about Lilliputians and Brobdingnagians * (neither
of which designations was available to the ingenious
Alexander Ross — remember *him?*). But the question is,
shall we find Swift using the figure of dwarfs upon the
shoulders of giants?

To ask the question is almost to answer it. With all
his ample opportunities for availing himself of the figure,
Swift stubbornly refuses to advantage himself of any. He
has five or six Lilliputians dancing on Gulliver's hand
and has the little Lilliputian girls and boys playing hide
and seek in his hair, but not once do they climb upon his
shoulders. Again, in Brobdingnag (or, if you puristically
insist, in Brobdingrag), Swift has Gulliver moved to all

> While Bentley and Wotton, our champions, he foils,
> And wants neither Temple's assistance, nor Boyle's;
> In spite of his learning, fine reasons, and style,
> — Would you think it? — he favours our cause all the while:
> We raise by his conquest our glory the higher,
> And from our defeat to a triumph aspire;
> Our great brother-modern, the boast of our days,
> Unconscious, has gain'd for our party the bays:
> St James's old authors, so famed on each shelf,
> Are vanquish'd by what he has written himself."

* I retain the now accepted spelling in spite of the correction
made by Captain Gulliver in his letter to his cousin [Richard]
Sympson, where he says that the "word should have been spelt"
Brobdingrag, not, erroneously, *Brobdingnag*. As usual in matters of language, centuries-old usage legitimatizes even error.

manner of places by the nine-year-old daughter of the farmer who first found him, but this gigantic girl (whom, you'll remember, Gulliver fondly named Glumdalclitch, or little nurse) never thinks of setting him high on her shoulders, nor, for that matter, do any of his friends or enemies at court.

The most I can get out of the *Travels* that bears on my central theme consists of some observations on the relativity of all things, and so, by implication, suggests that dwarfs are not always and everywhere dwarfs, nor giants, giants. Thus, Gulliver, the middle-sized man, is a giant in Lilliput and a dwarf in Brobdingnag. I take this to be a sociological allegory. Just as we sociologists say that social status is always relative to the social context, just so does Swift say that physical stature is always relative to the physical context. Swift, standing upon the shoulders of his predecessors and so seeing farther, generalizes this whole matter when he observes that "undoubtedly philosophers are in the right, when they tell us that nothing is great or little otherwise than by comparison." *

It's easy to understand why Swift didn't adopt the image of dwarfs standing on the shoulders of giants in the first two books of the *Travels*. For these deal only tangentially with matters of learning and natural philosophy. But that he elected not to make use of it in the third book, that piece of science fiction which details the voyage to Laputa, Balnibarbi, Luggnagg, Glubbdubdrib, and Japan and dwells on the work of the philosophers he

* This is not the place to develop Swift's idea of relativity at length. Should you want to study the entire instructive passage from which this one illuminating sentence is extracted, you'll find it in Part II, chap. I of the *Travels* (in my copy, on p. 112 of volume 11 of the *Works*, ed. by Scott, 1824).

found there, – this I can only put down to Swift's notorious recalcitrance. He was always kicking over the traces and refusing, as a reasonable Houyhnhnm should not refuse, to remain in harness.

Nevertheless, Swift, possessed by a genuine sociological imagination, has something for us, even in that third book. What he has is a little remote from my *main* theme but it bears, somewhat, upon a few of my collateral ones. In that book, for example, he anticipates some developments in modern scholarship, thus showing yet again that the Ancients, who by comparison with ourselves might be taken to include Swift, have sown what the Moderns have reaped. Consider his project – he attributes it to the professors of Lagado, but this is rank modesty on Swift's part – for inventing basic English (or, more accurately, basic Lagadan). In the Lagado school of languages, you remember, three professors serve as consultants, having been called in to improve the language of their country. Their very "first project," Swift has Gulliver report, "was to shorten discourse, by cutting polysyllables into one,* and leaving out verbs and participles, because, in reality, all things imaginable are but nouns." As with most pioneering efforts, this one is not faultless. We know today that the problem is a little more complicated than the good professors of Lagado thought. But the essentials are there, though it is not for me to suggest that C. K. Ogden and I. A. Richards had it from the Lagadans, through the courtesy of Gulliver and Swift (and, were we minded to return to the thorny and still

---

* Beyond all doubt, Swift was fixated on apocope, the distasteful practice of successively cutting off the tails of long words to make disgracefully short ones, as you will recognize by returning to my quotation, some 78 pages back, from Swift's anonymous contribution to *The Tatler*.

disputed problem of the *actual* progenitors of the *Travels*, perhaps by courtesy of Arbuthnot, too).

As you'll recall also, this project on basic language, being only the first, was soon displaced by another that threatened to settle the whole problem of making language efficient. This more drastic and so more promising project "was a scheme for entirely abolishing all words whatsoever." The merits of the proposal are self-evident. It is not understandable, therefore, why the Lagadans, through Swift, went on to present a rationale for this proposal. But they did and so I, as a faithful reporter of the facts, must, too. The abolition of words altogether would have an obvious advantage "in point of health, as well as brevity. For it is plain, that every word we speak is, in some degree, a diminution of our lungs by corrosion, and, consequently contributes to the shortening of our lives."

Now this sounds convincing, until you juxtapose it with another of Swift's observations, made some thirty-six pages later, after Gulliver had drifted from the flying island of Laputa * (where the Grand Academy of Lagado is located) to Luggnagg, with a short stopover in Balnibarbi. Of all the Luggnaggians, you'll recall, Gulliver found the social stratum of *struldbrugs*, or immortals, most interesting. Naturally enough, Gulliver's conversation with them soon turned to this matter of an enduring old age (thus anticipating, by quite a while, our currently

* I continue to follow the tradition of referring to "the flying island" of Laputa. But I should report that our Bob, examining Swift's text with the practiced eye of a mathematician and physicist, has found that Swift may have been putting us on. For the full story, see Bob's soon-to-be published paper. The full citation reads: Robert C. Merton, "The Motionless 'Motion' of Swift's Flying Island," forthcoming in the *Journal of the History of Ideas*.

enforced fascination with gerontology). In a particularly longwinded disquisition, Gulliver, who had been *listening* for so long that he was obviously aching to do some talking of his own, went on to suggest that an immortal existence might not be all it was cracked up to be. Immortality, he said, was not enough. The question was, under which conditions would this unending life continue? Of course, if it meant always being "in the prime of youth, attended with prosperity and health," then, there was little question that it was something worth having. But the real problem, Swift had Gulliver note with his (Swift's) usual insight, was how people "would pass a perpetual life, under all the usual disadvantages which old age brings along with it." In other words, how much decrepitude can a person stand? *

I have only two observations to make on this passage from the *Travels*. First, it shows great prescience. It is almost as though Swift had clairvoyantly recognized the great troubles that would confront so many of the residents of Florida and California as they found themselves forced to endure a long, long old age. The second is that Swift can't have it both ways. If he makes a case for his proposed abolition of all words by claiming that it would extend the longevity of man, thereby implying that this

---

* It's a pity that in his travels, Gulliver never came upon the thirteenth-and-fourteenth century theorist of longevity, Chia Ming (c. 1268–c. 1374). [I say Chia Ming; that is style Chia Wên-ting; his fancy name was Hua shan lao-jên, meaning old man of the Hua mountain (in Chehkiang; he was, after all, born in Hai-ning, Chehkiang).] He wrote his major treatise on diet and longevity — *Yin-shih-hsü-chih* (*Elements of Dietetics*) — to explain how he came to be a centenarian for, when he reached that august age, the emperor asked, naturally enough, how he had managed the feat. Chia answered, in effect: eat right and live longer.

is eminently to be desired, he can't then go on, as he forgetfully does, to argue that old age, with its decay of faculties proceeding more rapidly than the decline of ambitions and wishes, is anything but a happy condition. All I can conclude is that Swift, like most of us authors, is sometimes forgetful. As you know, it's hard to remember everything you have set down in the early part of a book when you're nearing the end, and it's just too much to expect an author to re-read what he has put behind him.

⟨ xliii

THERE'S really little more in the *Travels* that's germane to my subject — except, perhaps, for one thing. As I pointed out a few pages back, Swift was a member of the Scriblerus club and so was, in a degree, a member of a research-team. I realize, of course, that the term is slightly anachronistic but it's apt enough for even such strict historians as yourself to allow this little historical license. Now, it follows from one of the fundamental premises of the sociology of knowledge that the social relations in which a man is involved will somehow be reflected in his ideas. And this, evidently, is just what happened with Swift. Being able to draw upon his own experience in the Scriblerus group, he is quick to think in terms of research projects, requiring the collaboration of many minds in order to solve a complex problem. (Besides he had only to look about him and note the growing popularity of projects of every kind.) However all this might be — and I admit it's gross speculation, at best — the fact remains that Swift did dream up quite a number of promising projects calling for research. Again, what makes this fact pertinent is that, with what we now know to be his customary prescience, Swift anticipated the need for research on a lot of problems that some of us ignorantly suppose to be problems only of our time. (A little more of this sort of thing, and I'll be prepared to shift my allegiance from the moderns to the, comparatively speaking, ancients.)

I can't here recount all of Swift's prescient formulations of research projects that require doing, but perhaps two or three will suffice to make the point. For brevity's sake, I'll confine myself to the projects in "public administration" (the term being Swift's, not mine). There is, for example, the project dealing with what we now describe as the homeostatic mechanism (or balancing mechanism) of legislative bodies. Swift puts this in the form of a precept, but it's clear from the context that he intends it as something that still needs thorough and systematic investigation. The mechanism consists in this:

> That every senator in the great council of a nation, after he had delivered his opinion, and argued in the defence of it, should be obliged to give his vote directly contrary; because, if that were done, the result would infallibly terminate in the good of the public.

The hypothesis presupposed by this suggestion is evident: rhetoric, which need not express a close resemblance to the realities of the case, can and often does persuade. It can thus result in having senators vote in accord with activated sentiment rather than in accord with the dictates of reason. To counteract this untoward effect, which would lead to unrealistic legislation based upon emotion, it is necessary that the orators who stir up this emotion vote against what they propose. In this way, they may cancel things out and leave them as they would have been in the first place, a principle for the preservation of legislative equilibrium — sometimes mistakenly called legislative lethargy — that can scarcely be improved upon. Granted that the political arithmetic of votes presupposed by Swift's hypothesis seems a little peculiar at first, you must nevertheless remember that this is *only* an hypothesis, and when it is put to the test by rigorous research, the truth will out. But you must admit, surely, that it's an exceedingly ingenious — or, as current cant has it, an *insightful* — hypothesis.

Swift has another hypothesis about power politics, and this one too deserves research today as it did in Swift's day. But this is so complex an idea that it resists summary; you would be better served by turning directly to Swift's own account (which is on page 241 of my copy of the *Travels*; I do not give the full citation for you will find it in preceding footnotes).

It is a third hypothesis, however, that shows Swift at his prescient best. Contrary to what you may have supposed, and contrary to what Irwin L. Child reports in his chapter on "Socialization" in the authoritative *Handbook of Social Psychology*,* it is not, strictly speaking, the case that "interest in effects of toilet training has arisen

---

* Edited by Gardner Lindzey, compact in two volumes, and published by Addison-Wesley Publishing Company, Inc., in Cambridge 42, Mass. The quotation from Child will be found, interestingly enough, on page 666. (See the English divine, Francis Potter, who published nothing but his *Interpretation of the Number 666, wherein not only the manner how this Number ought to be interpreted is clearly proved and demonstrated; but it is also shewed that this number is an exquisite and perfect character, truly, exactly, and essentially describing that state of Government to which all other notes of Antichrist doe agree. With all knowne objections solidly and fully answered, that can be materially made against it.* The book was

largely from the psychoanalytic concept of the anal character (see, for example, Abraham, 1927; Fenichel, 1945)." The essentials are to be found in Swift, not only in the *Travels* but in much, too much, of his other writings. His fixation on matters stercoraceous has still to be probed by appropriate psychoanalytic studies. Now, it is all very well for you to rise to the defense of our contemporary moderns and argue that no one can read *everything*. But surely, knowing as they doubtlessly did of the Dean of St. Patrick's extravagant and sustained interest in matters fecal, the psychoanalytic originators of the "toilet-training theory" (or as Child puts it in a caption, the theory of "excretory behavior") should, at the least, have consulted Swift to learn what this distinguished predecessor had had to say on the subject. I don't intend to sound querulous, but there *is* such a thing as the scholarly obligation to consult the literature; in a way, that's what much of the quarrel of the Ancients and Moderns is all about.

After this long preamble, I'm inclined to say nothing more about Swift's thoughtful and situal (rather than pedestrian) hypothesis about the connection between the behavior of political men under conditions that are ordinarily of extreme privacy and their behavior out in the political open. Perhaps, if I say no more about it here, it

published at Oxford, in quarto, in 1642. Pepys bought his copy on the 16th of February, 1666 [*n.b.*], began to read it by the 5th of November, and finished reading it on the 10th of the same month. He reports that 666 "pleases me mightily"; that "I like it all along, but his close is most excellent; and, whether it be right or wrong, is mighty ingenious." Other readers seem to have agreed with Pepys; the book was translated into Latin, French, Dutch, and other languages. Potter would no doubt have had some perceptive analysis of the fact that Child's remark occurs on page 666; I find it simply baffling.)

will induce you to turn to the original source and that
is always worthwhile in itself.

One last research hypothesis from Swift's larger store
and I'm done. This one is so fully prophetic of problems
still requiring adequate study that I cannot bring myself
to omit it. Tell me, which time and place is Swift describing when he writes:

> . . . the bulk of the people consist in a manner
> wholly of discoverers, witnesses, informers, accusers,
> prosecutors, evidences, swearers, together with their
> several subservient and subaltern instruments, all
> under the colours, the conduct, and the pay of min-
> isters of state, and their deputies.

Not only is this description apt of a time he could not
know, but the hypothesis designed to explain the behavior
he describes is not entirely without merit. He writes, still
in the mood prescient, but evidently intending all this as
mere hypothesis:

> The plots, in that kingdom [of Tribnia *], are usually
> the workmanship of those persons who desire to raise
> their own characters of profound politicians; to restore
> new vigour to a crazy administration; to stifle or
> divert general discontents; to fill their coffers with
> forfeitures [for political witchhunting often seems to
> pay off in the most vulgar terms]; and raise or sink
> the opinion of public credit, as either shall best answer
> their private advantage.

I happen to think that these hypotheses are oversim-
plified but then, as everyone knows, *Gulliver's Travels* is
a children's book. Nevertheless, there's something here
still worth our notice. If Swift has failed us, in not saying
a blessed thing about dwarfs, pigmies, or gnomes, or

* Tribnia (of course) = Britannia.

even Lilliputians standing on the shoulders of giants, he
has reminded us, by works, not words, that not all wisdom
begins with the Moderns. But, then, except in the heat
of battle, who ever said it did?

ℂ *xliv*

NOT, SURELY, Alexander Ross. Even that angry conservative, as we have seen, could not, in the fullness of
his mid-seventeenth-century wrath, bring himself to claim
that the Moderns he so much condemned had in fact
downgraded the Ancients to the plane where they rejected
them entirely. The then modern dwarfs were not so
short-sighted as all that, even in Ross's jaundiced opinion. At any rate, we can understand why Ross, in searching out synonyms for the words "Dwarfs and Pigmies,"
could not have availed himself of the word, "Lilliipu-
tians." He had simply come along too soon.

But turning to the other component of the figurative
expression whose history we are tracing — the giant, sym-
bolizing the ancients — we have yet to explain why Ross,
and other Englishmen of the seventeenth century like him,
did not adopt the ready-to-hand symbols of Gargantua
or even Pantagruel. After all, a century before Ross and
his kind, Rabelais had devoted his middle years to writing his enduring work of genius and, just a year before
he died in 1553, had actually completed the full edition *
of *The Lives, Heroic Deeds & Sayings of Gargantua and*

* I stand by this statement, being one of those incorrigible die-
hards who refuse to acknowledge the sixth book, which appeared a decade later, as actually Rabelais'. It's too laboriously
Rabelaisian to be the genuine article.

Pantagruel. Why did Ross and the rest of that disgruntled company, with all their talk of giants and dwarfs, wholly ignore Rabelais and his work? Among a few other things, Rabelais had had a good deal to say about the bickering between modern philosophers and stand-ins for the ancient philosophers.

Once again, and somewhat to my regret, I'm afraid we must exculpate Ross and his ilk. Ross had gone into print with his *Arcana* in 1651, as I mentioned some 36 pages back, and it was not until the second year following that Sir Thomas Urquhart (or Urchard) had put in print his translation of the first two books of *Gargantua and Pantagruel.** As for the rest of that monumental work of genius, it did not get Englished until the editor Motteux, in 1693–94, published the first three books of Urquhart's translation, and finally, in 1708, himself translated books 4 and 5. It would really have been too much to expect the Rosses of the seventeenth-century English world to decipher Rabelais' own language; a translation was imperative. And Ross was long dead by the time that greatest of all translations from French *galimatias* into English was achieved by Urquhart and Motteux.

* Sir Thomas had long been in training to evolve a lingo adequate to the task of reproducing the grandiloquent farrago of Rabelais' masterwork. His mathematical treatise, *Trissotetras,* for example, instructs us in peerless double-talk that "The axioms of plane triangles are four viz. Rulerst, Eproso, Grediftal and Bagrediffiu," and that Rulerst actually branches into Gradesso and Eradetul, remaining all the while under the directory of Uphechet. Sir Thomas's later scheme for a universal language, *Logopandecteision,* hints darkly at "disergetic loxogonosphericals" while proceeding "to the catheteuretic operation" of something or other.

You will allow that this is inspired grimgribber. (Incidentally, can it have been *this* word Maury Maverick was searching for when he minted its synonym, gobbledygook?)

That, then, is why we hear no reverberations of
Rabelais in the writings of a Goodman or a Ross. That
"huge and mighty Gyant Gargantua" who "at the age of
foure hundred, forescore fourty and foure years begat his
sonne Pantagruel upon his wife named Badebec, daughter
to the king of the Amaurots in Utopia" — that Gargantua * might as well never have lived for all the attention
he gets from Ross and Goodman. If neither Gargantua
nor Pantagruel find mention, you might readily suppose,
and you would be right, that no echoes at all can be
heard of Panurge in those 17th-century writings about
Ancients and Moderns, giants and dwarfs. That, too, is a
pity. Somehow I can't but think that there must be something germane in such a man "of a middle stature, not too
high, nor too low" who, at five-and-thirty, had much to
commend him though it's true, as Rabelais reminds us,
that he "was naturally subject to a kinde of disease, which
at that time they called lack of money." Nor do we hear
a word of Pantagruel's "incomparable knowledge," based
on the works of both the Ancients *and* the Moderns. Nor
is anything heard, in the works of Ross, of that historic
debate between the renowned and learned Pantagruel
and his less famous antagonist, the English philosopher
Thaumaste. Now this fault cannot be left unremedied.
For this debate is historic in many more ways than one,
although of these many, I mention only two. First,
Thaumaste proposes and Pantagruel, in his proper confidence, agrees that the debate not be conducted "after
the manner of the academicks by declamation" but that it

* By the way, I have it on the authority of an almanac for 1697
that, just a century before, Gargantua and Tom Thumb fought
a duel on Salisbury Plain. The outcome is not recorded but
Tom evidently survived the unequal contest for popular tradition has it that he died at Lincoln, one of the five Danish towns
of England.

141

be conducted "by signes only without speaking, for the matters are so abstruse, hard and arduous, that words proceeding from the mouth of man will never be sufficient for [the] unfolding of them." In this proposal, you will at once detect the antecedent of Swift's scheme "for entirely abolishing all words whatsoever." What Swift has done, plainly enough, is to generalize Rabelais' suggestion, confined to the one episode of the debate between Thaumaste and Pantagruel, and so to give it a significance that quite transcends the original suggestion. We see here yet another instance of a Modern, that is, the early eighteenth-century Swift, climbing up on the shoulders of the so-to-speak Ancient, the sixteenth-century Rabelais.*

That is one historic aspect of the debate between Thaumaste and Pantagruel, as recorded by Rabelais. The other, and I cannot help but believe the more momentous of the two, is that the whole thing anticipates the Hooke-Newton-Merton sociological theory of the perverse effects of public debate upon intellectual clarity (not to say, integrity). If Vives anticipated Hooke, and Hooke and Newton anticipated me, then I argue that Rabelais anticipated Hooke, Newton, and me (though not, of course, Vives). (What is more, I have more than a sneaking suspicion that a lot of Ancients anticipated all of us comparative Moderns.) †

* The indebtedness of Swift to Rabelais is a matter of such common notoriety that I cannot bring myself to describe it in detail. Everyone knows, because Swift made no effort to conceal it, how much *Gulliver's Travels* owes to the famous voyage of Pantagruel. And that both Rabelais and Swift owe much to the *True History* of Lucian, "that fictitious journey through imaginary countries prefaced by an introduction, in an exquisite vein of irony, upon the art of writing history" — that this is so was known even before Sir Walter Scott set it all down in the lucid lines I have just quoted.

† Consider only the seeming intimations of the principle in the

The rationale of the proposed wordless debate and the corresponding great merit of a debate conducted wholly through gestures contrived for the occasion are both plain enough. The listeners (rather, the spectators) don't really know what's going on and so cannot interact with the speakers (that is, the gesturers), leading them to hold fast to opinions even though they privately know them to be untenable. The use of gestures, indecipherable by the audience (or rather, the lookers-on), cuts off such interaction and so allows each of the debaters to concede the truths gestured by the other. Rabelais doesn't put it in quite these words, in chapter xviii of the second book, but he does even better; he puts it in *his* words:

> [Pantagruel addresses the engaging but talkative
> Thaumaste] . . . although I ought rather to learn of
> thee, than thou of me; but, as thou hast protested, we
> will conferre of these doubts together, and will seek
> out the resolution, even unto the bottom of that un-
> drainable Well, where Heraclitus sayes the truth lies
> hidden: and I do highly commend the manner of
> arguing which thou hast proposed, to wit, by signes
> without speaking; [and now comes the decisive though

lost works of that ambiguous pre-Socratic pessimist, Prodicus, described by Aristophanes as a "bubbling brook," condemned by Æschines as a mere sophist and alternately praised and satirized by Plato (in the words of Socrates) as possessing "a wisdom . . . which is more than human and of very ancient date" (*Protagoras*, 340E). His wisdom enabled Prodicus to make "charming distinctions" between near-synonyms (such as "will" and "wish") while remaining cursed by a bent for pedantry quite as marked as that of Hippias. And of course Plato amply adumbrated the basic distinction between noisy contention in public and peaceful discussion in private; witness only *Protagoras* 337; *Gorgias* 457–8; *Republic* VI, 492; *Thætetus*, 168.

143

implicit sociological theory] for by this means thou
and I shall understand one another well enough, *and
yet shall be free from this clapping of hands, which
these blockish Sophisters make, when any of the
Arguers hath gotten the better of the Argument;* * Now
tomorrow I will not faile to meet thee at the place
and houre that thou has appointed, but let me intreat
thee, *that there be not any strife or uproare between
us, and that we seek not the honour and applause of
men, but the truth only* . . .

I'm sorry to insist on making the obvious manifest. But
I simply could not resist italicizing the crucial passages.
You see, Rabelais is not merely delivering himself of a
pious commonplace: let's seek truth rather than be concerned primarily with how we look in the eyes of men.
He is identifying the crux in such pious maxims, just as
Hooke, Newton and I were to do later, Hooke and Newton scarcely a century afterwards and I, creature of my
time, not until four centuries later. The crux, of course,
is this: how can one insulate the searchers for truth from
the responses of the mob, even of the scientific mob, to
say nothing of that promiscuous assemblage once known
as the *mobile* (which is in turn only an abbreviation of
mobile vulgus, the fickle or excitable crowd)? † Rabelais is
proposing an ingenious *mechanism* for insulating truth-
seekers from popular applause. Or, as he puts it in
descriptive rather than analytical terms, this device is
designed to protect the lovers of truth (*i.e.,* the philos-

---

* You hear here an echo of Plato (*Republic* VI, 492).
† Incidentally, we shouldn't be snobbish about use of the vul-
garism, "mob." It is all very well for Swift to ridicule this then
new-fangled word. It is even understandable that Burke should
apologize for its usage: "A mob (excuse the term, it is still in
use here) . . ." But Swift was writing in 1710 and Burke in
1790; today, it's quite admissible.

ophers) from "all the School-boyes, Professors of Arts, Senior-Sophisters, Batchelors [who will begin] to clap their hands, as their scurvie custome is." I'm fairly certain I've been able to generalize what I now discover to be Rabelais', not Hooke's, Newton's or my, principle, but I don't want to do that here. It's enough, perhaps, to say only that there are almost as many ways to insulate truth-seekers from the mob as there are to skin the cat.*

ℂ *xlv*

IT MAY seem a far step from the sixteenth-century giant, Rabelais, to the late seventeenth-century author and statesman of middling size, Sir William Temple. But, like Tristram, I shall not allow the prissy niceties of com-posing a tightknit account to shake my credit by forcing me to abandon a promise. You will surely remember that when we were exploring Dean Swift's possible contribu-tions to our saga, I promised to say more about his capricious patron, Sir William. There is no problem in

* As a proud and loving companion of some fifteen cats, I'd prefer that you not make the mistake of taking this idiom lit-erally. "Skin the cat" does not refer to a barbarous removal of the outer integument of one of the most admirable of domestic companions — one, incidentally, to whom we can rightly attrib-ute the birth of civilization, for if the very ancient Egyptians had not had cats, . . . Instead, and in its only acceptable sense, it is an idiom of gymnastics, referring to the various ways in which one can "grasp the bar with both hands, raise the feet, and so draw the body, between the arms, over the bar." I there-fore speak gymnastically, not sadistically, in the passage overhead.

redeeming that promise, for Temple enters our story through many doors.

But before we allow him to come into the thick of things, and there's no denying that that is where he belongs, we who take joy in the glories of the English language must acknowledge our enduring debt to him. We cannot permit his reputation to remain in the shadow just because he happened to make a notorious gaffe in assuming the *Letters of Phalaris* to be authentic. That reputation must be refurbished, – not least because we have been victimized in letting its original refulgence become dulled by the passing of time and the rendering of seemingly authoritative judgment. Let's face up to it: the contempt in which some of us are inclined to hold Temple stems not from our own reading of his works but from Macaulay's indictment of them. It was back in October 1838 that Macaulay trained his heavy guns, as any good Whig naturally would, upon the Tory's, the Right Honorable Thomas Peregrine Courtenay's, *Memoirs of the Life, Works and Correspondence of Sir William Temple*. The fact is that we've been living for much too long in the shade of Macaulay's unsparing appraisals of men of letters or action. Too many of us have for too many years allowed that considerable genius to do our thinking (or, at least, our judging) for us. There are even some scholars, you realize, who still believe that his diabolic anatomizing of the character of Bacon gives us a glimpse of the real man, hidden beneath his robes of state and his prophet's mantle. But let's not get started on that particular belittling of a genius who, like us lesser folk, had his faults, many of which he freely admitted and some of which he repented. The point is that once we recognize Macaulay's debating tactic of making us confess to be less instructed than his ubiquitous "schoolboy of

fourteen" should we dare to disagree with his judgments
of men, institutions and events, the recognition of this
truth can make us free. We can emancipate ourselves from
his authoritative control and need not repeat, as though
it were a judgment handed down from giant to pigmy,
his invidious account of Temple's limitations. After all, if
we were to assemble in one place all the knowledge and
understanding with which Lord Macaulay variously en-
dows his fourteen-year-old schoolboy, we would find this
astonishing youth a veritable sage, possessed of learning
and wisdom that surpass the length of numberless days.

Although Temple was not a man to Macaulay's taste,
it does not follow that he must also be a man not to ours.
Nor does it follow that Temple need be counted among
those "men of unquiet minds and violent ambition [who]
followed a fearfully eccentric course, dart[ing] wildly
from one extreme to another." Indeed, even Macaulay
had to acknowledge that "Temple was not one of these"
(although by skillfully placing Temple in close proximity
to them, he manages to have some of the tarnish rub off
on him). Nor need we be cozened by the great historian's
knack, exercised when he was so minded, of making the
most innocent activities seem downright suspicious as
when he manages to convert Temple's successful practice
of gardening into a serpent-like device for undermining
the virtue of those around him or when he seemingly
defends Temple, as Mark Antony defended the noble
Brutus, against the wicked charge that his sentences run to
excessive length, saying that "a critic who examines them
carefully will find that they are not swollen by parenthetical matters [this being clearly all to the good], that
their structure is scarcely ever intricate [this, surely, being
even better], that they are formed merely by accumulation [what's this, now? do we detect a change of tone?]

147

and that, by the simple process of now and then leaving
out a conjunction, and now and then substituting a full
stop for a semicolon [it's altogether clear now: we've
been had], they might, without any alteration in the order
of the words, be broken up into very short periods,
with no sacrifice except that of euphony. [And now
Macaulay is ready to climax his devilishly skillful defense
of Temple.] The long sentences of Hooker and Clarendon, on the contrary, are really long sentences, and cannot
be turned into short ones, without being entirely taken
to pieces." So does Macaulay pause for an instant to take
apart Temple's mere pretence to the art of writing a
genuinely *long* sentence.

But this, of course, is merely prelude. We have yet to
watch Macaulay bring Temple to heel on the very subject
which engages our unwavering attention: the battle between the ancients and moderns so far as this bears upon
the giant-and-dwarf Aphorism. If Macaulay can fault
Temple for seeming to write long sentences when, in
truth, he merely pastes together a congeries of short ones,
then we can rightly suppose that he will raze to the
ground Temple's jerry-built show of learning. He does
not disappoint us. In assured Macaulayan prose, he begins
by reminding the faithful subscribers to *The Edinburgh
Review* who waited for each new issue of that magazine
to learn what they must think about anyone or anything
Macaulay chose to discuss:

A most idle and contemptible controversy had arisen
in France touching the comparative merit of the
ancient and modern writers . . . [It] might have
been expected that those who undertook to decide the
point would at least take the trouble to read and
understand the authors on whose merits they were to

pronounce. Now it is no exaggeration to say * that, among the disputants who clamoured, some for the ancients and some for the moderns, very few were decently acquainted with either ancient or modern literature, and hardly one was well acquainted with both.†

And now Macaulay comes to that "evil hour" in which Temple undertook to defend the ancients, his prin-

* Properly translated, this phrase means that Macaulay is about to propose an exaggeration that would ordinarily surpass all credence. The cognoscenti will at once recognize this as a familiar abuse of "the of-course mood" (which the grammarians cannot ticket as indicative, imperative, subjunctive, *or* infinitive). The abuse consists merely in smuggling in disputable statements by a disarming preliminary phrase: "of course," "no doubt," or "it is no exaggeration to say." But this misuse must not be allowed to warn us off the authentic use of the of-course mood. This is a use in which the author announces a familiar fact or idea which must be stated in order to lay the foundation for some other facts or ideas that are anything but familiar. In such cases, it is both a matter of simple courtesy to the reader and a matter of self-protection for the author to signal by a qualifying "of course" that he too knows the fact or the idea to be unexcitingly familiar. In that way, he avoids the practice of Oliver Wendell Holmes's katydid who persistently says "an undisputed thing in such a solemn way." The of-course mood also keeps an author from flogging a dead horse, blowing down a man of straw or breaking through an open door, behavior that is almost as unattractive as it is wasteful.

† If you should want to read what precedes and what follows this passage, you need not turn to the October 1838 issue of *The Edinburgh Review* itself. Like me, you may not happen to have this particular issue at home. You can instead pick up your edition of Macaulay's *Critical and Historical Essays* and find it all there under the heading, "Sir William Temple." In my edition, the one published in 1864 by Longman, Green, Longman, Roberts, & Green, it appears as the very first essay in the second volume, running from page 1 to page 50. The essay is easily condensed into these few pages by the device of using 9-point type ("Bourgeois") and double columns. The extract above will be found on page 45 of this edition.

cipal qualification for the task allegedly being that "he knew not a word of Greek." What follows in Macaulay's essay is too painful to repeat. For, of course, he was in this instance on safe ground in directing his cannonade against the unhappily vulnerable Temple. That, among his other sins born of ignorance, Temple should have elected to cite the *Letters of Phalaris* as the best Letters in the world was bad enough. That he should then have gone on in a foredoomed effort to defend this judgment, and to get a confederacy of his friends and disciples to join in the defense against the learned proof by Bentley that the letters were not only very bad but forged – all this is too sad and painful a spectacle for us, of our own will, to look upon again.

And yet, look we must. For that arrogant, courageous and trenchant scholar, Richard Bentley, forces himself upon our attention in so many ways that we cannot deny him renewed entrance into our narrative. It is not merely that he showed, beyond all intelligent doubt, that the *Letters of Phalaris,* exultantly ascribed by Temple to a prince of the seventh century B.C., were in fact clumsy forgeries by a Greek rhetorician of the Christian era.*
Nor is it merely that in the first Boyle lectures (in 1692), he promptly took up the implications of his friend's, Newton's, *Principia* to prove, most scientifically, the exis-tence of an omnipotent and omniscient Creator. Nor even that, together with Bentham and Mill, he belonged to all that crowd (or, as Horace, might [and did in fact] say, *hoc genus omne*) of prodigious youthful scholars so that he was admitted to Cambridge at fourteen, wait-ing, however, another ten years before he used his spare time, which was not ample, to prepare a personal con-

* In truth, the *Letters* bore the stamp of their own negation, as with the celebrated ancient Greek coin, dated 500 B.C.

cordance of the Hebrew Bible listing every word alphabetically and in five adjacent columns, giving "all the various interpretations of those words in the Chaldee, Syriac, Vulgate, Latin, Septuagint, and Aquila, Symmachus, and Theodotion, that occur in the whole Bible." (I quote Bentley's own account of his pastime.)

The ambuscade of the *Phalaris Letters,* the adaptation of the *Principia* to theological purposes, and the precocity of his pansophistic learning would not have sufficed to bring Bentley within the orbit of this narrative.* But he unmistakably qualifies himself for admission through the faint echo of the Aphorism in his apology to his youthful grandson, Richard Cumberland, for his lifelong interest in classical studies; thus:

> . . . the wit and genius of those old heathens beguiled me, and as I despaired of raising myself up to their standard upon fair ground, I thought the only chance I had of looking over their heads was to get upon their shoulders.†

Which brings us directly to Bentley's friend, William Wotton,‡ who had his own share of precocity. At the age of four, he worked his way through the Gospel of St. John in the Vulgate (that old Latin version by St. Jerome) and a year later, when his father made the mistake of showing him the Testament in Greek, young William soon worked his way through that as well. The scholarly boy thereupon took a breathing spell for a

* In one respect, Bentley was anything but precocious: he was full of years — three score and ten of them — before he became addicted to tobacco.
† Richard Cumberland, *Memoirs,* Boston, 1806 edition, p. 10.
‡ Wotton also liked to smoke. As a matter of fact, he gave up a Roman urn, which had been dug up at Sandy, Bedfordshire, to Archdeacon Battely of Canterbury for a tobacco-jar.

couple of months, before plowing into Hebrew. Only then did he take up his studies in earnest, carefully rationing his day so that he could read English at eight every morning, Latin at eleven, Greek at two and Hebrew at four. Even so, he didn't get through the whole of "Batrachomyomachia" until he was six. As a result of such delays, he was not admitted to Cambridge until he was nearly ten and had to wait until he was thirteen for his B.A. This is the same Wotton who, on page 77 of (the third edition of) his *Reflections upon Ancient and Modern Learning*, defended the Moderns by attacking Temple's tendentious use of our Aphorism, while all the while managing to give one of the best popular accounts of the growth of physical science up to his day.* He is also the same Wotton, of course, who was jointly slain with Bentley in Swift's *Battle of the Books* by a "lance of wondrous length and sharpness" that transfixed them both, "till down they fell, joined in their lives, joined in their deaths; so closely joined, that Charon would mistake them both for one, and waft them over Styx for half his fare."

ℂ *xlvi*

RETURNING in more cheerful mood to Temple, let us remember Johnson's magisterial observation to Boswell

* Wotton is another of us who have suffered from the plague of being scooped (or nearly so) by someone else publishing our own best thoughts. On page xx of the Postscript, he writes nervously: "Since the Second Edition of my Book was Printed off, we have had an Account in the *Journal des Sçavans*, that Monsieur Perrault has Published a THIRD PART of his *Parallel between the Ancients and the Moderns* . . . The Book is not

that "Sir William Temple was the first writer who gave cadence to English prose [no doubt, in those clumsily contrived *pasticci* of seemingly long sentences that spurred Macaulay's contempt]. Before his time they were careless of arrangement, and did not mind whether a sentence ended with an important word or an insignificant word, or with what part of speech it was concluded." However all this may be, the salient fact for us is that in his *Essay upon the Ancient and Modern Learning* of 1690 (to be distinguished, of course, from the posthumously published *Defence of the Essay upon Ancient and Modern Learning* which was less Temple's than that of his circles of friends and defenders), Sir William moves directly to the point and promptly cites our Aphorism, thus:

The Force of all that I have met with upon this Subject, either in Talk or Writing is, First, as to Knowledge, That we must have more than the Ancients, because we have the Advantage both of theirs and our own, which is commonly illustrated by the Similitude of a Dwarfs standing upon a Gyants shoulders, and seeing more or farther than he. Next, as to Wit or Genius, that Nature being still the same, these must be much at a Rate in all Ages, at least in the same Clymates, as the Growth and Size of Plants and Animals commonly are; And if both these are allowed, they think the Cause is gained. But I cannot tell why we should conclude that the Ancient Writers had not as much Advantage from the knowledge of others that

yet, that I know of, in *England,* and possibly may not be procurable in some time. I thought it necessary, however, to take notice, that I have had a bare Intimation of such a Book, and no more; that so if in any Material Things we should happen to Agree, (as writing upon the same Argument, 'tis very probable we may,) I might not hereafter be thought a Plagiary."

153

were Ancient to them, as we have from those that are Ancient to us.*

And there we have the gist of Temple's contribution to our story. From him we learn more than the fact that the giant-and-dwarf figure is a familiar one; that much we had picked up from our old friend, John Hall, who, back in 1649, was describing it as a "common saying." Temple now informs us that the similitude *continued* to be "commonly" employed in his day, almost half a century later. This lends more support to our growing surmise that Newton, writing his letter to Hooke in 1675/6, had drawn upon and creatively adapted a saying common in his time and perhaps common enough to qualify as a commonplace. And it lends force to our growing conviction that even the worthy George Sarton, the dean among historians of science, sometimes nods, as when he hazarded the guess that Newton had it from Burton's *Anatomy of Melancholy*.

ℂ *xlvii*

TEMPLE tells us even more (and perhaps it is my gratitude for this tidbit that tempts me to support him against the assault by Macaulay). For the first time in all this history, we hear that the giant-and-dwarf similitude is being *talked* about; not only written about, mind you, but talked about. When Temple reports that he has come

---

* My notes locate this passage in Sir William Temple, *Works*, London, 1814, III, at page 46. But a more accessible source that rests on my bookshelves is the edition by J. E. Spingarn,

upon our figure "either in Talk or Writing," he brings
us full into the oral tradition. (If only Pepys or Evelyn or
Boswell had thought to record the spoken peregrinations
of the Aphorism in their circles of conversationalists, how
much more should we now know about the inferences
drawn from the Aphorism about the process through
which knowledge of all sorts accumulates. But then, in all
ages [and, as Temple would surely add, at least "in the
same Clymates"], literate men have set down in writing
only a small part of what was freely circulating in their
everyday talk.)

Although posterity is in general the loser when wit
and learning are ephemerally confined to conversation
rather than permanently congealed in writing (or, better
still, in print), you will agree that the loss is an especially
grievous one as we approach the eighteenth century, aptly
described as the greatest age of conversation. Here, as
before in this narrative, I refuse to be drawn away from
the strict history of the giant-and-dwarf similitude. But,
in all conscience, we must not pass over Temple's allusion
to the *talk* about giant-and-dwarfs with only an expression of sadness about our irrecoverable loss. The special
case must surely alert us to the general problem (a problem which afflicts you historians in particular). It's all
very well to point with pride to such records as Luther's
or John Selden's or Goethe's tabletalk, or to polish yet
again such a gem as that handed down to us by Boswell.
But I know, from painful past experience, how hard it is
to get a firm grip on the conversations of another time,
not least in collaborating with Elinor Barber on an in-

*Sir William Temple's Essays on Ancient and Modern Learning
and on Poetry,* Oxford: At the Clarendon Press, 1909. There
you will find it on page 3.

formal history of the travels and adventures of (the word) Serendipity.*

The sad fact is that, except for titillating samples, we know almost nothing about the conversation, polite and impolite, of that earlier day. Even Sutherland, who didn't really have tape-recordings of authentic talk in earlier times,† must confess his failure as he expresses his belief that his "is the first book to record at length how Englishmen and Englishwomen actually spoke from late medieval times down to the present day." We fare no better, I'm sorry to say, when we turn from the historian Sutherland to the sociologist Simmel, who manages to give a general theory of the sociology of conversation without having very much substance to go on.‡

Yet the canonists of conversation can't be all wrong. Surely, in Temple's time and immediately after, the art of

---

* In point of fact, this complaint about the loss of conversation, not merely the notorious loss of the conversational art, has been emphatically expressed in a carefully unpublished manuscript, the title page of which reads in its entirety thus: Robert K. Merton and Elinor Barber, *The Travels and Adventures of Serendipity: A Study in Historical Semantics and the Sociology of Science.* This would be the place to quote at length the supremely pertinent passages from that manuscript, were it not for the warning of its authors that it is "not to be quoted, abstracted, or reproduced without specific permission."

† You can discover this for yourself merely by turning to James R. Sutherland, *The Oxford Book of English Talk,* published, my tattered notes say, as recently as 1953.

‡ As himself a conversationalist of the first rank, it was perhaps inevitable that Georg Simmel should be tempted into formulating a sociological theory of good talk. But as you will find, in his *Grundfragen der Soziologie,* he has precious few facts on which to build his theory. You won't be much the wiser, if the truth be known, by turning instead to a later effort by W. Benjamin, "Probleme der Sprachsoziologie," *Zeitschrift für Sozialforschung,* 1935, IV, 2.

conversation must have flourished. Else, why the rivalry among salons,* both in London and Paris? I'm inclined to agree with Bernard Berenson's composite prescript and quantitative assessment (in his *Self-Portrait*) that "conversation should have the same privilege that is granted — reluctantly enough — to the other fine arts, the privilege of freedom from utilitarian purpose. The result may be of little consequence, as 18th-century conversation doubtless † was; the more so as in that least unhappy of centuries a larger number of people were enjoying talk than at any previous moment in history, even if we include the Athens of that greatest of all conversationalists, Plato's Socrates."

* Should you still entertain doubts, spend a little time with Glotz on *Salons* or, better yet, with V. Tornius on *Salons*, available in English since 1929.
† Having been forewarned, just a few pages back, about the dubious art of abusing the of-course mood, you'll recognize in BB's "doubtless" a signal that he lays claim to being most certain when he is, in truth, most unsure.

After all, BB must have known Swift's *Hints toward an Essay on Conversation* (*c.* 1709), which roundly lampooned his contemporaries who talk incessantly of themselves or who monopolize conversation (thus irresistibly putting us in mind of Darwin's amused report of a dinner at his house during which "Carlyle . . . silenced every one by haranguing . . . on the advantages of silence. After dinner Babbage, in his grimmest manner, thanked Carlyle for his very interesting lecture on silence"). And if BB somehow missed Swift's fugitive *Hints*, he must surely have come upon his later book (assigned to Simon Wagstaff, Esq.), *A Complete Collection of genteel and ingenious Conversation, according to the most polite mode and method now used at Court, and in the best Companies of England.* Wagstaff's unstinted report of the conversations of Lady Smart, Tom Neverout, Miss Notable, and Lady Answerall at least suggests that then, as now, we should look to quite other circles for the art of good talk.

ℂ *xlviii*

WITH Berenson's allusion to Socrates, we are back to
the quarrel of the Ancients and the Moderns and with it,
inevitably, back to Sir William Temple, the GYANTS and
the dwarfs. For Sir William will not leave the matter
alone. He converts a figure of speech into a literal reading
of history in which Gyants, both figurative and literal,
flourished, never, perhaps, to arise again. As in his
Phalaris misadventure, he plunges decisively into credulity
in order to make his case that, for both body and soul,
the olden times were the incomparably best times:

> In the growth and stature of Souls as well as Bodies,
> the common productions are of indifferent sizes, that
> occasion no gazing nor no wonder. But (tho') there
> are or have been sometimes Dwarfs and sometimes
> Gyants in the World, yet it does not follow that there
> must be such in every Age nor in every Country. [So
> far, impeccable logic and reasonable biological as-
> sumption: subspecies and varieties of men as of other
> animals and of plants *may* die out; when it comes to
> dwarfs at least, minimifidianism is unwarranted.] This
> we can no more conclude than that there never have
> been any, because there are none now, at least in the
> compass of our present Knowledge or Inquiry. [And
> now, the plunge] As I believe there may have been
> Gyants at some time and some place or other in the
> World, of such a stature as may not have been
> equalled perhaps again in several Thousands of Years
> or in any other Parts, so there may be Gyants in Wit
> and Knowledge, of so over-grown a size as not to be

equalled again in many successions of Ages or any compass of Place or Country.

Once having taken the plunge, Sir William joins the ranks of professional adumbrationists. He faithfully follows the adumbrationist's script: modern discoveries are not new; if new, they are not true; if both new and true, they are not useful. This is how he forthrightly puts it:

There is nothing new in *Astronomy* to vye with the Ancients, unless it be the *Copernican* System; nor in *Physick,* unless Hervy's * Circulation of the Blood. But whether either of these be modern discoveries, or derived from old Fountains, is disputed: Nay, it is so, too, whether they are true or no; for though reason may seem to favour them more than the contrary Opinion, yet sense can very hardly allow them; and to satisfie Mankind, both these must concur.† But if they are true, yet these two great discoveries have made no change in the conclusions of *Astronomy,* nor in the practise of Physick, and so have been of little use to the World, though perhaps of much honour to the Authors.

Almost, I suspect, you are ready to join forces with Macaulay to profane Temple's knowledge. But do hold your attack. After all, few of us are talented enough to achieve unflagging error and so, soon after he repeats the

* Do not cavil here, for spelling was then still an idiosyncratic art. Sam Johnson had not yet laid down the law, and Noah Webster was still far in the offing.
† How great our debt to Temple who once again demonstrates how easy it is for truth to provide an underpinning for error. That reason and sense must concur in science is indeed a truth beyond reasonable or empirical doubt; that Copernicus and Harvey have failed to meet the twin tests is at the least, disputable. Or do you consider this last an unforgivably *radical* claim?

catechism of the adumbrationists, Sir William hits upon a consummate truth (as you will see by inspecting my own account of how scientists are governed by a socially induced love of honor rather than of gain). Listen to his voice of truth and forgive him his occasional errors of prophecy, as he (slightly) anticipates me in tracing out the motive forces of recognition by informed peers among scientists and scholars:

> Now I think that nothing is more evident in the World than that Honour is a much stronger Principle, both of Action and Invention, than gain can ever be. That all the Great and Noble Productions of Wit and of Courage have been inspired and exalted by that alone. [A small truth has a way of inducing a large exaggeration; omit the enthusiastic conclusion, "by that *alone*," and you remain on safe ground.] That the Charming Flights and Labours of Poets, the deep Speculations and Studies of Philosophers, the Conquests of Emperors and Atchievements of Heroes, have all flowed from this one Source of Honour and Fame. The last Farewel that *Horace* takes of his Lyrick Poems, Epicurus of his Inventions in Philosophy, *Augustus* of his Empire and Government, are all of the same strain; and as their Lives were entertained, so their Age was relieved and their Deaths softened, by the Prospect of lying down upon the Bed of Fame.
>
> Avarice is, on the other side, of all Passions the most sordid, the most clogged and covered with dirt and with dross, so that it cannot raise its Wings beyond the smell of the Earth . . . 'Tis no wonder, then, that Learning has been so little advanced since it grew to be mercenary . . .

Touched with anger and melancholy, here is a proleptic diagnosis of the dangers confronting science in an age of affluence.

⟪ xlix

BUT ENOUGH of Sir William Temple, his version of the giants and dwarfs, his adumbrationist sins and his recognition of the motive powers of fame and glory. To continue further with these long, long extracts from his sagacity and his nugacity would be to ignore the immortal Shandean precepts laid down in chapter 14 of the first book of the *Life and Opinions* of our master, Tristram, and to justify the charge set out in chapter 1 of the fifth book (that barbigerous chapter long since known as the "Fragment on Whiskers").* You remember *no doubt* the rhetorical questions that so sharply make up that charge, but I nevertheless jog your memory and mine:

> Tell me, ye learned, [he prophetically asks] shall we for ever be adding so much to the *bulk,* so little to the *stock?*
> Shall we for ever make new books, as apothecaries

* I use the edition close at hand. This happens to be that of the four-volume *Works of Laurence Sterne* which, the title page proudly asserts, were printed in the London of 1819 "for Cadell and Davies; Lackington and Co.; Longman, Hurst, Rees, Orme, and Brown [Longman, as you may have noticed from earlier citations, evidently had a way of associating himself with a great variety of colleagues, none of whom seemed to last very long]; J. Cuthell; J. Nunn; John Richardson; S. Bagster; Black and Co.; J. Carpenter; W. Stewart; J. Asperne; Baldwin, Cradock, and Joy [this one, I should have guessed, an obvious invention of Dickens were it not that he was only a boy of seven at the time this edition appeared]; R. Scholey; J. Porter; R. Hunter; J. Walker; G. and W. B. Whittaker; J. Bohn; and B. Reynolds." In that day, at least, booksellers knew they could feed, in their way, "of the dainties bred" in this book.

make new mixtures, by pouring only out of one vessel
into another?
   Are we for ever to be twisting, and untwisting the
same rope? for ever in the same track, — for ever at
the same pace? *

Pause, now, to celebrate Tristram's awesome daring.
For I must report that this all-out opinion on plagiary,
this rhetorical assault on the practice of feloniously adopting others' words as one's own, is lifted straight out of
Burton. The audacity of this theft in broad daylight — for
surely those who cherished the eighteenth-century Sterne
would be apt also to cherish the seventeenth-century
Burton — is only compounded by the fact that the purloined passage appears in the same Introduction to the
Reader in which Democritus, junior (*i.e.*, Burton) so
fraughtfully quotes Didacus Stella on the giants and
dwarfs. Indeed, the looted language appears on pages 6
and 7; the decisive dictum on page 8. To spare you the
need for consulting Burton directly, that all unbelieving
you might make the comparison with the audacious
Sterne, I give you Burton's words just as he set them
down to the later benefit of Tristram:

   As apothecaries we make new mixtures every day,
   pour out of one vessel into another; and as those old
   Romans robbed all the cities of the world, to set out
   their bad-sited Rome, we skim off the cream of other
   men's wits, pick the choice flowers of their tilled gar-
   dens to set out our own sterile plots . . . we weave
   the same web still, twist the same rope again and
   again . . .

* You will find this on p. 408 of volume one of the *Works.*
The title page, I am happy to report, remains as in the original edition: *The Life and Opinions of Tristram Shandy, Gent.*

Now return to the text of Tristram, compare and ask yourself when you have last encountered a more sardonic piece of plagiary.*

To ask his appropriated trio of questions, as Tristram well knew, is to answer them. Draw upon the wisdom of the past, to be sure, or else the implicitly arrogant claim to knowledge beginning with yourself will stand self-condemned.† But do not confuse this dependence upon the corporate giants of the past with a merely learned repetition of what they have taught you. Instead, follow your bent where it leads for there is no better road to the writing of a history. Now, there is no profit in carrying coals to Newcastle (*Anon.*, 16th century), faggots into the wood (Horace), owls to Athens (Diogenes Laërtius) or historiography to the historian (Merton). Yet, haven't you historians sometimes erred in ignoring that manual of the historical method so compactly set forth in chapter 14 of Tristram's first book? I think you have. And to demonstrate this, I need only quote Tristram, for to para-

* It is surely of no interest, to you any more than to me, that, back in 1812, John Ferriar happened to note this same bit of plagiarizing of Burton by Sterne, this in his *Illustrations of Sterne with Other Essays and Verses,* pp. 94–5.

John Ferriar nevertheless achieves a triple relevance for us. He is the same Ferriar who misdated Burton's *Anatomy,* as I faithfully reported to you on page 8 and, like Aubrey, Ogden Nash, Sterne, Coleridge and myself, he had a connoisseur's eye for a truly striking eye. Witness his article, "Of popular illusions, and particularly of medical demonology," published in Volume III of the *Manchester Memoirs* where, on page 49, he reports that Mercatus "had seen a very beautiful woman break a steel mirror to pieces, by a single glance of her eyes, and blast some trees by merely looking on them; *solo aspectu.*" (It was John Livingston Lowes who put me on to this aspect of Ferriar.)

† I am mindful here of the question put by an indignant wit: "what has he done that he is so modest about it?"

phrase him is only to periphrase him (and for me, as
for Tristram's Yorick, periphrasis remains the cardinal
sin). Here, then, is the gist of his method, a method
which has guided me at every step in this narrative:

> Could a historiographer drive on his history, as a
> muleteer drives on his mule, — straight forward — for
> instance, from Rome all the way to Loretto, without
> ever once turning his head aside, either to the right
> hand or to the left, — he might venture to foretell you
> to an hour when he should get to his journey's end;
> — but the thing is, morally speaking, impossible: for,
> if he is a man of the least spirit, he will have fifty
> deviations from a straight line to make with this or
> that party as he goes along, which he can no ways
> avoid. He will have views and prospects to himself
> perpetually soliciting his eye, which he can no more
> help standing still to look at than he can fly; he will,
> moreover, have various
>> Accounts to reconcile;
>> Anecdotes to pick up;
>> Inscriptions to make out;
>> Stories to weave in;
>> Traditions to sift;
>> Personages to call upon;
>> Panegyrics to paste up at this door;
>> Pasquinades at that: — All which both the man
> and his mule are exempt from. To sum up all; there
> are archives at every stage to be looked into, and
> rolls, records, documents, and endless genealogies,
> which justice ever and anon calls him back to stay the
> reading of: — In short, there is no end of it . . .

But I do not call upon Tristram merely in his capacity of historical methodologist, concerned to find out what

the historian is doing when he is doing what he is doing. Were this alone his claim to relevance for our main business of the giants and the dwarfs, he would have remained in the antechamber, honored but uninvited. But as you have guessed and as I am happy to confirm, he provides us with a multiplicity of relevance. For one, here he is saying "that when a man sits down to write a history, — tho' it be but the history of Jack Hickathrift or [and *now* comes one ticket of entry into our narrative] Tom Thumb, he knows no more than his heels what lets and confounded hindrances he is to meet with in this way." Now we have touched upon Tom Thumb a little way back, but as you doubtless recognized, in only the most superficial fashion. And as Tristram's allusion reminds us, this most famous of diminutive beings is surely deserving of more. Remember only that Fielding contrived his famous burlesque, *Tom Thumb the Great*, in 1730, just thirty years before Tristram was born, and that Henry Carey promptly drew upon Fielding's work to write *Chrononhotonthologos*, "the most tragical tragedy ever tragedised." Carey, as a matter of fact, deserves better than the studied neglect accorded him. You may say, with Chappell and Cummings,* that there is no satisfactory evidence of his actually having composed "God Save the

* Were there space, I could explain why I find fault with W. Chappell's version of Carey's priority in this matter, at least as he presents it in volume two of his *Popular Music of the Olden Time*. Nor is W. H. Cummings altogether clear in his reading of the evidence in that series of articles he published in the *Musical Times* from March through August 1878. I suspect that Carey is being systematically short-changed, just because it is not thought meet that this national air should have been authored by one whose unauthorized birth shrouds his origins in mystery although it *is* definitely known that he died on the 4th of October, 1743.

Queen." But, if so, how do you account for J. C. Smith having told Dr. Harington of Bath, just fifty-three years after the tune had been anonymously published, that Carey had brought it to him "in order to correct the bass"? Surely, this is the sort of precise testimony that clearly bears the stamp of its own authenticity.

There are some who will tell you that Carey is the reputed author of "God Save the *King*" (not "the Queen").* Now it is not for me to get embroiled in a quarrel between scholars. Yet I do believe that I can straighten this one out to the satisfaction of all. The question whether it was the Queen or the King who was initially being celebrated may at first seem answerable by merely establishing a matter of fact: who was on the throne when the song was composed? Since the first known date of publication (in the *Harmonia Anglicana*) was 1742, this, apparently, is enough to clear things up. Caroline was five years dead and George II alone wore the crown. This would seem to settle the matter: "God Save the King" it was. But not so, for, and here I come to the heart of the matter, the issue turns not on a question of fact but on a matter of political sentiment. The devotees of the Queen *knew* that it was she who ruled while the King dallied with a string of beautiful favorites, chief among them being Amelia Sophia, "the young and beautiful wife of Adam Gottlob, count von Walmoden." (She was the occasion for George's saying to his queen, "you must love the Walmoden, for she loves me"; at least, that is how Hervey reports it.) All this lay behind one of the pasquinades of the time, thus:

* For example, Benjamin E. Smith, A.M., L.H.D., editor of the *Century Cyclopedia of Names,* first published by the *London Times* in 1894.

You may strut, dapper George, but 'twill all be in
   vain;
We know 'tis Queen Caroline, not you that reign.

But the sycophants of the King would scarcely acknowledge this. *They* remembered his early tribute to the
English when, as a new prince lately quitting Herren-
hausen in Hannover, he remarked that "I have not a drop
of blood in my veins which is not English," and then went
on to say, a little later, that the English are "the handsomest,
the best-shaped, the best-natured and lovingest people
in the world." This won him few friends in Hannover but
a good many in England. The followers of George
naturally took up the refrain "God Save the King" just as
the followers of Caroline took up the refrain "God Save
the Queen." And there, I submit, is the sociological truth
of the matter, long obscured by the historians' mistaken
formulation of the issue.

    However it may be with "God Save the Queen," there
can be no questioning of Carey having authored the poem,
"Sally in our Alley." This is the best known of his many
poems; moreover, it is the one which the divine Addison
had been pleased to praise more than once. As for the
denial of his priority in having composed "Namby-
Pamby," and so having thrust that expressive term into
our language once and for all, this, I think, borders on
persecution of a genius; – a genius, moreover, who is
anything but unsung (if he did indeed write the British
national anthem). "Namby-Pamby" is undeniably Carey's
coinage, even though some cavillers would jealously
argue that it is too good to be his. After all, we have it
on the unexcelled authority of Pope that Carey's appellation for that cloying versifier, Ambrose Philips, was as
original as it was apt. And since Pope was long engaged

in a "reciprocation of malevolence" with Philips, in
which he made repeated and searing use of the damaging
epithet, he should know.*

¶ l

POPE, of course, continues to hold interest for our account of giants and dwarfs, quite apart from his consummate vindication of Carey's priority. For one thing, he
gives us hope that we may not have missed very much,
after all, in having little access to the conversation of his
time. Remember only his confiding to Spence that "I had
rather be employed in reading than in the most agreeable
conversation." † For another, he shows through his own
behavior how the drive for recognition can become so
intense that even the ordinarily most honorable of men
will cut corners to assure himself, as he supposes, the
largest possible measure of fame. I need not remind you
of the sorry episode of the translation of the *Odyssey* in
which he tried first to suppress the details of his collaboration with Elijah Fenton and William Broome and then

* All of which highlights the unfortunate ambiguity of Sam
Johnson's observation that the poems of Philips which please
most are "those which from Pope or Pope's adherents procured
him the name of Namby-Pamby, the poems of short lines by
which he paid his court to all ages and characters, from Walpole, the steerer of the realm, to Miss Pulteney in the nursery."
Why, for heaven's sake, "Pope OR Pope's adherents"?
† On the dangers of an excess of reading, I have had a good
deal to say in the book I am writing on The Behavior of
Scientists. But perhaps it is otherwise with poets than with
scientists; erudition may not *really* curb originality when one
is in tune with The Muse. There may actually be Two Cultures,
you know.

persuaded Broome, that opulent son of a poor farmer, to write an obsequious statement giving the public the false impression that Pope was responsible for all but five books of the justly famed translation.* You will recall Henley's nasty couplet:

Pope came off clean with Homer; but they say
Broome went before, and kindly swept the way.

There's no pardoning Pope, I suppose, for succumbing to socially induced temptation, but we can try to understand him. True, Broome was by far the better Greek scholar, but he had no touch of originality, aping Pope so closely that he could counterfeit him, and owing the memory of his name exclusively to his underacknowledged collaboration with Pope. In the end, a sort of rough-hewn justice has been done.

But I must stop this bungling defense of the poet, for each new episode of misbehavior throws me off the guard I had painfully erected for the case just before. If only Pope hadn't gone on to doctor his correspondence with Curll and Cromwell! If only he had not assailed Addison, belittled Bentley, bludgeoned Bludgell, collied Cibber, cursed Curll, denounced Dennis, heckled Hervey,† mocked Moore, philippicized Philips and thumped Theobald, (although we can only commend him for having

---

* You'll find the whole unhappy tale in any of the lives of the poet, but perhaps you will consider it best told, not in Sam Johnson's classic biography but in the more recent one by R. K. Root, *The Poetical Career of Alexander Pope.*
† *This* Hervey, I need not tell you, is John, Lord Hervey of Ickworth, not to be confused with Sir William Temple's misspelled "Hervy" whom we met a while back. This is the one so amiably described by Pope as "familiar toad, half froth, half venom." Be that as it may, the DNB nevertheless assures us that "By his wife, Hervey had eight children."

made a butt of that scamp, Bubb Dodington). But he was a wrathful man, a perpetually angry man, and there was no halting him.

And here I simply must stop reporting the relevances of Pope for the history of the giants and dwarfs. To take up again, for example, the disputed authorship of *Martin Scriblerus* about which, as we have seen, even the experts agree to disagree, would serve only to open anew a wound now healed over. In this matter, Pope retains his place in the sun and Arbuthnot must remain content to stand in his shadow. At any rate, we have sifted a little more of that history of Tom Thumb restored to our attention by Tristram.

❲ li

FROM my having begun by picking up his passing reference to Tom Thumb, you might suppose that Tristram comes no whit closer to our abiding concern with the giant-and-dwarf Aphorism. If so, I have misled you. For though this most notable of Shandeans does not move in on the gnomic Aphorism in so many words, he marches around its periphery, pausing only to give us scholarly insight into one or another of the many problems tangential to it. Of these many, I can touch upon only a few, if I am to keep to the main course of our explorations.

ℭ *lii*

FOR one thing, Tristram almost persuades me that he
was secretly in search of the route taken by our Aphorism
among remote intellectual giants of the past. How else
account for the crucially pertinent names he includes in
the following memorable inventory?

> 'Tis either Plato, or Plutarch, or Seneca, or Xenophon,
> or Epictetus, or Theophrastus, or LUCIAN — or some-
> one perhaps of later date — either Cardan, or BUDAEUS,
> or Petrarch, or STELLA — or possibly it may be some
> divine or father of the church, St. Austin, or St.
> Cyprian, or BERNARD, who affirms that it is an irre-
> sistible and natural passion to weep for the loss of our
> friends or children . . .*

For another thing, Tristram treats the problem of the
incidence of genius and talent, a problem which, as we
have seen many pages back, was tackled by Bacon and
temporarily put to rest by the 17th-century Hakewill. But
note how much more adroitly Tristram handles the
issue! He is telling how the happy state of Denmark
differs from his own England, remarking the fact that
in the land from which Yorick came — Hamlet's Yorick,
of course, and not Tristram's parson Yorick who (in the
person of Sterne) can at best be presumed to have been
his lineal descendant — that, in Denmark, "nature was
neither very lavish, nor was she very stingy in her gifts of

---

* Tristram himself presents the list of quotables (Book V, chap.
3), but I have taken the liberty of emphasizing the pertinent
names.

genius and capacity to its inhabitants; — but, like a discreet parent, was moderately kind to them all"; then, going on to contrast the circumstance that Danes were "pretty near to a level with each other" * with the state of things in England where "the case is quite different: — we are all ups and downs in this matter; — you are a great genius; or 'tis fifty to one, Sir, you are a great dunce and a blockhead."

It must be just as evident to you as it is to me that once Tristram turned to questions of genius and lesser talents, he could easily have gone on to provide what would surely have been the definitive treatment of the giants-and-dwarfs similitude. (Moreover, as we know from his conscientious, recurrent and anything but surreptitious thefts from the *Anatomy of Melancholy*, Tristram was no stranger to Democritus junior, and so had been introduced to Didacus Stella.) He could have started with the graphic figure of dunces poised on the shoulders of genius, and then . . . But for reasons he uncharacteristically failed to make plain, he simply would not move the giant-dwarf image into the center of his stage. Yet if he does not make the figure central, he repeatedly skirts round it by dealing with its implications, both direct and subsidiary. Here he is, for example, recognizing the accumulative increments of knowledge:

> Thus — thus, my fellow-labourers and associates in this great harvest of our learning, now ripening before our eyes; thus it is, by slow steps of casual increase, that our knowledge physical, metaphysical, physiolog-

* You will hear in Tristram's phrase an echo of Bacon's celebrated (and, in some quarters, notorious) claim that his method of science will "place all wits and understandings nearly on a level." Thus we find Tristram, with his usual equanimity, refusing to take a stand on the Bacon-Shakspere confusion of iden-

ical, polemical, nautical, mathematical, enigmatical, technical, biographical, romantical, chemical, and obstetrical, with fifty other branches of it, (most of 'em ending as these do, in *ical*) have for these two centuries and more, gradually been creeping upwards towards that 'Ακμὴ of their perfections, from which, if we may form a conjecture from the advances of these last seven years, we cannot possibly be far off.

And then, in this same chapter XXI of Book I, Tristram virtually joins both his ancestor Rabelais, who, you'll recall, proposed that gestures be substituted for words, and his contemporary Swift, who proposed the abolition of all words, observing that when knowledge reaches perfection,

it is to be hoped, it will put an end to all kinds of writings whatsoever; — for the want of all kind of writing will put an end to all kind of reading; — and that, in time, — *As war begets poverty; poverty peace,* — must, in course, put an end to all kind of knowledge; — and then — we shall have all to begin over again; or, in other words, be exactly where we started.

So, in his distinctive way, all unknowing that Plato had long since promulgated the same doctrine, Tristram rediscovers the theory of cycles of rediscovery. It is only proper, then, that Tristram should have his father say, in connection with what is called the Shandean System, that *Amicus Plato,* although he goes on to add, *sed, magis, amica veritas.*

Since I, too, prefer truth to the piety of friendship, I

tities, allotting a distinctive role to each of them by expressly referring to Shakspere's Yorick and by resonating to Bacon's oft-reiterated phrase on the levelling of wits. Although he draws upon *Hamlet,* surely, Tristram, like Macduff, is here noble, wise and most judicious.

must confess to having no strict proof that Tristram is here of a piece with Rabelais and Swift. It is only an hypothesis. And I am thoroughly mindful of what Tristram reports about the singular behavior of hypotheses; that, "it is the nature of an hypothesis, when once a man has conceived it, that it assimilates every thing to itself, as proper nourishment; and, from the first moment of your begetting it, it generally grows the stronger by every thing you see, hear, read, or understand." But I am mindful also that he concludes: "This is of great use." * Since the truth of Tristram's doctrine is exemplified by its own enunciation, any further report of the versatile uses of hypothesis would be altogether superfluous. At any rate, these uses are recorded in chapter XIX of Book II and are thus open for inspection in every one of the uncounted editions of Tristram's memoirs.

Having taken note of Father Shandy's hypothesis about the nature of hypothesis, we cannot afford to forget the first of his unshakable axioms: "That an ounce of a man's own wit, was worth a ton of other people's." †

---

* It so happens that the particular hypothesis which gave birth to these general observations on the behavior of hypotheses comes close to our central subject. The originating idea, set forth by Mr. Shandy, Sr., holds that for sound anatomical, physiological and obstetrical reasons, Caesarian sections are bound to deliver men of talent or of towering genius whereas delivery in the ordinary way produces ordinary men, such as you and me. In few words, many "who figured high in the annals of fame, — all came *sideways*, Sir, into the world."
† Pause, if only for a moment, to ponder the peculiar beauty of this axiom, once it is seen in context. While Father Shandy pronounces this indisputable first principle, his son Tristram is busily engaged in pilfering the wit and wisdom of a motley array of forerunners: Montaigne, Rabelais and Bacon, Dr. Fludd (but not Cardinal Bentivoglio) and, of course, Robert Burton.

(The word "wit" must of course be understood here in that one of its many eighteenth-century senses which denotes "knowledge" and "information," as in the phrase *to get wit of*.) This axiom has guided me at every juncture in this untutored exploration into the tortuous history of our Giant-and-Dwarf Aphorism. You will have noted that I often prefer to rely on my own feeble resources rather than to turn invariably to the scholars on every side who could set me straight when ignorance threatens to lead me astray. Relying on the Shandean axiom, I regard an original error as better than a borrowed truth. For the first is part of me whereas the second remains alien, however much I may try to make it essentially mine. That is what the axiom asserts, thus manifesting in itself the saving grace of original error.

It is a pity that Shandy *père* did not address himself also to the problems of sociological methodology, rather than remaining an historical methodologist — pure and simple. Had he done so, I am confident that he would have anticipated my observations, long since put into print, of the difficulties facing the sociologist of today. Consider only the relations between the socially plausible, in which appearances persuade though they may deceive, and the true, in which belief is confirmed by appropriate observation. It may be enough to suggest that the independence between the two confronts the sociologist with some uncomfortable alternatives. Should his systematic inquiry only confirm what has been widely assumed — this being the class of plausible truths — he will of course be charged with "laboring the obvious." He becomes tagged as a bore, telling only what everybody knows. Should investigation find that widely held social beliefs are untrue — the class of plausible untruths — he is a heretic, questioning value-laden verities. If he ventures

to examine implausible ideas about society that turn out
to be untrue, he is a fool, wasting effort on a line of inquiry not worth pursuing in the first place. And finally,
if he should turn up some implausible truths, he must
be prepared to find himself regarded as a charlatan,
claiming as knowledge what is patently false. Instances
of each of these alternatives have occurred in the history
of many sciences, but they would seem especially apt to
occur in a discipline, such as sociology, that deals with
matters about which men have firm opinions presumably
grounded in their own experience.*

Keeping all this in mind, we can nevertheless learn
our method of exposition from that indefatigable and
pioneering Shandean, Tristram. Little wonder that he had
a quiet confidence in the sure touch of his art. For he
knew that ideas and subjects temporarily mislaid would
in the end find a place in his narrative, a place that might
at first seem ill-chosen, when judged by the irrelevant
canons of organized discourse, but one that would later
be found peculiarly well-advised, provided that the
reader's patience was coupled with confidence in the
axiom that ultimately there is an apt time and an apt
place for almost everything. That is why (in chapter XIX
of Book II) Tristram remarks, in manly, unapologetic
and telling fashion, that "What I have to inform you,
comes, I own, a little out of its due course; — for it
should have been told a hundred and fifty pages ago, but
that I foresaw then 'twould come in pat hereafter, and
be of more advantage here than elsewhere." And then,
he provides aspiring authors with decisive guidance:

* In the unlikely event that you want more of this kind of thing
you have only to pick up *Sociology Today* (edited by Leonard
Broom, L. S. Cottrell, Jr. and myself for Basic Books) and
scan my piece on problem-finding in sociology.

"Writers had need look before them, to keep up the spirit and connection of what they have in hand." Now, when Tristram speaks, I listen and inwardly absorb. That is why I had deferred, some thousands of words ago, any further account of Bernard of Chartres, for only now are we prepared to understand his unique place in the history of the giants-and-dwarfs Aphorism.

ℭ *liii*

IN SAYING that Bernard occupies a *unique* place in this narrative, I use the word "unique" in its old-fashioned, almost, one might say, in its unique sense.* Bernard

---

* Thus departing widely from the practice of your colleague, the Irving Babbitt Professor of Comparative Literature at Harvard, who, if I am to believe the indulgent *third* edition of Webster's International Dictionary, could bring himself to write at least once of the "less unique" just as the novelist Dorothy Canfield Fisher could write of the "more unique" and the playwright Arthur Miller could cap it all by writing of "the most unique" (though, by way of extenuation, or even special justification, it should be said that he was thus describing his singularly eumorphous bride of world-renown).

Plainly, we can only look nostalgically toward that once-upon-a-time when "unique" was an exceedingly powerful and precise word. *Nous avons changé tout cela.* Now we observe, with helpless dismay, the erosion of its meaning, which once strongly and exactly indicated the only one of its kind, having no like or equal. Just another victim of sloppy semantic change, it has deteriorated into a mere, rough synonym of *unparalleled, remarkable, unusual, peculiar, odd, curious* or even *quaint.*

This deterioration of meaning must of course be sharply distinguished from the precise and studied sense in which certain things may be strictly described as more (or less) unique than others. (We are not schoolmarms, holding fast and un-

177

stands alone, for it was he, and none other, who originated the simile of the giants and dwarfs. All others who make use of the figure — whether in the twelfth century, the thirteenth and fourteenth, the sixteenth, seventeenth and every century thereafter, — all these had it from Bernard, either directly or through mediating hands.

In making this strong statement, unweakened by carefully insinuated reservations, I lay myself open to the charge of unscholarly conduct. I know this, but I can do no other. There comes a time even in the life of an academic man when he must stand up and be counted. This is such a time. As a dedicated gnomologist, I maintain that Bernard of Chartres, and no one else, originally captured the idea of the cumulative though not steady advance of knowledge in saying "we are like dwarfs *******(*) upon the shoulders of giants, and so able to see more and see farther than the ancients . . ."

If only authentic scholarship were not a series of anti-climaxes. Having reached this climactic point in our quest, I should have liked to put Bernard's simile in univocal English. But the facts do not allow me this comfortable option. (That is why I have temporized by inserting the elliptical *******(*) in the foregoing quotation.) Shall we English-writing students of the subject report Bernard as saying that we are like "dwarfs *standing* on the shoulders of giants," or like "dwarfs *sitting*" on that eminence or even like "dwarfs *positioned*"

_____

thinkingly to unconsidered *rules*.) For, as George Gaylord Simpson is only the latest to observe, the more complex a thing is, evidently the more various the respects in which it can differ from all other things of its class. Thus, *Tristram Shandy* is clearly more unique than your favorite daytime serial on television.

there? Our authorities on the matter are of no great help. At one time, for example, Sarton's Englished version has us "stand" there; at another, he has us "sitting" there.* Our French colleagues serve us no better. Gilson has the dwarfs definitely *seated* on high — *"assis."* While Lavisse leaps nimbly over the entire problem: they are *hoisted* (*"hissés"*) onto the giants' shoulders. (Almost we catch a glimpse of the dwarfs standing on tiptoe, an engaging and functionally apt image arrived at by treating *hissés* as a cue to the idiomatic *se hisser sur la pointe des pieds.*) †

Nor can we take the formulations, such as Didacus Stella's ‡ or Newton's, which came long after in order to

* The first is in his *Introduction*, II, 196; the second, in his *The History of Science and the New Humanism*, 30. Nor do the dates of publication of these works help us to find out which was Sarton's considered judgment: both were published in 1931, although the latter work grew out of his Colver lectures given at Brown University in 1930. Furthermore, even had the two versions appeared years apart, could we then have responsibly assumed that the later one was the more considered reading? It might as well have been a lapse.

† I have engineered this direct confrontation of the two great authorities, Lavisse and Gilson, only to bring into the open what is hugger-muggered in the Aphorism itself. It is all very well for Bernard to advise us to locate ourselves upon the giants' shoulders. But which giants? Shall we sit upon Gilson or be hoisted high by Lavisse? In a word: Who shall decide when eminent doctors disagree? Shall we go with Étienne Gilson when he presents us with *"assis"* on p. 259 of his *La Philosophie au Moyen Age* (Paris, 1944) or go with Ernest Lavisse when he gives us instead *"hissés"* on p. 331 of the third volume of his *Histoire de France* (Paris, 1902)?

‡ Remember him? He is the *"Didacus Stella in Luc. 10, tom. 2"* cited in Burton's *Anatomy of Melancholy* and brought to our day by Bartlett's *Familiar Quotations*. But Didacus Stella is of no help at all on this crucial issue. He simply evades it. He writes, you recall, that *"Pigmæi gigantum humeris impositi*

179

decide what Bernard meant. That would be pure anachronism of the most virulent sort: *retroactive* anachronism.

And finally, we are not helped much by turning to Bernard's own version (as recounted by John of Salisbury), for he leaves the matter open — wide open. He said, John assures us, that "nos esse quasi nanos gigantium humeris *insidentis*" (the italics are mine). How are we to turn the versatile *insidentis* into English? True, we could say that its English equivalent is, in its prime intransitive sense, "sitting upon." But does that really settle the matter? For in its transferred sense, and let us remember that the word was part of a complex figure of speech, it could mean "resting upon" and, by no great stretch, "standing upon." How, then, are we to choose among competing alternatives to arrive at a firm English position on the problem? If only we had enough information to arrive at an appropriate behavioral context for the word in the twelfth century; according to the contextual theory of language, that would settle the issue once and for all. But search my library as I will, I simply cannot find out the position, in that century, usually taken by people precariously perched on another's shoulders. Apparently some sat; braver (and more far-sighted) ones stood; and some just *leaned.** With no firm evidence to guide us, I am inclined not to sit upon the issue but to stand right up to it and accept

---

plusquam ipsi gigantes vident." *Impositi,* indeed! "Placed upon" is an egregious dodge, for it tells absolutely nothing about the posture of the dwarfs. Of course, this is one way of coping with a problem, but what man of character can choose quick surrender to valiant defeat (let alone the promise of a difficult victory)?
* For the last, see the faint clue provided by *The story of*

established usage. Thenceforward, I shall accept the reading of Bernard which has dwarfs *standing* upon the shoulders of giants.

[Now that we seem to have cleared up the ambiguity of Bernard's *insidentes* and of Didacus Stella's backsliding *impositi,* I am prepared to admit that the good old Teutonic verb *stand* does not serve us much better. The OED requires 38 columns of tight-packed print to set out 104 meanings of the word (and its various formations). After studying a few dozen of these meanings, one suffers an attack of paronomasia. One doesn't know whether one is standing on one's head or on one's feet. In such cases, one must suppose, the only sound position is a stand-pat policy if one is to stand committed to truth and be prepared to stand the consequences. This may stand one a high price, but as things stand, to stand **firm may stand one in good stead and may** indeed be the only way to stand off abominable ambiguities. One must simply stand one's ground if one stands for something rather than nothing. If, I say, one stands for standards, if one is more than a stand-in for a scholar, if one wishes to preserve one's scholarly standing and to stand on good terms with one's peers, then one must take a strong stand. In the end, each of us stands under the heavy obligation to stand guard and to stand to our guns in the face of the standing threat to single-sensed clarity. To stand upon ceremony in these matters or to stand much upon

Genesis and Exodus, an early English song, c. 1250 (but based upon the *Genesis and Exodus [à 1000]* by the earliest English Christian poet, Caedmon, which gives us reason to suppose that leaning may have been the characteristic posture in the intervening centuries. The fact that Caedmon was himself a *seventh-*century master of Anglo-Saxon is beside the point; the only manuscript of his that I know of is tenth century and, I am told on good authority, is still to be found in the Bodleian.)

our dignity would only mean that we have little else to stand upon. United we stand, provided that we do not stand upon our differences but stand together, side by side, rather than stand apart, aside or astrut. We must stand by, not back, if we are to stand off the standing threat or at least bring it to a standstill. Only so, do we even stand a chance; only so, can we achieve a common understanding. This is no mean venture and the question is: can you stand it?]

ℂ *liv*

UPON deeper reflection, I simply cannot leave you standing there, confronted with a pseudo-solution by fiat rather than enjoying an authentic solution reached through scholarly investigation. On this complex question, I consider myself deputized to search out and collar the fugitive truth. Reluctantly but dutifully, therefore, I remove myself from the confines of my study and wander into the wider world to ransack Columbia's libraries, searching all the while for a definitively behavioral answer to the mooted location and posture of dwarfs in the Bernardian era. Goodbye, then, good friend — and *au revoir.**

---

* *Au revoir*, of course, in the secondary sense: I'm off to look anew.

ℂ *lv*

HOW blessedly right is Deuteronomy: I have searched
and I have found!!!

A spate of behavioral evidence, intricately fitted into
windows of colored glass and permanently frozen in
sculptured stone, tells us all we need to know. There
were characteristic positions, in those distant days, that
one took up whenever one was being borne on the
shoulders of another.

What is more — so much more that it overwhelms — a
substantial part of this behavioral evidence is located,
with surpassing aptness, at Bernard's favorite stamping
ground — Chartres itself! But I must not keep you any
longer from these choice finds, selfishly reserving them for
my own pleasure. Listen, then, — or even better, (since
voir c'est croire), look, see and believe for yourself.

Come first to Chartres and inspect the window in the
south transept. There (in Figure 1) are the four evangelists St. Matthew, St. John, St. Mark and St. Luke *
sitting on the shoulders of the four prophets Isaiah,
Ezekiel, Daniel and Jeremiah! Since a sample of one
will do well enough for the universe of four, I show you
here (in Figure 2), a close-up only of Isaiah bearing
the full seated weight of St. Matthew.

As though this were not enough, I can tell you, with
all the authority of that great historian of art, Émile
Mâle, that this representation of the four evangelists

* In the French of Chartres: saint Mathieu, saint Jean, saint
Marc, et ——————————— saint Luc. Saint Luc! Might
it be, could it be, that "Didacus Stella in LUC. 10. tom. 2" refers
to — *him?* But enough of such stray musings, and back to our
immediate search.

A

B

Figure 1, *left*. South Transept, Chartres.

Figure 2, *above*. St. Matthew on the shoulders of Isaiah, Chartres.

poised on the shoulders of the four prophets is a "symbolisme audacieux" (an audacious symbolism). For we are to understand by it that "although the evangelists find their base of support in the prophets, from this vantage-ground they can see farther and more widely." *

What Mâle broadly hints, Delaporte states in so many words, as he comes upon the statuary carved on the porch of the cathedral of Bamberg. He straightaway announces that this audacious symbolism of the Ancient Law preparing the way for the New expresses the essentials of Bernard's Aphorism, not only at Chartres but at Bamberg, too. But though the text is Delaporte's text, the claims are the claims of Mâle.†

And now, see for yourself, in Figure 3, the position of the apostles carried on the shoulders of the prophets in the Prince's Portal (*Fürstenportal*) at the Bamberg Cathedral. This time, the apostles are standing, not, as in Chartres, sitting. Should you doubt the evidence before your eyes, I add, in Figure 4, a close-up of an apostle-and-prophet pair.

Consider further visual evidence on the behavioristics of shoulder-climbers in those medieval times. The apostle-on-prophet motif of the Bamburger Dom was heavily influenced by the motif exhibited in the figures carved on the baptismal font in Merseburg at the end of the twelfth

* Source: Émile Mâle, *L'art religieux du XIII* siècle en France* (Paris, 1923), p. 9.
† As Yves Delaporte freely acknowledges in his work, *Les vitraux de Chartres* (Chartres, 1926–27, p. 432) when he quotes yet another of Mâle's prodigious volumes of scholarship (*L'art allemand et l'art français au moyen âge,* p. 193): "The idea is French; it may even be Chartrian, for the artist only applies to the Bible an adage about the ancients and moderns which was current in the schools of Chartres for more than a century."

Figure 3, *above*. Fürstenportal, Bamberg Cathedral.

Figure 4, *left*. Detail of Fürstenportal.

century. And now, the stance has changed back again. As you see in Figure 5, the apostles, some wearing the strange Gothic smile, are carefully and variously *seated* on the prophets' shoulders.

And if all this evidence is not enough – and I really must bring this behavioral report to a halt if we are to get on with the rest of our story – turn *finally* to the (tenth-century?) church of Payerne, in what is now Vaud canton, Switzerland. I say "finally" with reason. For here (in Figure 6) you will see, on one of the capitals of a pillar in the nave of the church, an array of seeming *dwarfs*, with inexpressive mien,* astride the shoulders of other rather dwarf-like figures, the legs of each super-posed dwarf wrapped tightly round the neck of his subordinate, who in turn holds fast to the legs of his superior. (Scanning the unavoidably blurred Figure 6, you may not detect all that I describe. You may even suppose that my scholar's wish has fathered an illusory perception. 'Tis not so. And to demonstrate beyond all doubt the veridicality of my reported perception, I pro-vide, in Figure 7, a line drawing that perspicuously

* Only rarely does a word so singularly apt with an apt aptness force itself into a sentence as the word "mien" does here. For is it not an act of poetical justice that this should be a word coined by Richard Bentley, so badly maligned by Swift, and even more, that it should appear in that work which thoroughly mauls Temple's folly: *A Dissertation upon the Epistles of Phalaris* (1697, 1699)? As Bentley happily reports his neol-ogism: "Another happy phrase, which he [Boyle] says, I have newly minted, is the Meen of a Face; which as he takes it, is much the same thing with the Behaviour of a Look or the Carriage of a Smile . . . Meen does not signifie behaviour, even when it's spoken of the whole Person, but the Air and Look that results from it." Can there *be* another word more apt than *mien* in this behavioral report on the positions taken up by medieval dwarfs?

Figure 5. Baptismal font, Merseburg.

delineates these figures sculpted on the Payerne pillar).

Now review the behavioral evidence: at Chartres, Merseburg and Payerne the superordinate figures *sit* on the shoulders of their supporters; at Bamberg, they *stand*. In short, no single position was uniformly prescribed in those days for men mounted high on another's shoulders. As students of behavior, we can go even further, for the conclusion is as clear as it is inescapable: sitting on shoulders was the *modal* position (probably because it is a position more stable for the superordinate and more comfortable for the underling); standing on shoulders was the *deviant* position (less frequent, probably, because it is more precarious).

In turning Bernard's *insidentes* into English, then, we

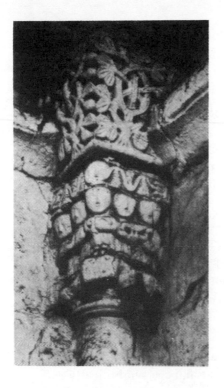

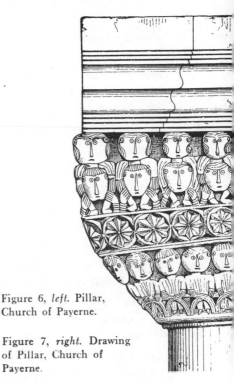

Figure 6, *left.* Pillar, Church of Payerne.

Figure 7, *right.* Drawing of Pillar, Church of Payerne.

can write that dwarfs are sitting *or* standing, according to our estimate of the character of the dwarfs in question. If we think of them, *a posteriori,* as preferring safety to far-ranging vision, we have them sit there; if we think of them as daringly prepared to sacrifice safety to greatness of vision, we have them stand there. I submit that seldom before in the behavioral theory of language has there emerged so compelling a solution to the contextual meaning of a disputed word. Translators of the Aphorism need no longer write "stand" or "sit" as the mood strikes them; now they have clear guide-lines for choosing the more appropriate translation.

Having worked through to this beautifully compelling solution, I wish I could let the issue rest there, and return to that history of the Aphorism which engages our abiding attention. But there is an untidy loose end in this behavioral investigation that demands to be tucked into place before we can conscientiously continue the narrative. Implied, and still unanswered, is the question whether the painters and sculptors of that medieval time were graphically reproducing the symbolic substance of Bernard's Aphorism.

Try as I might, I cannot evade this insistent question. Anxious though I am to avoid becoming embroiled in a wrangle among authorities, – for the Vives-Hooke-Newton-Merton principle still rings in my ears – the conscience of a scholar will not allow me to escape this unpleasant obligation simply by running away from it. But, at least, I can make short shrift of the controversy by treating it with distant and cool objectivity. (I *will* not wrangle!)

The authorities (of distinctly different grade) line up as follows: Mâle, of course, argues that the windows at Chartres and the sculpture at Bamberg symbolically express the Bernardian figure of speech. Delaporte happily subscribes to Mâle's opinion and Weese is even more outspoken, saying that the sculptor at Bamberg has not hesitated to take Bernard's metaphorical expression literally and to present it in the form of apostles standing on the shoulders of the prophets.* So, with this trio of authorities.

A quartet of other authorities achieve a dubious neutrality by maintaining a stony silence on the issue. Blavignac, who has much to say about the sculpture at

* Mâle and Delaporte you have met; Arthur Weese I introduce as the author of *Die Bamburger Domskulpturen* (Strassburg, 1914) where, on pp. 87–88, he writes in no uncertain terms: "Der Bildhauer hat sich nicht gescheut, den bildlichen Ausdruck, dass die Apostel auf den Schultern der Propheten stehen, wörtlich zu nehmen und wirklich darzustellen."

Payerne, has nothing at all to say about Bernard (possibly
because he writes of architecture only up to the tenth
century — a good two hundred years before Bernard).*
Georg Dehio, who writes of Bamberg at length, and
Georg Pudelko,† who is taken with the font at Merseburg,
belong in the same camp of a neutrality achieved by
silence. Joining them, most recently, is Valentiner who
manages to write a book entitled *The Bamberg Rider*
without saying a solitary word about Bernard although he
writes at length and with remarkable acuity about the
younger and older artists who created the statues of
apostles standing on the prophets' shoulders.‡

But the advocates of Bernard (*i.e.* Mâle, Delaporte
and Weese) enclitically notwithstanding, and the ab-
stainers (*i.e.* Blavignac, Dehio, Pudelko, and Valentiner)
unenclitically *not* withstanding, one authority, who engages my total respect, resolutely opposes even the slightest intimation that Bernard's Aphorism has ever been
metamorphosed into sculpture or windows of stained

* Blavignac is blameless; he could not have taken a stand on
this much-mooted problem had he wanted to, for he was writing
in 1853, long before anyone had even identified the problem
as a problem. (To realize the full force of this, examine, someday, my paper on "Problem-finding in Sociology.") Whenever
you want "des exemples très curieux de manuation," look for
them in J. D. Blavignac, *Histoire d'architecture sacrée du
quatrième siècle au dixième siècle* (Paris, 1853), especially at
p. 249.
† Unlike Blavignac, Dehio and Pudelko might have spoken out
— but didn't. I can say only this for them; they provide us with
magnificently clear plates of figures superposed on figures:
Georg Dehio, *Der Bamburger Dom* (Munich, 1924) contains
plates of the Prince's Portal; Georg Pudelko, *Romanische
Taufsteine* (Berlin, 1932) has a plate of the baptismal font at
Merseburg, as does
‡ W. R. Valentiner, *The Bamberg Rider* (Los Angeles, 1956)
in his Figure 12 on p. 53.

glass. Raymond Klibansky (the distinguished scholar then at Oriel College, Oxford) holds it "very doubtful" that the evangelists on the shoulders of the prophets in the window at Chartres have any connection with the similitude enunciated by Bernard of Chartres. He argues with compelling force. First of all, Bernard died before the building of the Cathedral actually began (an argument, I must confess, that leaves me cold since it assumes that traditions die at birth. It is almost as though Klibansky had never pondered Henry Adams' *Mont-Saint-Michel and Chartres* — surely a counterfactual assumption, if there ever was one). And second, says Klibansky, the painter could scarcely have dared to suggest that the saintly evangelists were merely dwarfs (thus, by implication, countermanding Mâle's claim to an "audacious symbolism").*

But all these premises of scholarly debate are mere prelude to the conclusive argument which you (and I) have already identified: before the Chartres windows were ever fashioned, apostles sat resolutely on the shoulders of prophets in a niche of the Merseburg font, to give symbolic expression to the continuity between the Old Covenant and the New, with the New being decidedly superior.

Happily, this scholars' debate leaves us untouched, however it is ultimately decided. For us behavioralists, concerned only to discover the stance customarily taken by those perched on another's shoulders, the debate is altogether beside the point. We have the answer. Modal dwarfs sit; deviant dwarfs stand.

* Raymond Klibansky intended to put all this, and more, into an edition of the works of both Bernard and Thierry of Chartres (which was announced to appear in the Winter of 1936). Unhappily, the edition has never reached print (or so

ℭ *lvi*

SO MUCH for the Englished version of Bernard's Aphorism; what, now, of the claim that he, and he alone, originated it? To be sure, the evidence for the claim is entirely circumstantial, but what else could it possibly be? And if we are not prepared to accept this sort of evidence, how shall we ever rest our case? The circumstances are these: first, we have the strong evidence supplied by Bernard's pupil, John, that he heard him state the Aphorism and second, we know that no one has managed, after all these years, to find it stated, in so many words, before Bernard's time. This is good enough evidence for Klibansky who, as prospective editor of the works of both Bernard and Thierry of Chartres, is as close to a final authority as we can hope to find, and so, it is good enough for me. He states his conviction (or, at least, his belief) in these forthright words: "I believe that the simile of the dwarfs is an original one and was invented by Bernard himself." I concur.

And now, you might suppose, our search is done. Having tracked down the giant-and-dwarf figure to its *fons et origo* in Bernard of Chartres, we might assume that the task is finished. But this would be both premature conclusion and rank heresy. It would deny the truth of the Aphorism itself. For when Bernard originated the Aphorism, he did so, of course, by locating himself upon the shoulders of *his* considerable predecessors. After all,

I am assured after an assiduous search). Klibansky's spirited arguments are outlined in his note published in *Isis*, December 1936, at pp. 147–9.

living as he did in the 12th century, Bernard was something of a modern in relation to those who went before.* The self-exemplifying character of the Aphorism is again demonstrated, at least in part, by Bernard's having leaned on if not precisely sat or stood upon the shoulders of that sixth-century Roman grammarian, Priscian (or, if you must be a precisionist, Priscianus).

Once again, Klibansky comes to our aid. For, however much he loves Bernard of Chartres, he loves truth more. And so it is that he directs us to Priscian who, six centuries before Bernard, came close to the giant-and-dwarf figure, even though, as a creature of his time, he could scarcely manage the notion of progress in approximating the idea embodied in the figure. Here is how Priscian put it (in the dedication of his work to Julian): †

> grammatica ars, . . . cuius auctores, *quanto sunt iuniores, tanto perspicaciores,* et ingeniis floruisse et diligentia valuisse omnium iudicio confirmatur eruditissimorum . . .

There's nothing here, of course, of giants or dwarfs, but still the essential element of the idea is there. *The*

---

* Should you doubt this, listen only to his devoted student, John of Salisbury, describing Bernard: "the most abounding spring of letters in Gaul in modern times . . ." This, from his *Metalogicus*, i, c. 24, according to my former teacher (and yours?): Charles Homer Haskins, *The Renaissance of the Twelfth Century*, Cambridge: Harvard University Press, 1933, pp. 135–6.

† Not having the source at home, I refer you to Klibansky's citation. He tells us that the passage is in the preface to the *Institutiones Grammaticae* of Priscian, in the dedication to Julian (ed. Hertzius, vol. I [= *Grammatici Latini*, rec. Kellius, vol. II], p. 1). (It turns out that Klibansky is precisely correct but he might have added that the comprehensive work he cites was published in 1855.)

younger (*i.e.* the more recent) *the scholars, the more sharp-sighted.* They can draw upon what went before and so advance true knowledge — even in the matter of grammar. Or so it might be misunderstood to say. Actually, Bernard and others of his twelfth-century colleagues had to misinterpret Priscian fruitfully in order to arrive at their distinctive idea of the progress of knowledge. Priscian himself had something quite different in mind. As a confirmed eclectic, he was engaged in scolding his Roman predecessors for having virtually ignored those younger Greek grammarians, Herodian and Apollodor, rather than correcting them and improving upon them to bring the art of grammar closer to perfection. But through a lucky mistake — or, as we scholars like to describe it, through a *felix culpa* — Bernard misread the significance of Priscian within the context of his, Bernard's, own progressivist frame of reference, and arrived at the conception of dwarfs seeing farther by standing high on the shoulders of that giant which represents accumulated culture.

Just because Priscian was the beneficiary of a fortunate error is no sufficient reason for shunting him to one side as the merely accidental catalyst of a truth he could not himself appreciate. After all, he was a considerable scholar in his own right. He was born, you remember, at Caesarea in the Roman province of Mauretania (I believe *after* it was overrun by the Vandals) but he really flourished, Sarton tells us, at Constantinople. As a humanist, you may know him best for his eighteen books of Latin grammar since these comprised one of the really popular textbooks of the Middle Ages, its popularity being attested by the thousand manuscript copies that still remain. But there are others of us, less learned in the ways of ancient grammar, who prefer to think of him as

the author of a treatise on numerals, weights, and meas-
ures (which naturally made a point of using by-then-
ancient Greek sources). But whether regarded chiefly in
his grammarian role or his mensurator role, Priscian cannot be counted out of this narrative, simply because he
achieved only a near-miss in reaching toward the giant-
dwarf simile (which, figuratively speaking, manages to
merge discursive language and symbolic figures in an
enduring figure of speech).

ℂ *lvii*

PRISCIAN cannot be counted out for the best of
reasons: he may really have been the one to stimulate
Bernard to create the unforgettable Aphorism. Consider
the evidence — again, every bit of it circumstantial — and
try to escape the ineluctable conclusion. We need hardly
pause to note that Bernard knew Priscian's work intimately: not only did Priscian (and Donatus) alone
among Latin writers continue to be prescribed in the
curriculum at Paris as late as 1255, but in the century
before, in Bernard's own time, Priscian's books transmitting the ancient learning were (together with those of
Martianus Capella, Boethius, Isidore and Bede) among
those " 'without which no gentleman's library is complete.' " * This was no newfound estimate of Priscian's
worth: a century before Bernard, two of Priscian's

* Haskins is once again my authority for this contemporary
estimate of Priscian and that is good enough authority for me
(although I should have enjoyed having him designate the
source he was quoting on p. 81 of his magisterial *Renaissance
of the Twelfth Century*).

volumes were bought by the bishop of Barcelona for a house *and* a piece of land. This popularity even withstood the censorious criticism of Priscian for omitting the name of God — "an omission," says Professor Haskins, "for which the Constitution of the United States and the multiplication table have likewise been blamed!" *

Priscian endears himself to us if only because he could quote with discriminating taste ten thousand lines from the ancients, thus establishing a pattern that would be adopted, a millennium later, by Robert Burton (who himself had the good sense to quote Priscian's quotations —— copiously). No doubt, Bernard followed the same practice, which was so much a part of the technique of medieval scholarship. I say "no doubt" (definitely in the "of course" mood) only because I cannot say with assurance, since Bernard's works have all been lost. But in view of the universal use of Priscian as a text during the Renaissance of the twelfth century, what else can one conclude? And, as if to support this cogent supposition further, Otto, Bishop of Freising, who was a near-contemporary of Bernard, quotes Priscian's crucial phrase — *quanto iuniores, tanto sint perspicaciores* (which is to

* Surely, we must appreciate the admirable restraint shown by Haskins. With this opening about Priscian's failure to mention the Creator, Haskins might easily have yielded to the temptation to quote, yet again, that miserably worn anecdote about Laplace's encounter with Napoleon after he had presented him with a copy of his magnificent *Mécanique céleste*. Needling Laplace, Napoleon upbraided him for a fateful oversight. "You have written this huge book on the system of the world without once mentioning the author of the universe." "Sire," Laplace swiftly replied, "I had no need of that *hypothesis*." But why · do I repeat this to you, who are bound to know it well and to remember, too, the response of Lagrange, when Napoleon told *him* about the episode: "Ah, but that is a *fine* hypothesis. It *explains so many things.*"

say, the more youthful the philosophers, the more per-
spicacious) — thus assuring us that this doctrine had not
been lost to sight in Bernard's time.*

And certainly not, soon after his time. About a
century after Bernard, Roger Bacon is writing in the first
part of his *Opus Majus* that

> additions can be fitly made to the statements of real
> authorities, and correctly applied in many cases . . .
> For this reason Priscian says in the introduction to his
> larger volume that there is no perfection in human
> discoveries, and adds, "The younger the investigators,
> the more acute," because the younger, that is those of
> a later age, in the progress of time possess the labors
> of their predecessors . . . For thinkers of a later gen-
> eration have always added to the work of their
> predecessors, correcting much and changing more, as
> is shown in the case of Aristotle especially, who dis-
> cussed critically all the philosophical propositions of
> his predecessors.†

What can be more symbolically apt than to have the
"Doctor mirabilis," Roger Bacon — that encyclopedic
predecessor, by almost four centuries, of his countryman
and near-namesake, Francis Bacon — pick up the Priscian

* Evidently, Otto (and so, I surmise, the even more scholarly
Bernard too) was impressed by the Priscian aphorism for he
quotes it not just once but twice in his major work, *Chronica
sive Historia de duabus civitatibus*, which I cite in its newest
edition — from *Monumentis Germaniae Historicis, Scriptores
Rerum Germanicarum*, edited by Adolph Hofmeister, Hannover,
1912 — rather than in its first edition — edited by John Cus-
pinian and published at Strassburg in 1515. You will find the
quotation first in Book II, chapter 8, at p. 75; then, in the
prologue to Book V, at p. 226.
† As I say, this is extracted from Part I of Roger Bacon's *Opus*

Paradox—the younger, the more acute—several centuries before Francis Bacon enunciated his Paradox— the antiquity of time is the youth of the world. Permit me here to juxtapose the two premises, — the one of Francis Bacon (which I place as the major premise) and the one of Roger Bacon (thanks to Priscian, which I place as the minor premise) — in order that you may draw for yourself, in strict accord with Aristotelian logic, the inexorable conclusion:

> Francis Bacon: Juventus mundi, antiquitas saeculi
> Roger Bacon (after Priscian): Quanto iuniores, tanto perspicaciores
> Ergo, ———————————————————————.

I shall not insult your intelligence by actually drawing the conclusion, for the essence of an Aristotelian syllogism is that, once given the premises, anyone of more than feeble mind can draw the correct conclusion. Once imprisoned in the ironbound logic of The Philosopher, you simply cannot escape from the premises. This is a universal truth, as you will at once see exhibited if I put the compact Latin syllogism into ordinary English:

> Francis Bacon: The antiquity of time is the youth of the world;

Majus, the part dealing with "Causes of Error." Tempting though it be, I shall say nothing here about the other Parts, not even about the sixth dealing with experimental science or the seventh and concluding one dealing with morals. For a quick check on the accuracy of my quotation of Bacon's quotation of Priscian, I refer you to the recent and faithful translation of the *Opus Majus* by Robert B. Burke (New York, 1962) which is based upon the corrected text of Bridge's edition (London, 1900). You will find it, precisely as I claim, on p. 15 in chapter 6 of Part I of Volume I.

Roger Bacon (thanks to Priscian): The more
youthful, the more far-sighted;
Therefore, The Ancients are more far-sighted than the
Moderns.

Somehow, this doesn't seem to come out as the advocates
of the Paradoxes (and most of their allies, the advocates
of the Aphorism) would prefer. But, then, that is the
strength of strict syllogistic synthesis. Yet, if we are adroit
enough, we can escape between the horns of the dilemma,
after the fashion of Aquinas (in his *Summa Theologica*),
by showing that the minor premise does not contain all
the alternatives so that we are not really impaled on
either horn or we can escape through the even more
acrobatic maneuver of taking the dilemma by the horns
and simply denying the truth of the major premise. In a
word, Aristotelian logic *can* be fun.

ℭ *lviii*

SO MUCH for Priscian who came before Bernard of
Chartres; what of those who came immediately after?
You'll remember from my fleeting references earlier in
this letter that we owe our knowledge of Bernard's
Aphorism entirely to his devoted student, John of Salisbury, who recorded it, either in Book 3, chapter 4 or in
Book 4, Chapter 3 of his *Metalogicon*. (I vaguely
remember having checked this, but no matter.) Wearied
by my explorations among Sarton's medieval Johns and
eager to get on with the period just before Newton fixed
the Aphorism permanently in the collective memory of

the modern world, I had made short work of this John. (I see no reason for turning pedantic and referring to him as Iohannes de Saresberia, just because the official papers of his time called him so, or as Joannes Sarisburiensis, just because scholars sometimes prefer this designation.) The main point is that he has earned a place in our narrative for a variety of reasons, all apart from his crucial role in having rescued Bernard's Aphorism from the oblivion that seemed inevitable since, as Sarton reminds us, all "his works are lost."

For one thing, John not only transmitted the giant-dwarf Aphorism, he quite evidently believed it. How else can we interpret his self-image as exceedingly small in its every aspect? True, he was encouraged in this diminutive self-appraisal by his surname, Parvus (perhaps "Little" or "Short"), but is that reason enough for John to describe himself as "parvum nomine, facultate minorem, minimum merito"? * In short, why does he see himself as a dwarf? Surely, this is an excess of submission to the humility demanded by Bernard's Aphorism. Surely, John is becoming, after the fashion of the convert, more Bernardian than Bernard himself. Otherwise, he might have lived with the fact that he was small in name and let it go at that. Instead, driven by the logic of the Aphorism, he must go on to decry himself as smaller in capacity and, hypercritically, as smallest in worth. John has plainly developed what must henceforth be known as

* This orgy of self-depreciation, I am reliably informed by R. L. Poole, occurs in his Letter 202 (CCII) which can still be found in the second of the five volumes of John's *Opera* collected by J. A. Giles back in 1848. Lacking access to this esoteric source, I must turn instead to volume 199 of the easily available *Patrologiae Latinae* (as edited by J. P. Migne in 1855) where we find the small-in-name, smaller-in-capacity and smallest-in-worth letter in columns 224–26.

the Parvus-complex (in clumsy English, the self-belittle-
ment complex).*

Such masochistic self-denial is far removed from the
moral alchemy of a later day which, as I have had
occasion to note elsewhere, declines a word such as "firm"
in sturdily self-serving fashion, so:

* Do not allow the homonym to mislead you. The Parvus-
complex has nothing at all to do with that combine comprised
by Rosa Luxemburg, Leon Trotsky and A. L. Parvus. Whatever
else can be said of the vigorous trio, it cannot be said that
they were given to self-disparagement. To avoid the dangers of
homonymic reasoning, you have only to re-read Appendix A
in *The Student-Physician* (edited, you will remember, by one
R. K. Merton together with George Reader and Patricia Kendall
and published in 1957 by the Harvard University Press). As
a pertinent example of the technique for penetrating the thin
disguise of homonyms — those quite distinct words that happen
to be "like in look but unlike in sense"; you will detect
Fowler's touch in the preceding quoted phrase — I quote from
the Appendix (itself a dead metaphor): "The bacteriologist,
come of age since the days of Koch and Pasteur, does not
hesitate to use the term *culture* simply because the anthropologist, from the days of Tylor and Kidd, has utilized *culture* in
quite another sense. Nor, rightly enough, does the anthropologist hesitate to speak of *material culture,* by which he means
generally the physical artifacts produced by man-in-society, for
fear that this might be confused, in the minds of some, with
a *bacterial culture.* The parallelism, which is not apparently the
result of borrowing, indeed runs to specialized formations of
the basic homonym: both bacteriologist and anthropologist, for
example, speak, in their several ways, of *subcultures.* And
neither denies himself the term because 'culture' is colloquially
still understood as fastidious self-cultivation, or, after the fashion
of Matthew Arnold, as the 'disinterested search for sweetness
and light.' " I do not give you the exact page number for this
informative quotation in the hope that this will require you to
read the entire Appendix in search of the passage and that, in
my opinion, would be all to the good.

I am firm,
Thou art obstinate,
He is pigheaded.*

We can conclude only that John of Salisbury used
the penetrating aphorism to victimize himself. For if this
is the self-diminishing judgment of the man described by
Stubbs as "for thirty years, the central figure of English
learning," and by Sarton as "one of the best educated
men of his time, and one of the most learned," what are
we to think of his contemporaries and the rest of us who
are his indebted successors?

Almost, I can hear you advancing an alternative
hypothesis to account for John's Parvus-complex. Mindful
of his *Policraticus* (in eight books), you are thinking, no
doubt, that he had cause to depreciate himself. You may
say that this treatise on the art of government — "The
Statesman's Book" — is permanently marred by his
inexcusable lapses into digressions, illustrations, after-
thoughts, and reminiscences. With this, I am of course
forced to agree. As I have tried to make clear throughout
this letter, when one is drafting a systematic exposition of
an important subject, there is simply no excuse for
departing from the strict continuity of the argument. On
this premise, fundamental to all sound scholarly work,
we are entirely agreed. John has clearly violated this
premise and so turned his *Policraticus* into "an encyclopedia of miscellanies [albeit] the aptest reflection of the

* It is only fitting that this declension of virtue into vice should
have been anticipated (in effect) by Tristram, as he says of
one of his father's many virtues: " 'Tis known by the name of
perseverance in a good cause, — and of obstinacy in a bad
one." This anticipation (of Jeremy Bentham and me and no
doubt others) will be found in Chapter xvii of Book I.

cultivated thought of the middle of the twelfth century." *
Yet, I continue to doubt that it was the guilt generated
by this crime against scholarship which led John to see
himself as small in name, smaller in ability and smallest
in merit. If we are to pull up the roots of his guilt and
his consequent aggression against self, we must look
elsewhere.

To supplement my favorite interpretation — to which I
nevertheless cling tenaciously — of John's Parvus-complex,
his over-acceptance of the dwarfy implications of the
Bernardian Aphorism, I supply the cushion of an alternative hypothesis in the unlikely event that the first one
proves to be untrue. I do so because the credo of the
authentic scholar and scientist requires it: we must be
prepared to reject our brain-children, no matter how dear
they are to us, or else they will die of too much love. My
evidence for what I may describe as the Bernardian
hypothesis of the Parvus-complex is enough only to suggest an explanation of John's manifest sense of guilt, not
enough to prove it true. In admitting this, I do not
consider that I have abandoned my brain-child. I simply
refuse to spoil it by an excess of indulgence. For we
know that the outer form of scientific or scholarly exposition may deceive. Who is to be judged thin and anemic
in his claims to validity: the self-assured author who
insists that he has truth by the tail, that what he says is
beyond all doubt, reasonable or unreasonable, that who-
ever disputes his evidence is convicted of error at best
and of motivated ignorance at worst, *or* the author who
cautions his reader, at every critical juncture, to recognize
the limitations of his evidence, the conjectural character
of his inferences and the provisional nature of his conclusions? The resounding firm statements of the first
class of authors may seem forthright and courageous

* This is how R. L. Poole ambivalently describes it.

when they are, in truth, only deceptive and outrageous.
The quiet and restrained statements of the second class
of authors may seem excessively cautious and timid when
they are, in fact, only careful and honest.

The general reader, that recipient of universal knowledge, often seems to prefer the first kind of formulation:
one that is definite, bold, and refreshingly assured. That
reader does not enjoy the self-restricting statements of
the scholar or scientist whose claims to knowledge are
hedged in by his acute awareness that he just could be
mistaken. But this path of scholarship has its dangers, too.
You and I know that it is not enough to provide the
mere appearance of provisional and tentative statement,
in which rote cautionary phrases are interpolated in the
text but stick out as an alien thing that the author himself
does not seriously adopt. The ritualistic intoning of
caution and restraint has nothing to commend it. It may
only hide the arrogant assertions of the dogmatist under
the cloak of pious but not seriously intended allusions to
the provisional character of what is being vigorously
announced. But in the matter of accounting for the manifest guilt expressed by John of Salisbury, we have no
choice: we must acknowledge that the scant facts before
us admit of more than one interpretation. On the face of
it, John's triple characterization of himself as a man of
small name, capacity and merit, is clearly the result of his
having lived too long with Bernard's deflationary
Aphorism that forced even a Newton into what some
regard as a temporary excess of modesty.* Yet I am
(reluctantly) prepared to entertain another hypothesis

* Which brings us, inevitably, to that other, equally memorable.
expression of modesty uttered by Newton, Brewster says (II,
407), "a short time before his death": " 'I do not know what
I may appear to the world, but to myself I seem to have
been only like a boy playing on the seashore, and diverting
myself in now and then finding a smoother pebble or a prettier

about John's behavior; I set it forth, not because it seems to me tenable, but only because I will not take the soft option of mistaking each idea that crosses my mind as an indisputable piece of truth.

This improbable alternative explanation would attribute John's profound sense of guilt and consequent self-depreciation to his behavior on that fatal 29th of December 1170 when Thomas à Becket was murdered. As an historian, you will be led, by this hypothesis, to the prosy documents of the time, and these, no doubt, will give you *some* access to the true lineaments of the event; * as a sociologist, I turn for insight to the empathy of the poet and ponder, once again, T. S. Eliot's *Murder in the Cathedral.* It is all there, the grounds for this hypothesis about John's Parvus-complex, entirely between the lines of Eliot's dramatic poem (except for one swift allusion by

---

shell than ordinary, whilst the great ocean of truth lay all undiscovered before me.' "

Evidently, this humble oceanic feeling § was current some considerable time before Newton gave unforgettable expression to it. Here is our old friend, Joseph Glanvill, reviewing a collection of his essays: "And now when I look back upon the main subject of these Papers, it appears so *vast* to my *thoughts,* that me-thinks I have drawn but a *Cockle-shell* of Water from the *Ocean:* Whatever I look upon, within the *Amplitude* of *Heaven* and *Earth,* is evidence of Humane *Ignorance.*" (You'll find the full citation to Glanvill's *Essays* on p. 68 of my narrative; his cockle-shell figure appears on page 32 of that work.)

§ In attributing an oceanic feeling to Newton and Glanvill, I of course do so in anything but the Freudian sense. For them, it is a feeling of oceanic ignorance; for Freud, in contrast, it is a feeling of oceanic omnipotence (and presumably omniscience).

* You would no doubt have me turn to the *Materials for the History of Thomas Becket,* replete in seven volumes and edited by J. C. Robertson in London from 1875–85 (Rolls series no. 67). Yet despite the undeniable authenticity of the *Materials*

Thomas * to "John, the Dean of Salisbury, Fearing for the King's name, warning against treason, [who] Made them hold their hands"). The plain fact is that, when he was confronted with the fatal event, John's courage left him. While Henry's four Knights were conscientiously murdering Thomas à Becket in the Cathedral at Canterbury, John, like almost all the other clerks, fled and took refuge under an altar.† And if we are to believe Thomas Eliot, John, just before he rushed to safety, must have overheard Thomas à Becket reject the pragmatism of success in these words:

> You argue by results, as this world does,
> To settle if an act be good or bad,
> You defer to the fact. For every life and every act
> Consequences of good and evil can be shown.‡

and the valuable Introduction by Robertson, I do not find that they get to the heart of the matter now before us.

* To avoid needless ambiguity in the double-layered allusion, I report that "Thomas" refers here to both the twelfth-century Archbishop of Canterbury and the twentieth-century archbishop of poetry.

† Not all in Becket's entourage fled in fear. I am happy to report that William FitzStephen and Robert, canon of Merton, courageously held their ground. You may be inclined to question the evidence for FitzStephen since he himself provides it but you cannot doubt the evidence for Robert who, with characteristic modesty, never advertised his courage. That is to say, FitzStephen stands witness for Robert, though he has no witness to stand for himself. On the case for Robert, consult FitzStephen's *Vita Sancti Thomæ*, first printed more than five centuries after the murder in Sparke's *Historiæ Anglicanæ Scriptores*, 1723.

‡ You will recognize this passage as a poetic paraphrase of the sociological axiom that all action has both functional and dysfunctional consequences. Unaware of this axiom, observers of the human condition are wont to tag every act as *either* functional *or* dysfunctional, thus achieving quick conclusions at the expense of complex truth.

And as in time results of many deeds are blended
So good and evil in the end become confounded.

John, secure in body owing to his flight, could
scarcely have been serene in mind, once he heard Thomas
speak out just before he was killed. And if John lingered
in the place of death — the evidence is far from clear —
he must also have heard one of the conscientious
murderers explain that their act was one of duty, not
personal gain. This is what John might have heard the
second Knight explain:

> . . . in what we have done, and whatever you may
> think of it, we have been perfectly disinterested. [*The
> other* Knights: "Hear! hear!!"] *We* are not getting
> anything out of this. We have much more to lose than
> to gain. We are four plain Englishmen who put our
> country first. I dare say that we didn't make a very
> good impression when we came in . . .

From the saintly Becket and his scrupulous murderers,
John thus learned about the moral complexity of human
action. Assessing his behavior in the cathedral, when he
succeeded in saving his own skin at the expense of
another's, John must have come to recognize that, in
contrast to the murderous knights, he had
behaved in wholly self-interested fashion. Naturally, he
came to see himself as a very small man indeed.

So now we have two alternative hypotheses to account
for John's running himself down: what I have come to
call the Bernardian hypothesis, which holds that the
giant-and-dwarf simile taken literally leads to a diminutive image of self, and the Cathedral hypothesis, which
holds that wholly self-interested behavior at the expense
of others leads to acute feelings of guilt and derivatively,
to self-depreciation. Both hypotheses fit the known facts

about John's Parvus-complex. Yet I continue to prefer the first and *not* merely because it reflects the central theme of this letter, but for much the same kind of reason that eventually led wise men to prefer the Copernican to the Ptolemaic hypothesis. It is with psychology as with cosmology: in the end, truth (and the better conceptual scheme) triumphs.*

⟨ *lix*

IT IS no fleeting surmise, then, that though Bernard of Chartres originated the simile of the giant-and-dwarfs, his disciple, John of Salisbury, transmitted it, paying the heavy price of a loss of self-esteem in the process. But if Bernard planted and John watered, who gave the in-

* Does this daring claim evoke a bitter and cynical smile? If so, you are far more expressive than a notable band of agelasts (from the Greek *â + gelastikos*, inclined to laugh). Your memory may not be prompt enough to recall the yarn that Newton reputedly laughed only once in his life. Then I pass on the story (the source of which now escapes me) to the same effect about Calvin, except that he was allegedly even more sparing of laughter, not having indulged himself in open risibility even once. Even more ascetic was the 19th-century poet and philologist, Giacomo Leopardi, whose philological work at age 22 elicited the unstinted praise of Niebuhr and whose poetry has been likened to Dante's; wracked his life long by sickness, he is said never to have laughed *or* smiled. At least, that is the claim in an article in the *Quarterly Review* (Mr. Gladstone, Editor), March 1850.

This straight-faced trio would of course not have found much in common with Democritus who owing to his lifelong incorrigible cheerfulness remains known to posterity by the nickname, "the laughing philosopher."

209

crease? A host of perceptive minds, from the twelfth century onward. To treat each of these scholars and scientists in deserving detail would require me to extend this letter to unconscionable length. Moreover, it would tempt me into byways far removed from the main path of this narrative and so make for circuitous rather than straightlined inquiry into the history of the aphoristic simile. You will understand, then, why I only touch upon some of the many who built the conduit for transmission of the simile during the five centuries that lay between Bernard of Chartres and Isaac Newton.

After the originator, Bernard, and his recording pupil, John, surely Alexander Neckam claims prime attention as transmitter of the giant-dwarf figure. This is the same man you may know as Alexander de Sancto Albano, though his contemporaries preferred their little joke and called him Nequam (= good-for-nothing) and he himself arranged to describe himself so in the epitaph on his tomb.* As you might suppose, the wags of the time couldn't resist the temptation to indulge in a lot of puny puns † based on the nickname. As one instance, when he applied for the mastership of the St. Albans school, the Abbot Warin replied punningly: *Si bonus es, venias; si nequam, nequaquam.* Now, it's all very well to say to an aspiring young man, if you're good, come along, but if you're bad, by no means, but I do hope the jest is worth the trauma in Latin, for it's a pretty sorry specimen of wit in English.

* Clearly, another version of the Parvus-complex. Is it the case that everyone who trafficked with the giant-dwarf simile came to appraise himself harshly?
† By this point it should be plain that I share Mr. Walter Shandy's loathing of puns, at best, a symptom of acute paronomasia. I refer, of course, to Tristram's report in Book II, chap. 12: "Denis the critic could not detest and abhor a pun, or

This mistreatment of Alexander leaves me seething, and for good cause. For any man who did as much as Alexander to light up one of the obscurities in Bernard's giant-dwarf simile deserves better. You recall how difficult Bernard made things for us by using the indeterminate word, *insidentes*. This left us free to visualize those dwarfs standing, sitting, or otherwise positioned on the giant's broad shoulders. But this is the kind of freedom which tempts scholars into license. Alexander does away with Bernard's namby-pamby verb, being altogether clear about the posture taken up by the dwarfs. He writes: Et, ut ait philosophus, nos sumus quasi nani *stantes* super humeros gigantium (the italics are of course mine).* And in adopting this forthright language, he would seem to clear up this issue once and for all; the verb formation, *stantes*, makes the position of the dwarfs evident to even the most captious and sophistical of readers: they are standing. What is more, they are standing in that distinctively emphatic sense of *stantes* which is *strongly opposed to sitting*.

Alexander, then, must be credited not merely with helping to transmit Bernard's figure, but with straightening it out. Ever after, the posture of the dwarfs remains unequivocally established (with only a few unfortunate relapses). Furthermore, by reminding us that we are thoroughly upright, Alexander heightens our self-esteem. This, in turn, gets us to draw ourselves up to our full diminutive height. And finally, as though all this were

the insinuation of a pun, more cordially than my father; — he would grow testy upon it at any-time . . ." So much for our pundit's punitive, punctual and pungent puncturing of puns, punsters and plain puniness.
* Ockenden has alerted me to this passage in the *De naturis rerum* of Neckam which can be found on p. 123 of Thomas Wright's edition of 1863, published in London.

not enough, Alexander's sturdy formulation gives us excellent advice for extending our horizons. Dwarfs in the perpendicular are naturally going to see a lot farther than dwarfs sedentary or dwarfs recumbent. It stands to reason.

As though this too were not enough, Alexander generously contributes a new and engaging context for our Aphorism. This he does in his short, short chapter 78 which is punningly entitled "Regulus" (which we can read alternately as "little king" or as "wren"). Now the best known example of the wren, of course, is technically known as *Troglodytes parvulus,* the very little brown bird "with its short tail, cocked on high — inquisitive and familiar, that braves the winter of the British Islands, and even that of the European continent." Although it is not strictly germane, we should remember too that "wrens have the bill slender and somewhat arched: their food consists of insects, larvae and spiders, but they will also take any small creatures, such as worms and snails, and occasionally eat seeds. The note is shrill. The nest is usually a domed structure of ferns, grass, moss and leaves, lined with hair or feathers, and from three to nine eggs are produced, in most of the species white." (As you see, I cannot resist drawing upon Alfred Newton's implicit prose poem to the wren, enshrined in the eleventh edition of the *Britannica.*)

Consider now the ingenuity with which Alexander arranges to have the wren provide a context for the Aphorism. He picks up the old fable — old as early as the late twelfth century — of how it was that the smallest of birds came to be the king of birds. The story, you may remember, goes something like this. The fowls of the air once decided to choose for their king that one of them who should mount closest to heaven. This the eagle seemed to do, and all were ready to accept his rule. But, suddenly, a loud burst of song was heard, and perched upon the head of the eagle was seen the wren, come out of hiding from its place of concealment under the wing of the giant bird which had borne it aloft. And so it was that the little wren came to be known as little king (*regulus*). Naturally enough, this charming tale leads directly to the quotation from "the philosopher" of the giant-and-dwarf aphorism, with the moral explicitly drawn that "we must therefore attribute to our predecessors those achievements which we sometimes venture to transfer to the glory of our own praise in just about the same fashion as the wren seems to have conquered the eagle with practically no effort at all." *

* The same tale has been put to quite other uses. You have only to turn to your copy of *The Tatler*, Nº. 224, which Addison published on Thursday, September 14, 1710, as I have just turned to my copy here at home and you will see the use to which he puts it. On second thought, I had better report the essentials here and spare you the effort of locating the thing for yourself. This issue of *The Tatler*, written, Addison typically reports, "From my own Apartment, September 13," is devoted to the collections of "ADVERTISEMENTS that appear at the end of all our public prints." In Addison's view, and now in mine, Advertisements plainly serve many purposes for the vulgar. They provide instruments of Ambition. Then as now, a man who is not big enough to get into the news can nevertheless creep into the advertisements (as today, a manufacturer will crow that his money has been accepted for an ad in *Life* – or even *Fortune*). In this way, a man of small consequence – say, an apothecary – can go down to posterity in the same paper as a man of great consequence – say, a plenipotentiary. "Thus," as Addison reminds his readers, "the fable tells us, that the wren mounted as high as the eagle, by getting upon his back."

Actually, Addison has much more to tell us about the utility of Advertisements, and the art of preparing – can one really say, writing? – them. He tells enough to make us realize that the more it changes the more it is the same thing. Quite

In the light of these many contributions to our psychic comfort and comprehension, you may begin to understand my irritation over those forgotten wags who dubbed Alexander Neckam, Nequam. He has done the tradition of giants-and-dwarfs much good, and I would not want it interred with his bones.

ℭ lx

IF ANYONE in that long tradition is to be the object of aggression, then a prime candidate is the next fellow in line of continuity, Peter of Blois, that vain, ambitious and discontented archdeacon of Bath who flourished toward the end of the twelfth century. (Yet, be it said in all fairness, he wrote much to keep the memory of Thomas à Becket green.) Wanting to be swiftly briefed on him, I naturally turned first to that omnisufficient treatise on scientific thought of the period, Sarton's *Introduction*. The index to the second volume lists 72 distinct Peters but unaccountably maintains a rocklike silence about our Peter, the one from Blois. It does direct us to Peter the Eater (the euphonious nickname referring to his bibliophilic polyphagia or insatiable appetite for books). But that literary gastronome is clearly not our man. He

---

evidently, the image-builders and image-merchants of Madison Avenue would not appear strange to Joseph Addison. Long before Gillette and Schick and Personna, he notes the polemical character of advertisements: inventors of " 'Strops for Razors' " "have written against one another this way for several years and that with great bitterness . . ." Or again, he recognizes that advertisements "inform the world where they may be furnished with almost everything that is necessary for life. If a man

was a diehard conservative who rejected the novelties
represented by the Platonism and rationalism of the
school of Chartres and, however small my knowledge of
Peter of Blois, I do know he wore that old school tie
with pride. Peter the Irishman (or, if you disdain the
vernacular, Petrus Hibernicus) is also indexed but we
needn't pause over him, since he rules himself out by
having lived at the wrong time (the 13th century) and in
the wrong place (this wandering Hibernian flourished,
naturally enough, in Naples). And so with the seventy
other Peters listed by Sarton; none is the man we seek.
Reluctantly, I must conclude that, this once, my mentor
has let me down.

But if Sarton is of no help, C. L. Kingsford is. He
gives Peter his due — at length and most instructively. I
had been ready, for example, to say that Peter must have
taken the Bernardian simile directly from John of Salisbury, but it turns out that Peter never was John's
pupil, contrary to the legend spread by Schaarschmidt.
(Yet who can say? Haskins, too, makes him out as John's
pupil.) But there's no question that he was a great letter-
writer (quite enough to endear him to us). Nevertheless,
I find it hard to credit his boast that he could dictate to
three scribes at once while he wrote a fourth letter in
his own hand. Yet, it might be argued that if Julius
Caesar could do it, why not Peter of Blois?

However his letters did get down on parchment (on

---

has pains in his head, colics in his bowels, or spots in his
cloaths, he may here meet with proper cures and remedies."
The great art and skill in an Advertiser "is chiefly seen in the
style which he makes use of. He is to mention 'the universal
esteem, or general reputation' [the public image?] of things
that were never heard of." In one respect, the writers of advertisements are like men of quality and unlike other authors:
they "give money to the booksellers who publish their copies."

paper?),* we can be sure of one thing: they constitute the most interesting of his works. Of course, they suffer from an excess of quotations, particularly from the ancients, and it must be plain to you by now that this is one vice I find it hard to condone. Luckily for us, Peter's propensity for quotation exposed him to damaging criticism and he lashed out in rebuttal. In spite of this "barking of dogs and snorting of pigs," as he testily rejoined, he took pride in plucking the choicest flowers of authors, both ancient and modern. And then comes the decisive moment when, in Letter 92, he goes on to say:

> Nous sommes comme des nains *hissés* sur les épaules des géants, qui voient grâce à eux plus loin qu'eux-mêmes, lorsque, nous attachant aux livres des anciens, nous ressuscitons et renouvelons leurs pensées les plus élégantes, que le temps ou la paresse des hommes avaient abolies et rendues comme mortes.†

* Paper mills *were* established in Spain as early as the middle of the twelfth century, but I suspect that Peter had little access to this newfangled writing material.

† It may strike you a bit odd that I seem to have Peter writing in reasonably modern French, but the explanation is not far to seek. It happens that I don't have a copy of Peter's epistles at home, not the folio volume first published at Brussels about 1480 nor the Jacques Merlin edition of 1519 nor even the 1837 Berlin edition, *Petri Blesensis Speculum Juris Canonici* (which all contain the crucial Epistola XCII). I was prepared to accept Kingsford's Englished quotation of the simile (and, as it turns out, I would have erred in doing so) just as I was prepared to accept the assertion by Bédier and Hazard, in their *Histoire de la littérature française* (Paris, 1923–24, I, 15) that Peter had picked up the Bernardian simile intact. But on this occasion as on a few others, I felt uncomfortable about confining this inquiry to the limited resources of my own library. Happily, the Columbia library does have a copy of L'Abbé A. Clerval, *Les Écoles de Chartres au Môyen-Âge* (Mémoires de la Société Archéologique, Chartres, 1895) which

The next link in this chain of transmission of the simile, one Henricus Brito, is something of an embarrassment to me. I have it on the good authority of Raymond Klibansky that he belongs in the story, but I can tell you nothing else about him. None of my sources at home pays him any attention (and I refuse to reach out for more about him since, strictly speaking, he was inconsequential). Were it not that Klibansky dug up the "hitherto unknown" *Philosophia* of this Henry (in *Cod. Corpus Christi Oxon.* 283, fol. 147ra), he might as well never have lived, so far as posterity is concerned. But one fragment of that philosophical work is enough to restore Henry to notice, at least for the specialized purposes of our inquiry. This one short passage can be mined for all manner of nuggets, as you will see at once from what follows:

> huic etiam consonat verbum Prisciani in principio Maioris, ubi dicit quod quanta moderniores tanto

contains a good chunk of Peter's letter. To provide an English translation of the French translation from the original Latin would be only to confound discrepancies of nuance and so I have retained the good Abbot's language.

Another foray into the Columbia library uncovered the original text of Peter's Letter XCII (as printed in *Opera omnia: Patrologiae cursus completus*, vol. 207, ed. Abbé J. P. Migne, 1855, all published in Paris). The original Latin does not improve upon the derivative French; the crucial passage still evades the issue of the exact position taken by the dwarfs upon the giants' shoulders, thus: "Nos, quasi nani *super* gigantum humeros sumus, quorum beneficio longius, quam ipsi, speculamur, dum antiquorum tractatibus inhaerentes elegantiores eorum sententias, quas vetustas aboleverat, hominumve neglectus, quasi jam mortuas in quamdam novitatem essentiae suscitamus." "Super" is of course no help at all: to say that we are almost like dwarfs ON the shoulders of giants tells us neither how we got there nor what position we assumed once we arrived.

217

perspicaciores et ingenio magis floruisse videntur.
Supra quod dicit Petrus Heliae, quod nos sumus sicut
nanus positus super humeros gigantis, quia sicut potest
videre quicquid gigas et adhuc plus, sic moderni
possunt videre quicquid inventum est ab antiquis et si
quid novi poterunt addere. Huic etiam consonat
Alanus, cum dicit: 'Pygmea humilitas excessu sup-
posita giganteo ipsius altitudinem superat.' *

Confronted with such concentrated riches, one hardly
knows where to begin. Note, first, how our thirteenth-
century Henry has picked up the adumbration by the
sixth-century Priscian of the *idea* embodied in the giant-
dwarf figure. We've been through that one, but it's good
to have this confirmation of the hunch that Priscian really
was a major predecessor of Bernard. Then, observe how
Henry ascribes the actual figure of speech to Petrus
Heliae, not to its originator, Bernard. This serves to show
once again that in the transmission of ideas each succeeding repetition *tends to erase* all but one antecedent
version, thus producing what may be described as the
anatopic or palimpsestic syndrome.† I'm not in a position

---

* Klibansky quotes this entire in his compact and immensely
informative note, *Isis*, December 1936, 147–9.
† Not for your benefit, but just to put the derivations clumsily
on the record: from anatopism (= a putting of a thing out of
its proper place, a faulty arrangement) and from palimpsest
(= a manuscript in which a later writing is written over an
effaced earlier writing).
  If only as a prophylaxis for this ailment endemic among
scholars, I should like to identify the anatopic or palimpsestic
syndrome in some detail. Naturally enough, most of us tend to
attribute a striking idea or formulation to the author who first
introduced us to it. But often, that author has simply adopted or
revived a formulation which he (and others versed in the
same tradition) knows to have been created by another. The
transmitters may be so familiar with its origins that they mis-

to know whether this Peter is our Peter of Blois and since a short frantic search (with soft hue and loud cry) has left me none the wiser, I'm ready to let the matter rest. Of far greater consequence in this passage is the introduction of an entirely new character in the story, Alanus.

takenly assume these to be well-known. Preferring not to insult their readers' knowledgeability, they do not cite the original source or even refer to it. And so it turns out that the altogether innocent transmitter becomes identified as the originator of the idea when his merit lies only in having kept it alive, or in having brought it back to life after it had long lain dormant or perhaps in having put it to new and instructive use. Thus, even one of the ablest among you contemporary historians, Joseph R. Strayer, attributes the idea-and-phrase "climate of opinion" to Carl Becker (presumably the author from whom he first learned it). Strayer had no cause to know that the phrase was coined by one of our seventeenth-century friends, Joseph Glanvill; that it passed out of use for a long time until it was brought back into currency by Alfred North Whitehead who generally knew a good thing when he saw it; and only then passed into the hands of Carl Becker, who put it to such impressive use.

Or take another case of the anatopic (or palimpsestic) syndrome more immediately germane to our central topic: Philip Hamerton, in his exploration of *The Intellectual Life*, writes: ". . . as Sydney Smith observed many years ago," that is, some 35 years before 1873 when Hamerton put this in print, "there is a confusion of language in the use of the word 'ancient.' We say 'the ancients,' as if they were older and more experienced men than we are, whereas the age and experience are entirely on our side. They were the clever children, 'and we only are the white-bearded, silver-headed ancients, who have treasured up, and are prepared to profit by, all the experience which human life can supply.'" (page 109) Hamerton faithfully expressed his debt to Smith, all unknowing, it seems, that Smith was indebted to Bacon and the troop of seventeenth-century Baconians for the paradox, *Antiquitas saeculi, juventus mundi*. What's truly past is evidently forgotten prologue.

Henricus Brito exhibits the same anatopic syndrome in the passage overhead.

ℂ *lxi*

AT THIS telling, the identity of Alanus is not exactly clear. It is possible that he is Alanus ab Insulis, de Insulis, or Insulensis, better known to most of us as Alain de Lille (or de L'Isle). This remarkable twelfth-century scholar came to be designated as "doctor universalis" for his varied attainments in works "exegetical, rhetorical, doctrinal, hortatory, homiletical, polemical, scientific, moral, and disciplinary." * Alain's accomplishments were considerable enough and his origins uncertain enough for him to be claimed as a German by the Germans and as a Frenchman by the French, to say nothing of the claims to him issued by the Spaniards and Sicilians. Understandably, since he was known as Alain of Lille (otherwise, Ryssel, in Flanders) he was also claimed as a Flamand by the Flemish.† However, the seventeenth century Scottish biographer, Thomas Dempster, set aside all these grasping nationalist claims as patently absurd and tagged Alanus as indubitably a Scot.

There's really nothing more to say about this particular Alanus who might have been the one cited by Henricus as having used the giant-dwarf Aphorism. But

---

* Mistaking the style for the man, you might suppose that this quoted string of largely -ical modifiers comes from Tristram. You would be mistaken; it is from the distinguished nineteenth-century biographer of Alain, A. H. Grant.

† Thus irresistibly reminding one of the ironic observation by Albert Einstein in an address at the Sorbonne: "If my theory of relativity is proven successful, Germany will claim me as a German and France will declare that I am a citizen of the world."

there is a good deal that can be said, and in all conscience, should be said, about Thomas Dempster,* who,

* It would be unforgivably digressive to clutter the text with
much more about this intriguing man. Yet, his ethnocentrism
notwithstanding, he deserves to be rescued from oblivion. By
segregating a few of the significant facts of his life in the depths
of this footnote, I can perhaps do simultaneous justice to the
accomplishments of Dempster and the continuity of the main
text.

His autobiography has much the same admirable flavor as
Baron Münchhausen's, which it antedates by 150 years. He
begins by pushing his birthdate ahead in order to make his undeniable precocity even more impressive. He would have us
know that he was the twenty-fourth child among twenty-nine, all
these the offspring of a single marriage. He soon acquired the
rudiments of knowledge, learning the alphabet to perfection in
one hour of concentrated study at the age of three. In his early
teens, he studied at Cambridge, Paris, Louvain and Douay, and
confesses to having become a professor in the Collège de
Navarre at the age of sixteen. Thereafter, he was truly a peripatetic scholar, taking up successive professorships at Toulouse,
Nîmes, Collège des Grassins, Pisa, and finally at Bologna
(then the most distinguished university in Italy). I suspect that
his inability to stay put resulted from an unstable family en-
vironment. As a child, for example, he witnessed the marriage of
his eldest brother James to his father's mistress, an episode
that naturally led his father to cut James off without a cent.
Gathering some of his new kin, James attacked his father's
forces in a pitched battle, the elder Dempster escaping with
seven bullets in the leg and a sword-cut on the head. All this
allegedly redounded to the advantage of young Thomas who,
though he was the twenty-fourth child of his father, was named
heir to the barony. The wicked brother, incidentally, met his
comeuppance, years later, when he was drawn apart by four
horses.

Thomas was a virile scholar, aptly described as "a man
framed for war and contention, who hardly ever allowed a day
to pass without fighting, either with his sword or with his
fists." He escaped a half-dozen murderous attacks on his life,
attacks typically mounted by outraged rivals in the world of
scholarship. In the peaceful interludes, he read fourteen hours

in his best-known work, *Historia Ecclesiastica Gentis Scotorum,* claimed Alanus as a Scot, through and through. The fact is that this book is remarkable more for its inventiveness than for its authenticity. As Alanus' later biographer, A. H. Grant, indignantly sums up the matter: "Dempster's object was to exalt the renown of his native country, and with this view he claims a Scottish origin for every distinguished person mentioned in history who has ever been supposed to be a native of Britain, supporting himself often by quotations from imaginary authors, or garbled extracts from real ones. Many of the persons whose biographies he relates seem to be absolutely fictitious." I leave it to you: are you prepared to find Alanus Scottish on the testimony of this man who invariably cries Scot?

Of course, the Alanus quoted by Henry as having made use of the giant-dwarf simile may not be this one at all; he may be Alan of Tewksbury (who had the advantage of being undeniably English). Indeed, I am inclined to believe that Tewksbury is our man, since the only work which can be attributed to him with certainty is a "life of Becket" expressly written to supplement the life by John of Salisbury. On this circumstantial evidence, it is hard not to cast one's vote for the Tewksbury Alan.

Yet there is an alternative, if we would but seize it, which altogether spares us the difficult choice between the two Alans. We need only accept the judgment of Dom Brial that Alan of Lille and Alan of Tewksbury were

---

every day and, having total recall, enjoyed the game of giving the context of any passage from any Greek or Latin author quoted to him. He liked to improvise Greek or Latin verses on any subject given him and, somewhat like Peter of Blois, boasted that no one scribe could take his thoughts down fast enough. We shall not soon see his like again.

one and the same.* The reasons for this judgment are
fairly complex and so I do not go into them here. But it
does offer us a quick way out which I'm prepared to take
if only to get on with the story. It was Alan of Lille and
Tewksbury, then, who, on the authority of Henricus
Brito, said somewhere: *Pygmea humilitas excessu sup-
posita giganteo ipsius altitudinem superat.*

⟨ *lxii*

AFTER this prolonged siege of ambiguous identities,
hardwon inferences and virtual surrender to expediency,
it is a relief to find myself on the safe ground of amply
documented fact. For there is no question that the simile
was picked up and used to effective purpose by the early
fourteenth-century French surgeon, Henri de Mondeville
(or, variously, Henricus de Armondavilla, Amandavilla,
Armendaville, Hermondavilla, Mondavilla, Mundeville
and, most disconcerting of all, Mandeville †). Personal
surgeon to Philip the Fair and then to Louis X, he was
honest and independent, thus remaining poor throughout
his life in spite of his great reputation. He was also

* Dom Brial makes his case for merging the twain into one in
Hist. Litt. de la France, ed. 1824, xvi, 396–425; at least, J. Bass
Mullinger cites him so, and Mullinger was an honorable man.
† Disconcerting, obviously, because there might be those who
will take this as evidence enough for linking up this Henry
of Mandeville with the eighteenth-century Bernard Mandeville,
of *Fable of the Bees* fame; this, despite the absence of any
connection, genealogical (Henry never married), ideological or
aphoristical, between them.

something of a woman-hater * and was somewhat para-
noid about patients. Withal, he managed to compose a
veritable medical encyclopedia for surgeons, the *Cyrurgia*,
begun in 1306 and concluded (though not finished) by
1320 or so.

The encyclopedic *Cyrugia* refers 1,308 times to 58
authors (the computation being Sarton's, not mine).
Among these were giants, both ancient and contemporary,
as we see from this count of principal citations:

Hippocrates (68), Aristotle (47), Galen (431),
Mesuë Major (24), Serapion Senior, al Rāzī (45),
Abū-l-Qāsim (18), ʿAlī ibn ʿAbbās (12), Mesuë
Junior (13), ʿAlī ibn Riḍwān (38), Ibn Sīnā (307),
Constantine the African (13), Serapion Junior, Ibn
Rushd (17), Theodoric Borgognoni (113), Lan-
franchi (17).†

Seeing Henry poised upon this human pyramid of
citations, you might suppose that he would resonate to
the Bernardian Aphorism and you would be right. He
reproduces every component meaning of the complex
original saying and adds one observation of his own:

* Misogyny is notoriously difficult to diagnose for it is not easy
to tell where valid criticism leaves off and phobic distortion
sets in. Complicating the problem of diagnosis in the case of
Henry, moreover, is his inconsistent treatment of women. He
remained resolutely unmarried but, as Sarton reports, he did
advise women on methods of simulating virginity, this being,
perhaps, his expression of contempt for the assumed deceitful-
ness and cunning of women.
† I am indebted to Sarton for this quantification of citations
(*Introduction to the History of Science*, Vol. III, Part I, 870).
The count makes it evident that for Henry, the most significant
giants were Galen and Ibn Sīnā (quoted more often than the

Modern authors are to the ancient like a dwarf placed [*placé*] upon the shoulder of a giant: he sees all that the giant sees, and farther still. Thus can we know things which were unknown in Galen's time and it is our duty to consign them to writing.*

Thus, almost 400 years before the bitter Battle of the Ancients and Moderns, we find this Henry quietly assigning both the old and the new their distinctive places in science. He pays all respect due the authors of the past, including the respect of recognizing that, being human rather than divine, their ceiling of vision was not unlimited; then, in the vein of progressivist optimism, he announces the enlarged vision open to the modern beneficiaries of the ancients; and finally, this being his distinctive contribution to the history of the Aphorism, he proclaims the duty of recording newly-acquired knowledge, thus adding still another cubit to the stature of dwarfs become giants with the passage of time. (For I read his final expression of duty to say: The dwarfs of each age become giants for the next age, as contemporaries inevitably become ancestors.)

Knowing nothing more of Henry than this, one would be led to suppose that he was the complete idealist, far

other 56 authors together) and, then, after a long interval, the thirteenth-century Theodoric Borgognoni (of Cervia).
* This is the Sarton translation from the modern translation by Edouard Niçaise, *Chirurgie de Maître Henri de Mondeville, chirurgien de Philippe le Bel*, traduction française avec des notes, une introduction et une biographie (lxxxii + 903 p., Paris 1893), p. 745. (You will find more of the same on p. 3.)

The Niçaise edition, it turns out, is quite adequate for our purposes and so you need not consult the two-volume edition of *La Grande Chirurgie* prepared by Dr. A. Bos and published some five years later (1897–98) by the Société des Anciens Textes Français.

removed from the rough-and-tumble of everyday life. But this superb practitioner of the surgical art was also something of a practical man, as we discover from the introduction to his *Cyrurgia*. Evidently having suffered from mistreatment by patients, he looks upon them with jaundiced eye, vents his spleen, and emerges with a recipe for neutralizing their scurvy tricks. Henry is particularly incensed by rich patients who cloak their affluence in shabby dress. These patients, poor in spirit rather than in purse, should be cuttingly advised that the surgeon gives better attention when the fee is ample and sure. Stingy patients present quite another problem for "the longer we treat them, the more will we lose." It is advisable, therefore, to expedite their cure by using "the best medicines." With miserly patients, "who prefer that their bodies suffer rather than their purses," the indicated course of action is quite the other way: they should be administered "medicines that work slowly and gently in the hope that they will pay us in proportion to the time." There is more to Henry's psycho-economics of medical therapy but this may be enough to give you the general idea: this new discipline is designed to cure all diseases of the purse.

ℂ *lxiii*

HENRY is only prologue to the man later described as "the Father of Surgery" by Fallopius, himself variously eponymized in the Fallopian tubes and the aqueduct of Fallopius (though few still remember him for having coined such anatomical designations as vagina, placenta, cochlea, labyrinth, and palate). I refer, of course, to Guy de Chauliac (identifiable also as Guigo de Chaulhaco, Guido de Cauliaco, de Caillat, and de Chaulhac). Like Henry's lesser work, Guy's *Chirurgia magna* * is an avowed compilation from just about every previous author of consequence, citing 88 authorities, with Galen inevitably far in the lead (890 times), followed at a short distance by Ibn Sīna (661 times) and at a long distance by Abū-l-Qāsim (175) and ʿAlī ibn ʿAbbās (149).†

With such a heavy reliance upon the surgical learning of the past, Guy, like Henry before him, had no option but to declare his enforced modesty. Like Henry, also, he had the wit to draw upon the Bernardian simile.‡ But Guy evidently felt compelled to leave his mark upon the simile by ringing in some vivid changes:

Car les sciences sont faites par additions, n'estant

* The full title is *Inventorium sive collectorium in parte chirurgicali medicine* (1363). You will note that this inventory antedates the current interest in "propositional inventories" (in the behavioral sciences) by some six hundred years. It is encouraging for us behavioral scientists to read that Guy's inventory (according to Sarton) "remained a standard work in Western Europe up to the time of Ambroise Paré (died 1590)" and (according to Ralph H. Major) "was the authoritative text in surgery until the eighteenth century." It was a distinctly popular inventory of surgical knowledge, with 16 known editions in Latin, 43 in French, 5 in Italian, 4 in Dutch, several in German, five in Spanish and even one in English. For the count of editions, I'm indebted to Major, *A History of Medicine,* I, 311.

† Once again, I have drawn upon Sarton's arithmetic of citations; III, 1691. (Why does Sarton take no notice of Guy's use of the Aphorism?)

‡ Nor is there much doubt about the source of the aphoristic simile for Guy; he quotes Henry some 86 times.

possible qu'vn mesme commence, et acheue. Nos
sommes comme enfans au col d'vn geant: car nous
pouuons voir tout ce que voit le geant, et quelque peu
dauantage.*

Having perceptively noted that science grows by
unending increments of knowledge, with neither
beginning nor end, Guy then proceeds to transform the
figure. The dwarfs are changed into children, thus veto-
ing in advance Francis Bacon's effort to describe the
moderns as patently advanced in years and the ancients
as mankind's infancy. As though this were not enough,
Guy moves these youngsters from the comfortably wide
shoulders of the giant to a precarious and mutually
uncomfortable position on his neck. No doubt I am
merely a creature of our hedonistic age, but it does seem
to me that the minor gain in altitude is more than offset
by the major loss in comfort, to children and giant alike.
In all fairness to Guy, however, I must admit that his
elegant variation originates a trend, becoming marked in
our own time (as we'll see shortly), toward remarkable
transformations of the Bernardian figure.

   The forty-three French editions of Guy's treatise
meant, of course, that the giant-dwarf (or giant-child)
similé became a virtual commonplace among French
writers on medicine. To parade every occurrence of the
simile in that medical tradition would be mere pedantry,
but you might want to look up a couple of choice

* You'll find this, I am assured by R. E. Ockenden (*Isis*, 1936,
xxv, 451) on page 4 in the prologue to *La grande chirurgie* de
Guy de Chauliac (which, like Mondeville's treatise, was edited
by Edouard Niçaise, in 1890).
   (It is just as Ockenden says; although it appears in what I,
and Guy himself, would prefer to describe as the Dedication,
rather than the prologue.)

citations: the *Traicté et response de Alexandre Dionyse Maistre chirurgien & barbier à Vendosme sur la question proposee par d'Angaron et Martel* (Paris, 1581) and François Martel's *Apologie pour les chirurgiens* (Lyon, 1601).

The main conduit, apparently, through which Guy's child-centered version of the Aphorism flowed into seventeenth-century England was supplied by that argumentative iatro-chemist and member of the medical faculty of Paris, Joseph Duchesne (better known to you and to most of his contemporaries as Josephus Quersitanus, Quercetanus, or simply Quercetan). (Remember the allusion of that scoundrel Marchamont Nedham to the "famous Quercetan"?) The Latin of Quercetanus was translated, with something less than full fidelity, into free-flowing English as early as 1605 by that otherwise completely forgotten man, Thomas Timme:

> For (to use the words of learned Guido) we are infants carried upon the shoulders of those great and lofty gyants, from whose eminence we do behold, not only those things which they saw, but many other misteries also, which they saw not, for no man is so sottish as to imagine that those first founders of Physicke had attained to the exact & perfect knowledge of Medicine, or of any other science which *Hypocrates* himselfe acknowledged in his Epistle to *Democritus.**

Surely, you see what is happening. Guy's children are further diminished into infants through the combined

---

* Here is the complete citation: Josephus Quersitanus (Joseph Duchesne), *The Practice of Chymicall and Hermeticall Physicke, for the preservation of health,* translated into English from the Latin by Thomas Timme. London, 1605. The quoted passage, as is usually the case with the Aphorism, practically opens the volume: Book I, Chapter I, pp. 1–2.

talents of Quercetanus and Timme while his idiosyncratic reference to the giant's neck is restored as a reference to the traditional shoulders. What we have here, I must suppose, are swirling currents and counter-currents in the diffusion of the original imagery, with no one able to say, at any moment, just how it will all come out. But one thing the historical record clearly attests: Guy's switch from dwarfs or pigmies to children never really took hold in England, possibly because it was at odds with Bacon's image of his contemporaries as oldsters and the so-called Ancients as actually the youth of mankind. There appears to have developed a reciprocal neutralization of imagery so that Guy's innovation (more or less transmitted by Quercetanus) is cancelled out as the Aphorism returns to its traditional form of giants-and-*dwarfs* rather than becoming a pristine variant of giants-and-*children*.

Yet, as you and I both know from my detailed analysis of his ingenious text, early on in this narrative, there was one who did skilfully avail himself of Guy's imagery: the rich and irascible neo-conservative, Alexander Ross. You will recall — or if not, you can refresh your memory by turning back to page 103 — that Ross converted the moderns into "children *in* understanding" before going on to describe them also as both dwarfs *and* pigmies. We can now see that Ross did not create this commingled imagery. He simply drew upon what was there for the taking, shifting from children to dwarfs as best suited his polemical purpose. We can only marvel at his adroit technique of converting the progressive imagery of a Guy de Chauliac designed to give credit to modern increments of knowledge into a neo-conservative imagery designed to downgrade the moderns in favor of the ancient fathers of knowledge. However grudgingly, we must credit Ross with a prophetic and consummate metathesis centuries before Tennyson was to state the thesis: The new order changeth, yielding place to old.

⊄ *lxiv*

AND NOW the time has come for me to confess to a fault in this circumstantial History of the Bernardian Aphorism. I do so in anticipatory self-defense. If I do not admit it here and now, your acute scholarly eye will soon detect it for yourself and moved by your exacting scholarly conscience, you will charge me with conduct most unbefitting a scholar. A confession in advance may soften the impeachment. What is more, if I acknowledge my sin against scholarship in so many words and myself listen, I may take heed, reflect and mend my ways to the point of patching the fault before I reach the point of no return.

With much candor and no little discomfort, then, I admit to having been indefensibly parochial in drafting this account of the travels and adventures of the Aphorism. As though I were a committed Anglophile, I have spent almost the entire journey in England, eager to explore every by-way even into the backcountry of a Goodman, Ross or Hakewill, to say nothing of rolling along the king's highway that leads directly from Bacon to Newton. Contrast my leisurely journey throughout that scepter'd isle with my quick forays into France lasting only long enough to pillage Rabelais, Henri de Monde-ville and Père Mersenne (although, my extended stay at

Chartres should extenuate to a degree) and with my excursion to Spain lasting just long enough for me to meet Vives and to escort him first to France and then, of course, on to England. Upon reviewing this unbalanced itinerary, I can only conclude that I have been suffering from a bad case of peregrinity (or as I should perhaps refer to it: peregrinosis).*

* In the use of this term, at least, I have broken free of all anglophilic provincialism. In his *Journal of a Tour to the Hebrides* (p. 140, 2d ed.) Boswell reports that Johnson coined the word, "peregrinity," and that upon being asked if it was an English one, he replied "No." (This, I believe, is the most succinct quotation from Sam Johnson that was ever achieved.) §

§ A disturbing addendum: But the Rev. H. J. Todd — that chorister at Magdalen College, Oxford; that tutor and lecturer at Hertford college, Oxford; that librarian at Lambeth Palace and royal chaplain; that rector of Settrington and archdeacon of York; and, most of all, that continuator of Johnson's *Dictionary* — corrects Boswell's Johnson, saying that peregrinity is in fact "an old English word; and, being inserted in the vocabulary of Gockeram, early in the seventeenth century, may be presumed to have been in use." Todd concludes, and *this* opinion I am prepared to debate with him — while still carefully avoiding an outright wrangle — "but it is [a word] not worthy to be revived." (I may be doing Todd an injustice here; I sincerely hope I am; for I quote his opinion not directly from his edition of Johnson — for I do not have it at home — but indirectly from the only edition I do have at home, the one by Robert Gordon Latham which is *founded* on the *Dictionary* of "Dr. Samuel Johnson as edited by the Rev. H. J. Todd, M.A." This edition was published in London, in 1866, by "Longmans, Green, & Co. [a thoroughly ubiquitous pair]; W. Allan & Co.; Aylott & Son; Bickers and Son [that Dickensian touch again]; W. & T. Boone; L. Booth; T. Bosworth; E. Bumpus [here, surely, truth is stranger than Dickens]; S. Capres; J. Cornish; Hatchard & Co.; J. Hearne; E. Hodgson; Houlston & Wright; J. Murray; D. Nutt; Richardson & Co.; J. & F. H. Rivington; Smith, Elder, & Co.; Stevens & Sons; Whittaker & Co.; Willis & Sotheran; G. R. Wright." When the *Dictionary* was published in Edinburgh, however, only Maclachlan & Stewart were needed to turn the trick.)

Actually, of course, Todd is mistaken; it is not an old English word. Rabelais coined *pérégrinité* to denote the con-

Having diagnosed my condition, perhaps I can manage a home-fashioned remedy. Actually, there is no alternative if I am to be returned to a state of cosmopolitan health for the *materia medica* * does not so much as mention the ailment of peregrinosis.†

There is only one way to attack this spiritual ailment and that is head-on. I shall lift myself by my bootstraps, cross the Channel, and travel south by east until I arrive in that glorious land where the Renaissance reached its highest flower, there to meet a *cinquecentista* who plucked the Aphorism, root and all, from a tradition we have not yet even hinted at.

ℭ *lxv*

OUR sixteenth-century Aphorist of the Italian Renaissance is the Jewish historian, Azariah de Rossi.

————————————Hold your fire! You would have me ignore Azariah as one who stands beyond the pale.

You will tell me that this impractical non-utilitarian, this prolix scholar, this *commentator,* should not be allowed to enter our narrative. And I reply, in the words of Salo Baron, with the trenchant though modest and

dition of a *peregrinus* or foreigner: a kind of feeling-out-of-place-ness.
* Can it have been the omission of peregrinosis that prompted Dr. Oliver Wendell Holmes to observe: "I firmly believe that if the whole *materia medica* as now used could be sunk to the bottom of the sea, it would be all the better for mankind — and all the worse for the fishes"?
† The nearest we come to it in Osler is foot-and-mouth disease, and that's just not close enough.

guarded rejoinder that "malgré sa prolixité . . . le ton est tout à fait modeste et réservé." *

You will tell me that Azariah was marred by a faulty scholarship that cannot be lightly dismissed by a discreet silence; that he only rarely gave an exact and literal citation of his sources, thus leaving the rest of us at a loss, unable to follow up for ourselves what he had tracked down for us. As Azariah's self-appointed advocate, to this charge I enter a plea of — *nolo contendere*. That is to say, I do not admit my client's guilt even though he be convicted, for this will allow me to deny the essential truth of the charge in a collateral proceeding — which follows at once.

The charge levelled at Azariah is true only in a Pickwickian sense rather than being essentially true. To be sure, he did not always give exact citations to the copious literature that occupies such an inordinately large place in his writings. But the crucial and altogether extenuating fact is that this scholar Azariah de Rossi — he was not, like Alexander Ross, a rich man — had a library even more impoverished than my own. Often, therefore, he was obliged to cite from memory. It was not intellectual laziness that prompted his seeming misbehavior, but plain poverty. Like Rabelais' Panurge, Azariah suffered from lack of money to support his scholarship. He had no manuscripts, no incunabula, no library of books at his elbow. Often, his sole resort was to memory (rather than an amply financed citation index), a memory good enough to lead us directly to the Italianate peregrinations of our Aphorism.

* It is a great comfort for a sociologist to enlist the support of such a historian as Salo Baron. See his monograph, *La méthode historique d'Azariah de Rossi* (Paris, H. Elias, 1929) where on page 15 he lends me this aid and comfort in the face of your impending attack.

Azariah plainly belongs to the progressivist wing of
the Aphorism's users. Pious defender of the Jewish
tradition though he was, he was prepared to consider that
the ancient Sages, like the modern ones, were occasionally
subject to error. This composite of traditionalism and
modernism landed Azariah in a sea of contradiction. On
the one shore, as our guide to Azariah tells us, "it seemed
obvious [to him] that the later commentators of the Bible
could not have 'seen more' than the Talmudic authorities." * On the other shore, his scientific inquiries had
shown him that later investigators typically improved
upon their predecessors. Caught up in the turbulence of
this seeming contradiction, Azariah, like so many we have
met before him, escapes to a secure conclusion by artfully
drawing upon the Aphorism. Thanks to Salo Baron, I
can quote Azariah's decisive passage exactly in the note
below,† while providing a reasonable paraphrase here

* To our ears, become increasingly sensitive to every undertone
and overtone of the Aphorism, the optical phrase "seen more"
speaks volumes. Salo Baron perspicuously quotes only this
phrase from Azariah in the sentence I have taken from his
monograph, "Azariah de Rossi's Attitude to Life (*Weltan-
schauung*)" in the *Israel Abrahams Memorial Volume*, Vienna,
1927, p. 48.
† Baron (p. 49, fn. 131) notes that Azariah has this to say
immediately after he has quoted many Talmudic sentences
about the superiority of the Ancients:

האמנה אחרי הגיע אל האחרונים מה שהשיגו הראשונים לבד מהשתתם
עצמה, נראה דהוה ליה כמשל הנס הרוכב על הענק שזכר בעל שבולי
הלקט בהקדמתו על שם אחד מחכמי קדם, באופן שיאות להאמר כי היתרון
אשר אמנה נמצא לקדמון על האחרון בדברים הנתלים בנבואה מצד
היותו יותר קרוב לבעליה הנו לאחרון על הקדמון בדברים אשר חטרם
יצא מגזע העיון והנסיון, יען היותו תמיד הולך ומוסיף חבל לחבל ומשיחה
למשיחה עד כי בעזר הראשונים עצמם אשר נלאו סביבות היאורים
להוציא להם מים אמור יאמר הכורה אחר כורה אני קרתי ושתיתי ...

235

above. This is how Azariah unites his loyalty to
tradition and his belief in a progressively enlarged truth:

> The tradition reaching later generations augmented
> by their own freshly fashioned perceptions can be
> illumined by the story of the dwarf * astride the
> giant cited by the author of שבלי הלקט (*The
> Gathered Sheaves*). In the introduction to that work,
> says Azariah, the author quotes one of the ancient
> savants in a manner that prompts us to say that the
> advantage accruing to earlier generations over later
> ones is confined to matters of revelation alone (since
> they were closer to the source of revelation). The
> advantage of later generations, in turn, resides in
> matters stemming from reflection (shall we say,
> philosophy) and from experience (empirical science).
> In these matters, there is an ongoing process that adds
> link to link and strand to strand, finally reaching the
> point where, with the indispensable help of earlier
> generations who themselves despaired of success, the
> well-digger who follows after these earlier unsuccessful
> efforts, can now labor successfully and exclaim: '*I*
> have dug and *I* do drink!'

With this concluding anecdote of the egotistic well-
digger, Azariah points the moral and puts all of us
Johnny-come-latelies in our diminutive places.

* You will have noted in the preceding footnote that the word
Azariah uses for "dwarf" is "nanas," decidedly not of Hebrew
origin, but derived from the Greek *nanos* which also gave
rise to the Latin *nanus*. Can it be that Azariah is clearly signal-
ling his indebtedness for the simile to his predecessors by this
terminological resort to nanism (an English word derived
directly from the Greek)? Not likely, since *nanos* or *nanas* had
gained currency in Hebrew for over a millennium before the
time of Azariah.

ℂ lxvi

AZARIAH, you have observed, will not allow us to remain in his own sixteenth century. By referring to the *Shibbole ha-leket,* he forces us to retrace the Italo-Hebraic tradition of the Aphorism back to the late thirteenth-century author of that treatise on ritual, Zedekiah ben Abraham ʿAnav (ʿAnaw or, as some still call him, Anavi.) *

'Anav, like Azariah long after him, is given to the odious practice of quoting from a great number and variety of authorities, whose occasional errors he promptly sets aright. A basically modest man, 'Anav is a little worried that he might be thought presumptuous for improving upon his many learned predecessors. So, in the preface to the *Shibbole ha-leket* — he has no "Epistle Dedicatory" in which to put it — 'Anav apologetically introduces his version of the Aphorism. Compared with the great scholars of the past, he appears to himself like a dwarf. He dares to correct these authorities only because he is their successor, *standing* on their shoulders and therefore, in spite of his diminutive stature, able to see farther than they.†

* You should have no great trouble in locating a copy of the *Shibbole ha-leket.* It was often re-printed; for example in Vilna, 1886, and in Venice, 1546 (I should imagine that Azariah had something to do with this edition). As for myself, I prefer the abridged edition that was turned out in Mantua (in 1514).
† The fact is that during the past several days I have been unable to locate any of the editions of the *Shibbole ha-leket.* Rather than delay any longer, I have turned to Hermann Vogelstein and Paul Rieger who (in their *Geschichte der Juden in Rom,* Berlin, 1896, in vol. I at p. 383) provide a paraphrase of the crucial passage from ʿAnav. (They call him Anaw.)

And so, Azariah de Rossi had the Aphorism from
Zedekiah ben Abraham 'Anav who in turn had it from
another to whom we shall turn in a minute. But before
going on with the Italo-Hebraic phase of the story, we
must pause for another spectacular *insight* — which
deserves a chapter to itself.

ℭ *lxvii*

DO YOU remember John's Parvus-complex, his propensity for regarding himself in most diminutive terms,
and my favorite Bernardian hypothesis accounting for the
complex, which holds that continued immersion in the
Aphorism turns giants into self-imagined dwarfs?
Consider, then, the theoretical import of my further
discovery, made *after* I had set out this theory of the
Parvus-complex, that the surname 'Anav derives from the
Hebrew word transliterated as 'anaw and that — so apt a
fact that it is scarcely credible — 'anaw means meek or
modest!

Surely, I need not develop at length the significance of
this dramatic finding. Who, among all the many Hebrew
scholars of the late thirteenth century, resonated enough
to Bernard's Aphorism to adopt it entire and so transmit
it to his successors? Was it Zedekiah ben Abraham
'Anav's contemporary Abū-l-Munā Ibn abī Naṣr ibn
Haffāẓ al-Kūhīn al-Hārūnī al-'Aṭṭār al-Isrā'īlī? Of course
not, for the core meaning of this cognomen translates
into "the Jewish druggist of priestly descent" and what
has that to do with the giant-and-dwarf Aphorism? Or,
was it that other Hebrew contemporary scholar, Todros
Abulafia, which freely translated from the Arabic means

"the father of health, the healthy one"? Or perhaps Don Abraham Alfaquin (the wise or learned man)? To ask the question in the light of my hypothesis about the Parvus-complex is almost to answer it. None of these scholars could masochistically enjoy the harsh implications of the Aphorism for self-esteem. But it was altogether otherwise for 'Anav, prepared almost from the beginning of his conscient self to be meek, modest, and mild.

This new finding, then, both supports my initial hypothesis about the Parvus-complex and requires me to amplify it. It is not only that exposure to the Aphorism shrinks the ego but also that those previously disposed to self-derogation resonate to the Aphorism once they encounter it. This is not a simple matter of cause-and-effect in which the ideological content of the Aphorism produces a contraction of self-image among those exposed to it but a far more complex matter of endlessly interacting forces in which prior disposition makes for both exposure and response to the Aphorism which in turn reinforce subsequent exposure and response. In short, if you have modest pretensions to begin with, you are going to have smaller pretensions still after you've probed the full import of being only a dwarf hoisted onto the shoulders of giants.*

* It might help these exceedingly humble men to remember that shoulders can be put to other use. A wise man, for example, will arrange matters so that he has a head upon his shoulders and, preferably, will start on this early enough in life to ensure his having an old head on young shoulders. An unwise girl, in contrast, is apt to suffer a slip of the shoulder (meaning, as Halliwell reminds us, that she listens too much to the persuasions of the other sex). Whether wise men or foolish girls, however, all of us having purposes in concert should close ranks and march shoulder to shoulder, particularly if we want

ℂ *lxviii*

AFTER this telling confirmation of my theory, we are
ready to pick up again the short Italo-Hebraic strand that
threads its way into our story. The sixteenth-century
Azariah has acquired the Aphorism from the thirteenth-
century Zedekiah; now we find Zedekiah taking it directly
from his teacher, Isaiah (ben Mali of Trani). Or to
express the latter historical relation with deadly mathematical precision:

> Isaiah : Zedekiah = Bernard of Chartres : John of
> Salisbury

This Isaiah ben Mali of Trani is quite often known as
Isaiah of Trani, the Elder, in order to distinguish him
from his daughter's son, Isaiah ben Elijah of Trani or
Isaiah of Trani, the Younger. (Once so distinguished, the
younger Isaiah need concern us no further, for he
apparently never bothered to do anything at all with the
Aphorism.)

Isaiah of Trani was by all odds the greatest Italian
Talmudist of his time. He was born around 1180 — about

---

to make our collective point straight from the shoulder. We
must also be prepared to shoulder the burdens of our time and
to put our shoulder to the wheel, rather than carry a chip on
our shoulders or merely shrug our shoulders over the whole
business. In this way, perhaps, we can keep others from giving
us the cold shoulder. It is understood, of course, that only those
who shoulder responsibilities have a moral right to shoulder
shirkers out of the way. Still, we must not become smug and
isolated. We should be willing to rub shoulders with *hoi polloi*,
while avoiding the politician's vulgar fault of becoming, in the

half a century after Bernard of Chartres died – and
founded a school of Jewish studies in Trani (on the
Adriatic, 26 miles WNW of Bari delle Puglie, Apulia).
He lived (probably) in Venice and died about 1250.

Just as we know about Bernard's creation of the
Aphorism only from his pupil, John of Salisbury, so we
know about Isaiah's subsequent use of the Aphorism
from his pupil, Zedekiah ben Abraham 'Anav. Actually,
it is not quite accurate to say that Isaiah *employed* the
Aphorism; rather, with consummate Socratic skill, he
deployed its content in the catechistic style that is the
hallmark of the true Talmudist. Here is how Zedekiah
reports his master's, Isaiah's, version of the giant-and-
dwarf simile:

> . . . how does it occur to a man to contradict the
> words of the early masters whose hearts were as open
> as a great hall? He answered him with the following
> tale which he heard from the gentile scholars [*n.b.*].
> The philosophers interrogated their most learned col-
> league, saying: "Do we not grant that those of earlier
> generations were wiser and more learned than we? Yet
> we contradict them in many instances and the truth
> is with us. How is this possible?" The philosopher
> answered: "Who can see farther, a dwarf or a giant? I
> would say the giant – for his eyes are situated in a
> much higher place than the eyes of the dwarf. And if

---

words of a giant, "a back-friend, a shoulder-slapper." You
may not like to shoulder the psychic expense of doing all this,
yet you must if you are not to have guilt laid upon your guilt-
less shoulders. And finally, as we have ample reason to know, if
you are a giant, considered shoulder-wise (archaic), you must
ready your shoulders for the onrushing ascent of familiars and
dwarfs. And though we have it on good authority that auld
acquaintance should not be forgot, the really basic question is:
should aulder?

the dwarf were astride the neck [!] of the giant – who then would see farther? I would say the dwarf for now the eyes of the dwarf are higher than the eyes of the giant. Thus we are dwarfs astride the necks of giants because we have seen their wisdom and from the strength of their wisdom we have grown wise (enough) to say all that we do but not that we are greater than they.*

So there you have it. As a moderate Talmudist – of neither the far right nor the far left – Isaiah of Trani unhesitantly drew upon the Bernardian Aphorism, though he left unclear (possibly because it was so thoroughly known by his knowledgeable contemporaries) from just which "Gentile scholar" he learned it. At any rate, I have managed to overcome my bout of peregrinosis sufficiently to leave the insular version of the Aphorism in England in order to track down the peninsular version in Italy.

As Vanessa is fond of saying: *A rivederci!*

ℂ *lxix*

AND NOW, having travelled through England, France, and Spain, Germany, Switzerland and Italy in pursuit of the Aphorism;

having traversed every century from the twelfth through the nineteenth to hunt down the genealogy of the Aphorism;

having studied the seven arts, the *trivium* of grammar, logic and rhetoric and the *quadrivium* of arithmetic,

---

* This passage from the *Shibbole ha-leket* (the Büber edition published in Vilna, 1886, p. 15) has been Englished for me by *my* pupil, Paul Ritterband. Had I attempted it on my own, I should never have come to the end of this letter.

geometry, music and astronomy that I might better understand the import of the Aphorism;

having recovered the Baconian Paradox and discovered the Parvus-complex;

having evolved the Bernardian Hypothesis and defeated the Cathedral Hypothesis;

having newly discovered those two endemic ailments of scholars: the anatopic (or palimpsestic) syndrome and peregrinosis;

having identified anew that malignant disease, the itch to publish (*insanabile scribendi cacoēthes*), having discovered the Merton test for susceptibility to it and having rediscovered the Fuller abirritant;

having freely acknowledged that Newton anticipated me; and Hooke, Newton; and Vives, Hooke; and a host of medievals and ancients, the entire lot of us moderns, in fashioning the Kindle Cole Hypothesis;

having gambolled with Gargantua, gulled with Gulliver, and ranted with Ross (to say nothing of having godfreyed * Goodman);

---

* You have probably mislaid your copy of the *London Gazette*, 29 July 1695 and so cannot check for yourself the origins of the then current phrase, "to be godfreyed." The story, with its pointed moral, is worth retelling. It seems that Michael Godfrey, the first Deputy Governor of the Bank of England, appeared out of nowhere on the battlefield at Namur § while the conflict was still raging. King William was much distressed at the sight of the civilian Godfrey and reasoned with him that his presence served no good purpose at all. Just as he reached the climax of his composite plea-and-demand that the banker take himself elsewhere and just as the brave banker replied that "I run no more hazard than your Majesty," a cannon ball

§ Will apt coincidences never cease? The Battle of Namur! The very battle — indeed, the very attack of July 17/27, — in which Captain Shandy received the memorable wound in his groin.

243

having composed this hendecachordal anaphora;
having, in short, done all that befits a scholar bent
upon solving an enigmatic problem, I can no longer
evade that deep mystery which confronted us in the very
first footnote to this letter.

I refer, of course, to the identity of Didacus Stella (in
Luc. 10, tom. 2), first quoted in the seventeenth century
by Burton * and derivatively by many another since that
time. Had it not been for the curious mishap of Didacus
Stella having been transmogrified by Bartlett's *Quotations*
into part of a book title, I should never have begun the

from the ramparts laid Godfrey dead at the King's feet. This
episode led to the cant phrase: "the fear of being godfreyed"
(meaning not to expose oneself to needless dangers, when to do
so is of no help to anyone). Incidentally, if you really do
not have your copy of the *Gazette* close at hand, you can find
the story in Macaulay's *History of England,* Volume IV, Chapter XXI. (That is, I hope you can find it. This is one of
Macaulay's longer chapters, running, by a modest estimate, to
some 50,000 words. In the edition of the *History* I have here at
home — the one published in 1864 by Longman, Green, Longman, Roberts, & Green — the Godfrey episode appears on
p. 101.)
* And not, perhaps, only by Burton. For Donne reportedly
wrote: "Though there were many giants of old in Physics and
Philosophy, yet I say with Didacus Stella: a dwarf standing on
the shoulder of a giant may see farther than the giant himself."
Whether Donne actually put it so, I cannot say with confidence,
for I have this from a book which cites neither chapter nor
verse: Alexander Lindey, *Plagiarism and Originality* (Harper &
Brothers, 1952), 236. Perhaps, Donne was another to have
picked up the Didacus source; perhaps, Donne had it from
Burton and leaped over this intermediary to the Spaniard; or
he may have had it from the gloomy Godfrey Goodman, who, as
we have seen, provided Donne with not a few figures of
speech; finally, perhaps Lindey confused Donne with Burton
and so unwittingly contrived another mystery to strain our skills
of literary detection. But I'll not take the bait for, unhooked,
I remain free for other searchings.

chase after the Aphorism with that roister * of a footnote. Plainly not, for Didacus Stella would then not have become a man of mystery. Even so, had I not been a *forgetful* inquirer and instead turned again to George Sarton's piece in the December 1935 number of *Isis,* I could have promptly dissipated the mystery created by Bartlett's inadvertence. For that piece gives us the thumbprint facts of identity: Didacus Stella is the exegetist, Diego de Estella, born in the northern Spanish town of Estella in 1524 and dying at Salamanca in 1578.

So much for Didacus Stella. Plainly, he was a man, not a fragment of a book title.† But what about the book itself, the book where, all these several centuries, a troop

---

* "Roister" is employed here in its secondary, dialectal sense: "a hound that opens on a false scent."

† This sort of thing has happened before, if only in reverse. At least, so Sterne tells us. In a critical and typically informative footnote, he takes exception to the following observation by Tristram: "My father, who dipped into all kinds of books [a practice some of us would do well to reinstitute], upon looking into *Lithopœdus, Senonensis de Portu difficili,* published by Adrianus Smelvgot . . ."

The sternly critical footnote observes of this passage that "The author is here twice mistaken; — for *Lithopœdus* should be wrote thus, *Lithopœdii Senonensis Icon.* The second mistake is, that this *Lithopœdus* is not an author, but a drawing of a petrified child. The account of this, published by Athosius 1580, may be seen at the end of Cordæus's works in Spachius. Mr. Tristram Shandy has been led into this error, either from seeing *Lithopœdus's* name of late in a catalogue of learned writers in Dr. ———, or . . ." (*Tristram Shandy,* vol. ii, chap. xix)

Should you think this just another invention of Sterne's parturient imagination, you would be badly mistaken. There actually was an ignorant physician and man-midwife, William Smellie, who did indeed, somewhat as Bartlett was to do later with Didacus Stella, mistake the caption of the drawing of a petrified child just taken from its mother's womb

of scholars, marching in the footsteps of Burton, have
enjoined us to look for the Aphorism? What of the effable
ineffable citation: Didacus Stella, in Luc. 10, tom. 2?

ℭ *lxx*

WHEN I first came upon this citation – in Burton, More,
Koyré and all the rest – I was not a little confused by
the truncated reference to "Luc." Was this a shortened
allusion to Lucretius or Lucullus, to Lucilius or Lucretia,
to Luke, Lucan or Lucian? Was it an abbreviated Latin
reference to a treatise on "light" (*lux*)? or to a treatise
on a kind of sausage (Cicero's *Lucanica*)? or perhaps one
on the elephant (*Luca bos*)? In a word, who was Luc.?
What was he? That all our savants condense him?

I thereupon turned to my copy of Bartlett's *Quotations*
– it happens to be the eleventh (1939) edition – and
found, with a distinct feeling of gratitude, that Bartlett
had fully expanded the cryptic allusion (for such readers
as myself) and spelled it out thus: Lucan.

Thanks to Bartlett, my ignorance was cured by this
heady potion of a little knowledge. Quite evidently,

(*Lithopædus Senonensis*) as the name of an author. The unfortunate error was noted by Dr. Smellie's inveterate enemy, Dr.
John Burton of York (himself the original of Sterne's unforgettable portrait of Dr. Slop) and Sterne promptly seized upon
this heaven-sent bit of pedantry self-confounded. The point
is, of course, that neither Smellie in his fashion nor Bartlett in
his had any business to draw a red herring across the path
of our understanding. I should judge that the good Dr. Smellie
was incorrigibly solemn; else, he could scarcely have brought
himself to establish an estate called Smellom.

Didacus Stella had introduced the Aphorism in Volume II, Chapter (?) 10 of a book on Lucan (or, more precisely, Marcus Annaeus Lucanus, the much admired poet and nephew of the philosopher, Seneca). This seemed reasonable enough. After all, this short-lived poet, about whom mere legend has it that he had to do away with himself in order to escape the wrath of Nero after having made the fatal mistake of besting him in a public contest of poetizing (although, if the truth be known, it was altogether otherwise: Lucan had recklessly expressed his abhorrence of tyranny in his *De Bello Civili*, which, though often extravagant and riddled with digressions, remains one of the most beautiful and thoroughly outspoken poems of antiquity and then, following words with action, had even more recklessly engaged in the Pisonian conspiracy against the Emperor, an involvement which, once uncovered, required him, as it did Piso, in accord with the practice of the time, to kill himself) — this talented, generous and brave poet was held in much esteem in the sixteenth century, as he was for centuries before. What more natural, then, than for Didacus to have been one of that numerous breed who sang Lucan's praises? *

This compelling inference left only one further ques-

---

* And who, in those earlier centuries, were especially taken with Lucan? Lacking the precise information, you might almost infer it. Most particularly Bernard of Chartres who, as Haskins puts it, was "full of Virgil and Lucan" and John of Salisbury for whom "Lucan, indeed, [was] the *poeta doctissimus*" (or, as we would now say, "a very learned poet"). You can see, then, why Bartlett's expansion of the cryptic "Luc." into the unmistakable "Lucan" earned my immediate gratitude. For Lucan did, in truth, wrap himself around the principals who initiated and transmitted the Aphorism in the renascent twelfth century.

tion to be answered. Was it John Bartlett himself who had contributed the clarifying expansion of Burton's abbreviated "Luc." into the forthright reference to Lucan? Or was it, perhaps, Christopher Morley and Louella D. Everett, the co-editors of the posthumous eleventh edition of the *Familiar Quotations?* (Bartlett had passed on 34 years before.)

The answer to this question could not be far to seek. I knew, of course, that Bartlett had published the first edition of his compendium of the world's wit and wisdom in 1855, soon after he became the owner of the University Book Store and a little before he took up residence on Brattle Street in your own adopted town of Cambridge.* I knew also that his extraordinarily useful handbook ran to nine editions during his lifetime (far fewer than the twenty-eight editions of the *Thesaurus* that appeared during Roget's lifetime, though considerably more than the five editions of the *Anatomy of Melancholy* that brightened Burton's years). To discover the identity of the benefactor who had put me on to Lucan, therefore, I had only to thumb through earlier editions of the *Quotations* to find when the Aphorism was first quoted from Burton's *Anatomy* and when the illuminating extended citation of Lucan was first introduced.

This, I have done. (Or to be perfectly candid, this I have had done by proxy, through the kind offices of Harriet Zuckerman and David Michael Levin, since I prefer the rusticity of my library at home to the urbanity of the libraries at Columbia.) The results of this explor-

---

* I also happened to know that Bartlett liked to play whist and to fish for trout. As a matter of fact, his ardent love of fishing became a matter of common notoriety, ever since James Russell Lowell published his piscatory poem: To John Bartlett, Who Had Sent Me a Seven Pound Trout.

ation are eye-opening. To begin with, it was John Bartlett himself, not his posthumous co-editors, who first quoted Burton's quotation from Didacus Stella. Evidently, this did not come easily for Bartlett waited 36 years after his first edition until the ninth edition (in 1891) * before spotting the Aphorism by Burton out of Didacus. And it is in this first reference that Bartlett, clearly wanting to stand on the shoulders of Burton, supplies the vastly extended citation: *Didacus Stella in Lucan 10, tom. ii.*

What Bartlett himself delivers to us in the 9th edition, Nathan Haskell Dole, editor of the 10th edition, repeats intact and Christopher Morley and Louella D. Everett, editors of the 11th and 12th editions, reiterate with only a nuance of variation:

9th edition:	*Didacus Stella in Lucan 10, tom. ii*					
10th edition:	"	"	"	"	"	"	"
11th edition:	"	"	"	"	"	*Tom. II*	
12th edition:	"	"	"	"	"	"	"

By directing us to Lucan and so releasing us from the chore of probing the identity of the cryptic Luc., Bartlett and his successors have put us so greatly in their debt that we, in turn, can only forgive them for the misadventure which led them to make Didacus Stella part of a book-title. Yet, for all their help (down to the detail of converting the diminutive and possibly obscure "tom. ii" into the strapping and conspicuous "Tom. II"), our

* As early as the fifth edition, in 1868, Bartlett quotes the versions of the Aphorism set forth by the seventeenth-century Thomas Fuller and George Herbert and by the early nineteenth-century Coleridge (who knew and loved his Fuller well). These quotations remain in all later editions. But not so, I am sorry to say, with the quotation from Edward Young's *Night Thoughts* (vi, line 309) which is tangent to our Aphorism: "Pygmies are pygmies still, though perched on Alps;/And pyramids are pyramids in vales."

249

family of compilers have left one crucial matter unsettled. *Was it Didacus Stella himself who mustered the Aphorism in his writing on Lucan or was Didacus simply quoting Lucan's own use of the Aphorism?* You will recognize at once that in this textual crux we have arrived at the most decisive moment in our entire inquiry. For if it should turn out that Lucan himself stated the Aphorism, then I shall have pushed back its origins to the first century of our era — more than a millennium before Bernard of Chartres! Could I establish (with the devoted assistance of Bartlett *et al.*) that Lucan said it first, this would be a literary discovery comparable to Colonel Isham's discovery of the Boswell papers at Malahide Castle or Leslie Hotson's discovery of the actual circumstances of Kit Marlowe's death!

The prospect of *such* a discovery frightens almost as much as it beckons. But, ambivalence notwithstanding, how am I next to proceed? Where in the ten books of Lucan's epic *Pharsalia* (on the civil war between Caesar and Pompey) shall I look for the Aphorism?

And now, once again, Bartlett's *Familiar Quotations* comes to my aid. For in the newest, the 13th, indeed, the Centenary edition of 1955, the answer to this crucial question is provided in full circumstantial detail. Bartlett's original citation to *Didacus Stella in Lucan 10, tom. ii* is decisively enlarged and expanded to read:

DIDACUS STELLA in LUCAN [A.D. 39–65]: *De Bello Civili, 10, II*

Understandably, my first impulse is to rush off to the Columbia libraries to end my quest in unexpected triumph. But common decency requires me to pause and express my thanks for the riches so unobtrusively bestowed upon me. Lest I have any doubt about the identity of Lucan, the 13th edition of Bartlett encases in brackets his birth- and death-dates, (which are, of course, almost as idiosyncratic as a fingerprint, — particularly when coupled with his name).* Even more: lest I have difficulty in discovering the book in which Lucan may be deploying the Aphorism, Bartlett xiii directs me to his beautiful work on the Roman civil war. And finally, as though all this largesse were not enough, Bartlett xiii informs me that the Aphorism is to be found in the tenth book of that work, in the second chapter, paragraph or verse.

How can I pay sufficient tribute to the editors of the 13th edition of Bartlett's *Familiar Quotations?* How can I sufficiently praise their scholarly modesty (for the title page no longer names the editors, requiring us to attribute the entire edition to the publishers in your nearby Boston: Little, Brown and Company)? How, then, can I thank Little, Brown and Company enough for directing us, not merely to Lucan, but to Lucan's *De Bello civili, 10, II?*

In the only way a scholar can. By swiftly availing myself of the literary treasure trove so quietly (and anonymously) deposited in my lap and rushing off to the Columbia libraries to examine the cited source for myself.

*

And now that I have made the journey into scholar-ship, —— O Bartlett! O Christopher Morley and Louella D. Everett! O Little, Brown and Company! In your benevolent zeal, in your well-meaning wish to be helpful by not allowing the abbreviated *Didacus Stella in Luc. 10, tom. ii* to remain cryptic and obscure, you have created a ghostly source through a ghostly error. You

* I say "*almost* as idiosyncratic" only to retain scholarly exacti-tude. A set of Lucan twins of identical longevity would naturally neutralize the value of this identification.

have joined the ranks (though, unlike them, in total innocence) of those other creators of fabricated sources: the Golden Boy, Thomas Chatterton, who at age twelve composed the "Rowley poems" which he attributed to a medieval monk, Rowley (poems which for a time elicited the enthusiasm of Horace Walpole); the Scottish poet, James Macpherson, who concocted ostensible translations from the Gaelic which he attributed to the Irish bard, Ossian (an epic that never fooled Sam Johnson for a minute); and William Henry Ireland, that consummate inventor of Shaksperian manuscripts (whose *Henry II* Edmund Malone promptly spotted as a brilliant forgery).

—— There is not a glimmer of the Aphorism in Lucan's *De Bello Civili*.

—— Didacus Stella never wrote a line about Lucan.

—— Burton's curtailed citation to Didacus Stella *in Luc.* refers not to the pagan Roman poet Lucan but to his thoroughly Christian near-contemporary, the friend and companion of St. Paul and St. Mark, the saintly Luke.*

ℭ *lxxi*

THE SAD truth is, Burton's citation to Didacus Stella *in Luc. 10, tom. ii* refers to the tenth chapter of the second volume of Didacus Stella's

In sacrosanctum Jesu Christi Domini nostri Evangelium secundùm Lucam Enarrationum.

* By this point, I must reluctantly recognize that you cannot possibly decipher my scribblings. But Dorothy Edi-Ale uncannily can. I turn this postscript over to her so that she can turn it into legible copy.

ℂ lxxii

—IT IS a vexing thought that I should have allowed the
industrious Bartlett to take me with him as he drew the
natural inference from the popularity of Lucan that
Didacus' "Luc." must refer to him, and him alone. At
best, it was an unfruitful error concocted out of a lazy
citation.

What makes this natural misconception even more
disconcerting for me is the undeniable fact that I could
have throttled it at birth by putting my hand on Sarton's
paper where he gave the clue to Didacus' true identity
and to the actual subject of his book. This I failed to do
and so lived, for much too long, with the twin mystery of
Didacus and *in Luc. 10, tom. 2.* (Bartlett didn't help
matters, either.)

But now that I have climbed upon the shoulders of my
one-time mentor, Sarton, I find, to my further embarrassment, that I see farther. For one thing, Sarton provides a
decidedly truncated title for Didacus's book: *In sacrosanctum Evangelium Lucae enarratio.* No longer bottled up
in my study and having searched, researched and re-
researched the evidence available in the libraries of New
York, I can report that this title is *incomplete* and should
read (as I repeat in the interest of total scholarship):
*In sacrosanctum Jesu Christi Domini nostri Evangelium
secundùm Lucam enarrationum.* Lucae or Lucam, it
matters not; it is the biblical Luke of whom Didacus
writes.

Nor is that all. For centuries now — ever since Burton
— scholars have instructed us to look for the Aphorism

253

in "Didacus Stella, *in Luc. 10, tom. 2,*" thus beginning a
tradition that was to become obsolete before it became
ancient. For let me put it to you plainly (and without
that false modesty which is the height of arrogance):
who, before now, has followed that scholarly injunction
and actually looked into Didacus Stella for the Aphorism?
On the evidence, none. Even the incomparable Sarton
was evidently willing to repeat Burton's footnoted
directions without following them in actual practice. As
he put it, with his characteristically full integrity,
"Burton's reference is *probably* to Diego's *In sacrosanctum* . . ." No one can mistake the force of the "probably"
(and I have supplied the emphasis of italics to ensure
this universal recognition). Thorough-going scholar that
he was, Sarton was announcing that he had not tracked
down the reference for himself. As with Sarton, so, manifestly, with More, Koyré and the myriad of others (including Bartlett) who have routinely cited Burton's
Didacus Stella, *in Luc. 10, tom. 2.*, without themselves
looking into the cited source. But I have.

Prowling through the archives and rare books in our
local libraries, I came upon a treasure: a 1622 edition,
published in Antwerp, of Didacus' portentous work.*
Next, I looked into Capvt x of the book in search of our
Aphorism and made a spectacular find, another discovery
that frightens me by its magnitude. The fact is — how
shall I tell it to you without seeming to be that most
obnoxious of scholars: a sensation-monger? — the newly
uncovered fact is that in ascribing the Aphorism to
Didacus Stella, Robert Burton quoted out of context
and, in a most literal sense, actually misquoted
Didacus' version of the Aphorism.

* That you might recognize the book when you come upon it, I
give you here a copy of its title page.

REVERENDI
PATRIS FRATRIS
DIDACI STELLÆ,
EXIMII VERBI DIVINI
CONCIONATORIS,
ORDINIS MINORVM
REGVLARIS OBSERVANTIÆ,

Prouinciæ fancti Iacobi, in facrofanctum
IESV CHR,ISTI Domininoftri
Euangelium fecundùm Lu-
cam enarrationum

TOMVS SECVNDVS.

Editio vltima ab authore recognita.

ANTVERPIÆ,
Apud Petrum & Ioannem Belleros.
M. DC. XXII.

Cum Gratia & Priuilegio.

⟦ *lxxiii*

THE PRECEDING chapter ended with strong words.
Yet the evidence, which has lain hidden and unregarded
for three centuries and more, is unequivocal. Knowing
how this will flutter the dovecote of contemporary scholarship, I give you that evidence, piece by piece, as I drag
the reluctant truth into the light of day from the shadows
where it lay enduringly obscured. I give you only the
circumstantial details and hope that you too will come
to the same, to me inexorable, conclusions. Burton quoted
Didacus out of context and Burton did not quote with
complete fidelity.

First, as to the context. It is a familiar enough story:
another case of the anatopic or palimpsestic syndrome.
Like many another, before and after him, Burton nar-
rowed his quotation from Didacus and so obliterated the
comparatively ancient past of the Aphorism. This indis-
cretion jelled into a myth that was eventually regarded as
a fact. As a result, from Burton's time until ours, with
Bartlett serving as accomplice and with eminent and
cultivated scholars inadvertently contributing their share
to the myth, Didacus Stella has been regarded as *the*
principal source of the Aphorism for men of the seventeenth century and later. All this came to pass simply
because Burton wrote that "I say with Didacus Stella, 'A
dwarf standing on the shoulders of a giant may see farther
than a giant himself . . .' " Burton's multitudinous
readers of the many, many editions of the *Anatomy of
Melancholy* could then only assume that the Aphorism
originated with Didacus, and as the years rolled on, this

Burton-induced assumption became fossilized into seeming and unquestioned fact. Yet what is the authentic fact we find on first looking into Didacus' commentary? Only this: that Didacus reluctantly sets himself in opposition to the advocates of ancient wisdom as the best and most inclusive wisdom, introducing the Aphorism with the words: "Far be it from me to condemn what so many and so great wise men and learned men have affirmed; nevertheless, we know it well, that Pigmies . . . [follows then the Aphorism]."

In a word, then, Didacus aligns himself on the side of the moderns. And though he does not say straight out that the Aphorism has served this polemical purpose *before him,* any faithful reader of what is hidden *between* the lines of his discourse could readily surmise as much. Yet there is not a hint of all this in Burton's quotation from Didacus.

You may consider all this purely inferential, since I rest my case about the excluded context on what is implied by Didacus rather than on what he said in so many words. If so, I shall not debate this part of my discovery with you. But I do maintain that you cannot have it both ways. If you insist that sound evidence must be literal evidence — set down in print for all who run to read — then I turn to the second part of my discovery which is nothing if not literal. For I can now demonstrate that though Burton retained the spirit of Didacus' version of the Aphorism, he unquestionably sacrificed the letter.

As you assuredly know, but what I now repeat in order to jog your memory, Burton "quoted" Didacus as follows:

Pigmei Gigantum humeris impositi plusquam ipsi Gigantes vident.

257

But what did Didacus actually write (at least in that edition of his book which, published in 1622, was sandwiched between the first edition of Burton's *Anatomy* published in 1621, which did *not* contain the Aphorism, and the second edition, published in 1624, which did)? The printed text is unambiguous:

Pygmæos gigãtum humeris impositos, plusquam ipsos gigantes videre.

Now, to extinguish any last lingering doubt, compare the two: Burton's alleged transcription and Didacus' actual language. You will tell me, no doubt, that the two are fully equivalent statements, particularly when transformed into English. This I shall not debate. But I ask you to consider the full import of the here demonstrated fact that Burton did not literally quote Didacus and that generation after generation of scholars have blandly perpetuated his mis-quotation by lazily neglecting to examine the original source. If you reject the first part of my discovery as "merely" inferential rather than literal, you cannot, in all conscience, also reject the second part as being "merely" literal rather than consequential. At the least, then, half of my discovery must stand intact: either the inferential or the literal part, I care not which. (As for myself, I happen to believe, with as much detachment as I can summon for the occasion, that *both* parts of my discovery can withstand the most incisive criticism. But perhaps it is not for me or for you to judge: I confidently leave the verdict to posterity.)

ℂ *lxxiv*

WE MUST not leave the matter of Burton and Didacus before tidying up one loose end which has been left dangling in our narrative. I refer to the connection between Burton and Newton in the matter of the Aphorism: is it the case, as Sarton maintained, that "Burton obtained [the] maxim from Diego de Estella, and Newton probably [*n.b.*] obtained it from Burton, whose *Anatomy* was already appearing in its eighth edition in the year of (1676) Newton's letter to Hooke"? Now, as you know, I yield to no man in my respect for Sarton's scholarship just as I yield to no man in my pleasure over the *Anatomy of Melancholy*. (To say nothing more, Burton's *Anatomy* has explained more than one bout of my melancholia and "inward desolations" that the intellectual descendants of Freud would hardly dare touch.) But there comes a time when personal attachment must give way to scholarly commitment, and this is just such a time. My teacher and friend, George Sarton, notwithstanding, it is the merest of inferences — and in the light of the evidence I have assembled, a rather far-fetched inference at that — that Burton was indeed the source for Newton's use of the Aphorism. We cannot even say, with assurance, that Burton was the principal disseminator of the Aphorism in that century of England's genius. Both before Burton, and after him, philosophers, poets, physicians, theologians, translators, hacks and political turncoats were busily making a commonplace of what Newton was to immortalize by his one use of it. Before Burton, and before Didacus too, the Aphorism had been

259

broadcast on every side, from its ultimately singular source in Bernard of Chartres. As for what happened after Burton, I need not remind you that it is simply not the case that *post Burtonum, ergo propter Burtonum.*

ℂ *lxxv*

NOW THAT we are back in our century of origin, with its pigmies Goodman, Hakewill, Ross, Carpenter and all the rest, and its singular giant, Newton, there's no need to retrace the further peregrinations of the Aphorism in detail. Should you want a specimen entry from the early nineteenth century, I give you Coleridge's: "A dwarf sees farther than the giant when he has the giant's shoulder to mount on." * Note the characteristic literary skill with which Coleridge avoids committing himself either to the "standing" or the "sitting" schools of thought on the Aphorism; the dwarf can simply "mount on." Note, further, and this is only another example of Coleridge's capacity for fine and deepcutting distinctions, that he makes the behavior of the dwarf contingent rather than determined; the dwarf sees farther *when* he mounts the giant's shoulder, this clearly implying that he does not invariably climb that eminence, either because he is too short-sighted to perceive the opportunity for extending his range of vision or because, as in under-developed cultures, the giant is simply not available.

Moving from the realm of poetic philosophy to that of science and moving from the 12th century to the middle of the 19th century, we come full circle from one

* You will find this in Samuel Taylor Coleridge's *The Friend*, Sec. I, Essay 8.

Bernard (of Chartres) to another Bernard (Claude), who equates the giants to great men of science rather than to the accumulation of scientific knowledge:

> Great men have been compared to giants upon whose shoulders pygmies have climbed, who nevertheless see further than they. This simply means that science makes progress subsequently to the appearance of great men, and precisely because of their influence. The result is that their successors know many more scientific facts than the great men themselves had in their day. But a great man is none the less, still a great man, that is to say, — a giant.*

At about the same time — long after his celebrated precocious years of childhood — John Stuart Mill was prophetically raising the question "whether our march of intellect be not rather a march towards doing without intellect, and supplying our deficiency of giants by the united efforts of a constantly increasing multitude of dwarfs"? Evidently, the attack on teams of intellectual workers had been mounted long before today.

❡ *lxxvi*

AS THE Aphorism moves toward our own century, the figurative language becomes more and more truncated while the informing idea persists. There develop what the social psychologists describe as two reciprocal processes

---

* First published in 1865, Claude Bernard's *Introduction to the Study of Experimental Medicine* remains an unexcelled account of how talented physiologists go about their work; he comes to the giant-dwarf figure on page 42.

in the transmission of rumor: the process of leveling, in which the original version becomes shorter, deprived of details and so more easily grasped, and the process of sharpening, in which the surviving details are given particular emphasis. This is just what happens to our Aphorism. The giants and the dwarfs both are leveled to the ground with nary an allusion to them while the shoulders are retained as the only recognizable part of the original Bernardian figure.

Thus, we find that most erudite scholar of Greek thought, Theodor Gomperz, writing of Lucian — NOT, be it noted, our Lucan but the Greek wit and satirist whose parody of adventure stories, *The True History*, influenced both Rabelais *and* Swift — that he, Lucian, was "a scoffer who, much as he disliked the Cynics, may often be observed standing on their shoulders." * Thus glimpsing Gomperz' barely disguised dislike of the scoffing Lucian and knowing that those mounted on the shoulders of others are either self-confessed dwarfs (who are apt to be, in fact, giants) or self-imagined giants (who, failing to realize that they do stand on the shoulders of others, are apt to be, in fact, dwarfs) — knowing all this, we may perhaps not be rushing into too wild a conjecture to suppose that Gomperz is indeed making curtailed use of our Aphorism, for he surely regards Lucian, with all his cleverness, as having dwarfish traits. So perhaps we can count the great scholar of Greek thought as another in the long line of those who have taken up the figure. At any rate, we had better count him so, for *Hofrat* Professor

* Gomperz describes Lucian so in the second volume (p. 165) of *The Greek Thinkers*, the volume translated from the German into English by G. G. Berry (not, as the first volume was, by Laurie Magnus who, cognominally speaking, would of course have been the more symbolically appropriate translator).

Gomperz and his wife, Elise, repeatedly interceded in
Freud's behalf when Freud was seeking to be elevated
to the rank of professor in his native Vienna and, as we
shall see at the very end of this letter, it is Freud who
unquestionably has the last word in the long tradition of
the giant-and-dwarf simile.*

You need not search far to find Sir Michael Foster
observing (in his *History of Physiology*, 1901) that "it is
one of the lessons of the history of science that each age
steps on the shoulders of the ages which have gone before.
The value of each age is not its own, but is in part, in
large part, a debt to its forerunners."

That sage among your New England philosophical
brahmins, Charles Sanders Peirce — whose surname I too
know should, in strict Bostonian style, rime with *hearse*
— introduces a truly acrobatic twist to the figure when he
writes that philosophy must be rescued and brought "to
a condition like that of the natural sciences, where investigators, instead of contemning each the work of most
of the others as misdirected from beginning to end,

* Do you consider these credentials not enough to include
Gomperz in our history? If so, consider this: he edited a volume
by John Stuart Mill — who, as we know, *did* adapt the simile
— and this volume was translated into German by Freud,
while he was still a student.
Angered by the dwarfs who denied him his place in the academic sun, Freud was profoundly grateful to Elise Gomperz
for her unflagging efforts to get a professorship for him,
affectionately addressing her as "Dear Protectrix" and "Your
Highness" and respectfully describing his memory of her
"unforgotten husband . . . when I, young and timid, was
allowed for the first time to exchange a few words with one of
the great men in the realm of thought." All this and more
will be found in The [315] *Letters of Sigmund Freud,* which
were selected and edited by his son Ernest L. Freud and published in this country by Basic Books in 1960.

cooperate, *stand upon one another's shoulders,* and multiply incontestable results . . ." *

By the twentieth century, the Russians have joined the ranks of the Bernardian Aphorists, albeit of the truncated variety. So it is that we discover Nikolai Ivanovich Bukharin, at the time of writing in 1931, Member of the Academy of Sciences of the USSR, Director of the Industrial Research Department of the Supreme Economic Council, President of the Commission of the Academy of Sciences for the History of Knowledge, later brought to public trial for treason and exonerated in 1936, only to be re-arrested and put to death in 1938 for counter-revolutionary plotting of which, we are recently assured by the post-Stalin authorities in the USSR, he was wholly innocent — we find Bukharin adopting a similarly abbreviated version of the figure as he asserts that "experience, representing the result of the influence of the external world on the knowing subject in the process of his practice, stands on the shoulders of the experience of other people." †

* He argues for this feat in *Pragmatism and Pragmaticism,* this being volume V of his posthumously *Collected Papers,* published by your Harvard University Press in 1934, at pages 274–6.
† This was in his paper, "Theory and Practice from the Standpoint of Dialectical Materialism," presented to the International Congress of the History of Science and Technology held in London in 1931 and published in the collection of papers by delegates from the USSR under the title, *Science at the Cross Roads.*

It was probably no accident (as the Marxists say) that Bukharin adopted the truncated expression, "stands on the shoulders of . . ." After all, Friedrich Engels had reiteratively adopted the same expression in the second part of the prefatory note to *The Peasant War in Germany* (the part written in June, 1874, not the first part which he had prepared for the then-new edition in 1870), when he observed: "Just as German

In the same year, Frank Harris is truculently asking on page 265 of his libellous biography *Bernard Shaw*, "what basis Shaw has for his claims that he stands on Shakespeare's shoulders."

It will come as no surprise to find echoes of the Bernardian Aphorism reverberating in the works of George Sarton as when he writes of three illustrious botanists of the sixteenth century, Flemings all, that "they were standing on the shoulders of the German fathers and did better what the latter had done before them" and writes also of that Bolognese jurist and equine anatomist of the sixteenth century, Carlo Ruini, that he "was standing on the shoulders of Vesalius and others and applying their methods to the horse." *

Still another twist is given the Aphorism by your fellow historian and my Columbia colleague, Herman Ausubel, who probably reflects the mass society in which we (are said to) live when he vastly multiplies the number of standees in describing the Victorians as "giants with massive shoulders on which subsequent generations

theoretical socialism will never forget that it *rests on the shoulders* of Saint-Simon, Fourier and Owen . . . so the practical workers' movement in Germany must never forget that it has *developed on the shoulders of* the English and French movements, that it was able simply to utilise their dearly-bought experience, and could now avoid their mistakes, which *in their time* were mostly unavoidable." (The italics, of course, are all mine.)

* I should perhaps add (after Sarton) that Ruini did NOT discover the greater circulation of the blood, despite that plaque to the contrary put up by the veterinary school of Bologna. You can discover the grounds for rejecting this mistaken claim to priority and the truncated similes in Sarton's *Appreciation of Ancient and Medieval Science during the Renaissance,* as published in 1955 by the University of Pennsylvania Press, pp. 123 and 100.

of English – and other people – have been able not only to stand but to stand comfortably." *

The rapid advance of science has enabled at least one philosopher and historian of science to break out of the seeming impasse over the thorny problem of the exact position taken by us dwarfs upon the eminence of giants. For as Gerald Holton, Derek J. de Solla Price and then many others have estimated, some 80 to 90 per cent of all scientists known to history are alive today. To capture this strongly modernist thought that much of what is now known in science has been discovered in our own time, Holton introduced a symposium at which distinguished physicists were to report the history of their major discoveries with the "disastrously mixed metaphor: in the sciences, we are now uniquely privileged to sit side-by-side with the giants on whose shoulders we stand." †

Lately, the Aphorism has brought mingled comfort and despair to my fellow sociologists. On the optimistic side, Howard Becker says of our guild that "we do stand on the shoulders of our forerunners, and we consequently see farther, in many important directions, than they conceivably could." ‡ On the pessimistic side, another

* Herman greatly enlarges the figure in his book on the reformers among the late Victorians: *In Hard Times* which happily the Columbia University Press issued in 1960.
† The composite sit-and-stand figure will be found in Gerald Holton, "On the recent past of physics," *American Journal of Physics,* December 1961, 29, 807. A further context for the figure is provided by Derek J. de Solla Price on the very first page of his big little book, *Little Science, Big Science,* published, naturally enough, by the Columbia University Press in 1963.
‡ The paper in which Becker expresses this opinion (on page 380) is symptomatically entitled "Vitalizing Sociological Theory." It was printed in the *American Sociological Review* in August 1954.

(who should perhaps go nameless) has acrobatically
adapted the simile, to highlight "one of the differences
between the natural and the social sciences . . . [I]n the
natural sciences, [we are told] each succeeding generation stands on the shoulders of those that have gone
before, while in the social sciences, each generation steps
in the face of its predecessors." *

ℂ *lxxvii*

BUT NOW, time runs out and there's little prospect of
my being able to answer your question in required detail.
When you come right down to it, the essential point is
that the dwarfs-on-the-shoulders-of-giants Aphorism is a
rough equivalent to the twentieth-century sociological
conception that scientific discoveries emerge from the
existing cultural base and consequently become, under
conditions that can be reasonably well defined, practically
inevitable. We now know that the Aphorism really was
originated by Bernard of Chartres (as he stood on the
shoulders of his predecessors, primarily Priscian). And,
as you can see from the small sample of occasions I have
mustered, the Aphorism then made its way slowly into the
seventeenth century when it was picked up by Newton, to
be associated forever after with his name. For your
convenience, here is a swift listing of a few (though far

* Since anonymity will not be preserved in any case, I had
better tell you straight out that David Zeaman is responsible for
this observation in his paper on "Skinner's theory of teaching
machines" published in Eugene Galenter, ed., *Automatic
Teaching: The State of the Art* (New York: John Wiley & Sons,
1959), 167.

from all) usages of the Aphorism before and after
Newton's which I have managed to track down (chiefly
in my study at home with later assists from sources in the
New York Public and Columbia libraries).

c. 112€	BERNARD OF CHARTRES
12th century	John of Salisbury
c. 1150–1200	Alexander Neckam
1180	Peter of Blois
c. 1190	Alan (of Lille? of Tewksbury?)
13th century	Henricus Brito
13th century	Isaiah ben Mali of Trani
c. 1280	Zedekiah ben Abraham 'Anav
1306–20	Henri de Mondeville
1363	Guy de Chauliac
1531	Johannes Ludovicus Vives (Juan Luis Vives)
1574	Azariah de Rossi
1578	DIDACUS STELLA (Diego de Estella)
1581	Alexandre Dionyse
1601	François Martel
1605	Josephus Quercetanus (Joseph Duchesne)
1616	Godfrey Goodman
1621	Nathanael Carpenter
1624	ROBERT BURTON
c. 1625	John Donne (?)
1627	George Hakewill
1634	Marin Mersenne
1642	Thomas Fuller
1649	John Hall
1651	Alexander Ross
1665	Marchamount Nedham (peripheralist)
1667	Thomas Sprat
1676	ISAAC NEWTON
1690	Sir William Temple

1692	Sir Thomas Pope Blount
1705	William Wotton
1812	Samuel Taylor Coleridge
1865	Claude Bernard
1868	John Stuart Mill
1874	Friedrich Engels
1901	Sir Michael Foster
1902	Theodor Gomperz
1905	Charles Sanders Peirce
1931	Frank Harris
1931	Nikolai Ivanovich Bukharin
1942	Robert K. Merton
1954	Howard Becker
1955	George Sarton
1959	David Zeaman
1960	Herman Ausubel
1961	Gerald Holton
timeless	SIGMUND FREUD

ℂ *lxxviii*

THE FULL story must wait for another letter but perhaps I can call a temporary halt by reporting the episode which caps all earlier uses of the Aphorism. Properly enough, it was another giant, this time, Freud, who clarified its import, once and for all. It came to pass when Stekel, that unwanted disciple of Freud and regarded by him as a conscienceless pretender to science, tried to make self-interested use of the Aphorism.* Stekel had

* Freud's image of Stekel can be reconstructed from this episode: Ernest Jones "once asked Freud if he regarded an 'ego-ideal' as an universal attribute, and he replied with a puzzled expression: 'Do you think Stekel has an ego ideal?' "

269

become thoroughly persuaded that his ideas surpassed those of the master. He liked to express this by saying, with arrogant modesty, that a dwarf on the shoulders of a giant can of course see farther than the giant himself. Comes then the giant's grim crusher when he hears of this claim: "That may be true, but a louse on the head of an astronomer does not." Exit Aphorism.

Yours,

P.S.

AS THIS history has drawn to a close, I should tell you about the working title, as distinct from the formal title, that soon imposed itself upon me. You, as an author always at work on a book (or very briefly in between books), will not be surprised to hear that I hit upon a private tag for the manuscript as it lurched into being. Every writer has this sort of experience. In my case, it happened that I came upon the formal title almost at the beginning. But as the days devoted to the writing of the letter lengthened into weeks, this long tag served no immediate purpose. After all, you would scarcely expect me to say as I settled down each morning to write fresh but preordained pages: "Now, back to *On the Shoulders of Giants*." This would have been a little like addressing an old friend not, say, as "Bud" but as "Mr. Bernard Bailyn."

And so, as was perhaps inevitable in this age of acronyms, *On the Shoulders of Giants* soon became contracted into OTSOG. There is, of course, a superabundance of precedent for beheading the words of a title in

this fashion and then collecting the decapitate-letters
into what might seem to be a nonce-word. Just about
every department of social life has its own complement of
such titular decapitations. I say nothing of CBS and IBM
in the world of business or of UNICEF and NATO in the
world of international affairs or of SEC and HEW in the
pacific branches of our national government. But I do say
a little something of the ultimate step taken in this
direction (a step unforeseen even by such prescient
students of the vagaries of language as Rabelais, Swift
and Sterne): the abbreviation of abbreviations in the
military branches of our government. Take only the one
case furnished by Bergen and Cornelia Evans (the genial
brother-and-sister team of lexicographers known fondly to
a few of us as B&CE). This is the case of CSCN/CHSA. You
will promptly recognize this as an acronymous
version of the euphonious collocation of syllables,
COMSUBCOMNELM/COMHEDSUPPACT (which is, evidently
enough, itself an abbreviation of the title of Commander,
Subordinate Command, U. S. Naval Forces Eastern
Atlantic and Mediterranean, Commander, Headquarters
Support Activities).

This dazzling gem of abbreviation, this macronym,
manages to contrast the shining valor of the military man
and the dull timidity of the scholarly man. And so, I
made no effort to enter into the unequal contest. I did
not try to best that grand configuration of syllables
COMSUBCOMNELM/COMHEDSUPPACT by the hopelessly
inferior construct, ONTHESHOFGITS. Instead, I modestly
stuck by OTSOG as quite enough for my purposes. And,
this I must tell, the longer I have lived with OTSOG, the
more I have felt at home with it. (The very contraction
seems to carry a positive affective tone. In fact, we may
have gotten hold of a considerable generalization of

human experience here. For notice that though we speak affectionately of FDR and JFK, we seem, interestingly enough, never to have brought ourselves to speak of WGH and his laconic successor, CC. As for the self-styled conservative BG, we can only boggle.)

OTSOG has many and varied virtues as an apt descriptive word. Consider only these few:

— It is an ugly word. Its very ugliness arrests the attention and so makes it a memorable word.

— It is a startlingly unique word. Remote in sound and look from all other words in the language, it cannot easily be confused with any one of them. This has the further advantage of maintaining my imprescriptible right to being its originator (although not its perpetual owner, for I now place it in the public domain).

— It is bound to be an unmodish word. Ugly and unique, it will escape the ill fate of being battered down by incessant use into a wornout cliché.

— It is a short word. It splits decisively into two syllables before even the most unpracticed philological eye. It remains, therefore, easy to spell and to pronounce.

— It is a self-made word. Put more sociologically, it enjoys an achieved status rather than one merely ascribed to it on the basis of its antecedents. Yet

— it is an unambitious word. It has no need of a conjectural etymology designed to establish makebelieve lordly beginnings. In a word,

— it is an ordinary word, homely and unaffected. It is not distinguished by rank or position, but belongs, now and forever more, to the commonalty of words. There is nothing here of an ostentatious derivation from the

aristocratic Greek or the patrician Latin. It remains
reminiscent in look and sound of the unassuming and
simple Anglo-Saxon and Scandinavian.

— It is a plain word, — open, manifest, and unmistakable; downright, mere, sheer, flat and absolute;
simple, not ornate; unembellished and undec-
orated; compounded of very few ingredients, neither
rich nor highly seasoned; free from duplicity or guile;
a word honest, candid and frank, avoiding all ambiguity, evasion or subterfuge; a straightforward and
direct word.

— It is a variously onomatopœic word. Its first syllable
calls to mind the Corsican dwarf born on the mountain of Stata Ota, and its second the Grave of Giants,
a cromlech of long stones at Lugna Clogh, near Sligo,
or the oval cromlech at Ballymascanlan near Dundalk
in Louth (which, we now know, was brought there by
the giant, Parraghbough M'Shaggean).

— It is also and faintly an onomatopœic word in a
thoroughly symbolic sense. What other word catches
better the tone and flavor, the technique and æsthetic
character of that kind of exacting scholarship which,
never diverted by red herrings drawn across the track,
is dedicated to the chase of an elusive problem (that
parthenogenetically manages to spawn numerous other
problems), the inquiry being all the while disciplined
by an enduring sense of the ultimately relevant?

— In short, what word, other than OTSOG, can fully
capture in its every lineament that kind of scholarship
which is composed of
>   displays of demonstrative accuracy,
>   bouts of peripeteia,
>   ingenious wordmaking,
>   the debris of forgotten history,

an abundance of historical and sociological
   shibboleths,
agreeable incongruities,
equitable divisions between the sinister and the
   dexter,
careful sobriquets and little or no stock pathos,
the various grammatical stops (, ; :), ellipses
   (. . .), aposiopeses (- - -) and even (when need
   be) against the powerful opposition of Lord
   Macaulay, the needed interpolations (— —,
   () and []), though carefully avoiding an
   excess of apostrophic emphases!
the subdued enunciation of basic truths in that
   middle ground that lies between shouting and
   total silence which I think is called meiosis,
   and
just a soupçon of Gallicisms, a modicum of Latin-
   isms, an iota of Græcisms, a smattering of
   Scotticisms and a great stock of Anglo-Saxon-
   isms?

   All this is caught up in the word OTSOG, as much in
its sound as in its look. Yet even these do not exhaust
the seemingly inexhaustible virtues of the word. I have no
doubt that many times before words of a like versatility
have sprung into the fevered brain of a writer only to
end as nonce-words, used for the one precious occasion
and never again heard from or of. But happily, OTSOG has
yet another virtue that immunizes it, I believe, against
this harsh and lonely fate. For, as you must have noticed
for yourself, OTSOG is admirably suited to all the various
word formations: nounal, adjectival, verbal and ad-
verbial.

otsog, *n.* a close-knit narrative that pays its respects to scholarship and its dues to pedantry; also, an exceedingly diversified (and thoroughly parenthesized *) piece of dedicated scholarship

otsog, *v.* to engage in this form of scholarship

otsogable, *a.* capable of being converted into an otsog

otsogal, *a.* of or pertaining to otsogs or otsogers

otsogally, *adv.* in an otsogal manner

otsogalore, *a.* abundantly otsogal

otsogamy, *n.* 1. the condition, rule or custom of being wedded to otsogery;
2. a dangerous state of mind and condition of the psyche;
3. a marriage of otsogers (apt to be unstable);
4. (illiterate, but apt to become common usage) having the flavor of a piece of otsogery that has been kept until it is "high"

otsogarian, *a. rare* relating to an otsog or to otsogery

otsogashed, *a.* cut to the quick by an otsog

otsogasp, *sb.* a convulsive catching of the breath, induced by exhaustion or dismay while reading an otsog (this is the full acronym, including title *and* subtitle)

otsoger, *n.* one who commits an otsog; particularly, a confirmed practitioner of the art of otsogery

otsogerist, *n. syn.* of otsoger (a more elegant form)

otsogerize, -ise, *v.* to convert into an otsog

otsogery, *n.* the general practice of otsog-type scholarship (as distinct from a particular specimen, let alone a minute piece [which is an otsogism])

otsogesce, *v. rare* to assume the appearance of an otsog

otsogfidian, *n.* a true believer in the art of otsogery

* and heavily footnoted

275

otsogging, *vbl. sb.*   the action of otsog, *v.*

otsogiana, *n.*   a collection of otsogs

otsogify, *v.*   to render a scholarly problem in the
otsogal fashion

otsogild, otsoguild, *n.*   a brotherhood of otsogers

otsoginess, *n.*   a general state, or condition, of (a
piece of) scholarship, (as in: This book is just
loaded with otsoginess)

otsogirl, *n.*   young unmarried female otsoger; extended to include the middle-aged, married, female
otsoger

otsogism, *n.*   the doctrine of otsogery; also, a sliver of
otsogery

otsogist, *n.*   *syn.* of otsoger (not preferred usage)

otsogity, *n.*   the fact of being an otsog; also, an instance of this

otsogiverse, *n.*   a world created by otsogery

otsoglad, *a.*   otsog-happy

otsogle, *v.*   to cast admiring or insinuating glances at
modest men perched on the shoulders of giants; to
"make eyes" at them

otsogling, *n.*   a young or petty otsoger

otsogloom, *n.*   the sombre melancholy sometimes
induced by a severe dose of otsogiana

otsogre, *n.*   a monstrous otsog of frightening aspect

otsogress, *n.*   an otsogre of the female persuasion

otsogurient, *n. obsolete, rare*   a subject that just begs
to be otsogerized

These few entries barely scratch the surface of the
word-formations to which OTSOG swiftly lends itself, but
they may be enough to give you the general idea. We can
add the usual complement of word-compounds: for casual
examples, mock-otsogery (but decidedly *not* the barba-
rism, pseudo-otsogery), otsoglike, otsogwards, and
otsogcraft. As medical science continues its progress, we

shall need new words to designate newly identified ills; not least, the otsogopsychoses (which at the moment divide neatly into otsogomania and otsogophobia, with the latter occurring on so vast a scale as to create a really serious problem for us committed otsogers).

Yet I must not violate the sense of our Aphorism by pretending for even a moment that this puny seizure of alphabetitis is peculiar to our own time. In contriving OTSOG, I have, once again, only clambered onto the shoulders of our cultural forbears. For you will remember the legend of the special meaning assigned the acronym, CABAL, back in 1672 when the five ministers of Charles II who signed the Treaty of Alliance with France for war against Holland chanced to be *C*lifford, *A*rlington, *B*uckingham, *A*shley and *L*auderdale. Ever since, we have known how to describe, most economically, a secret or private intrigue of a sinister character formed by a small body of persons. I thank the Muse for having led me instead to the sweet innocence and honesty of OTSOG.

Onomasticon OR A Sort of Index

Persons and Personages

ADDISON, JOSEPH: anachronistic critic of Madison Avenue, 167, 212, 214, 213–5n

AITKEN, GEORGE ATHERTON: G. A. Aitken, M. V. O., partial to Arbuthnot, 121–3

ALAN OF LILLE (DE L'ISLE): Alan of Tewksbury?, 219–23

ALAN OF TEWKSBURY: Alan of Lille?, 219–23

'ANAV, ZEDEKIAH BEN ABRAHAM: modest Italo-Hebraic transmitter of The Aphorism; vulnerable to the Parvus-complex, 237–41

ANTONY, MARK: defender of Brutus, 147

ARBUTHNOT, JOHN: may have authored Pope's *Memoirs of Scriblerus*, 120–3

ARISTOTLE: a Graeculus?, 99

ARNOLD, MATTHEW: cultured critic and poet, full of light and a little sweetness, 127, 203

AUBREY, JOHN: sprightly 17th-century observer and man-about-town, 13–7, 22, 26, 83–4, 95–7

AUSUBEL, HERMAN: a multiplier of standees, 265

AZARIAH DE ROSSI: Italo-Hebraic commentator, 233–7

BACON, FRANCIS: William Shakspere?, 17, 62n, 80–1, 172n, 198–9

BACON, ROGER: "Doctor mirabilis"; remarkable predecessor of his 17th-century namesake, Francis Bacon, 198–9

BAILYN, BERNARD: Harvard historian, the occasion for it all, xx, 270

BALDWIN, CRADOCK, AND JOY: not a Dickensian law firm but an authentic firm of publishers, 161n

BARBER, ELINOR: co-author of an important unpublished work, *The Travels and Adventures of Serendipity*, 156n

BARON, SALO: a scholar, 234–5

BARTLETT, JOHN: he helped make a familiar quotation unfamiliar, 3, 4, 7, 12, 244, 248–51, 253

BECKER, HOWARD: a sociologist, 266

BENTHAM, JEREMY: a child prodigy and adult colossus, 109, 112–9, 150, 203

281

PARVUS, A. L.: partner of Rosa Luxemburg and Trotsky; has nothing at all to do with the Parvus-complex, 202*n*

PASCAL, BLAISE: master of paradoxy (wrote: "Writers who condemn vanity enjoy the glory of having written well on the subject: and their readers like it to be known that they have read them: and I who write this perhaps have this disposition, and possibly those who read it . . ."), 75, 75*n*

PEIRCE, CHARLES SANDERS: Father of pragmatism (which he branded as pragmaticism, a term "ugly enough to be safe from kidnappers"), 263

PEPYS, SAMUEL: tailored fifty volumes of diary manuscript, 55*n*, 85, 155

PETER OF BLOIS: a rock which the scholar strikes with his rod, 214*ff*

PETER THE EATER: literary gastronome. 214

PETER THE IRISHMAN: resident of Naples, 215

PHILIPS, AMBROSE: the archetypical namby-pamby, 167

PHOCION: Athenian general; like Socrates, a victim of hemlock owing to an excess of virtue, 63*n*

POPE, ALEXANDER: a contentious genius, 120–1, 167–9

POTTER, FRANCIS: an expert on the number 666, 136–7*n*

PRICE, DEREK DE SOLLA: distinguishes big science and little science, 266

PRISCIAN: acute sixth-century grammarian and mensurator: a priscianist, 194–8, 200, 218

QUERCETANUS: *see* Duchesne, Joseph

RABELAIS, FRANÇOIS, a giant, 54, 139*ff*, 173–4

AL-RĀMĪ, SHARAF AL-DĪN AL-ḤASAN IBN MUḤAMMAD: the Persian literary man with a flair for gynecic figures of speech, 98*n*

RITTERBAND, PAUL: he brightened a dark passage, 242*n*

ROBERT, CANON OF MERTON: a very brave man, 207*n*

ROGET, PETER MARK: inventor of a slide rule: also creator of a Thesaurus, 107*ff*

ROMILLY, SIR SAMUEL: Bentham's candid friend, 118

ROSS, ALEXANDER: rich, irascible neo-conservative of the 17th-century, 83, 92, 98*ff*, 139–40, 230–1

SARTON, GEORGE: the dean among historians of science, 5, 37*ff*, 224*ff*, *passim*

SCALIGER, JOSEPH JUSTUS: a bottomless pit of erudition and son of Julius Caesar Scaliger, 50–2

SCALIGER, JULIUS CAESAR: father of Joseph Justus Scaliger, 52

SCOTT, SIR WALTER: editor of Swift's collected works, 122, 142*n*

SELDEN, JOHN: master of table talk, 21, 155

AL-SHĀDHILĪ, ṢADAQA IBN IBRĀHĪM AL-MIṢRĪ AL-ḤANAFĪ: the Egyptian ophthalmologist with a keen eye for ocular phenomena, 97*n*

SHAKSPERE, WILLIAM: Shakspere (inveterate plagiarist of 20th-century psychological knowledge), 43, 106*n*, 125*n*, 265

SHANDY, CAPTAIN: *see* Toby, Uncle

285

Places, Things, and Non-things *

* Non-things = unreified concepts

Afterword

IN AUGUST 1957 Robert K. Merton delivered the Presidential Address at the annual meeting of the American Sociological Society. I assume that the Address did not include all the material subsequently published in the *American Sociological Review*, Vol. XXII, No. 6, December 1957, under the title "Priorities in Scientific Discovery: A Chapter in the Sociology of Science"—but only the gist of it. Merton proposed to account for the eruption, from time to time in the history of science, of quarrels about priority. Who discovered what when? He referred to several famous conflicts, including these: Galileo asserting his claim against Father Horatio Grassi in the invention of the telescope for use in astronomy, Newton at loggerheads with Hooke on optics and celestial mechanics, the same Newton against Leibniz on the invention of the calculus, Henry Cavendish against Watt and Lavoisier on the discovery of the compound character of water.

Several reasons offered themselves. Perhaps it was enough to point to egotism, natural to the human species. But Merton wasn't impressed by that consideration. Or by the notion that scientists are peculiarly given to egotism: not enough evidence. In the end, he settled upon a different explanation. Science, he remarked, is a social institution, and therefore sensitive to the violation of intellectual property. The property of particular concern to science is originality. Merton spoke of "the institution of science, which defines originality as a supreme value and thereby makes recognition of one's originality a major concern." Such recognition is especially crucial because the discovery, as soon as it is made, becomes common property, and the discoverer's rights in the matter consist thereafter only in the recognition he receives for it. The supreme recognition is eponymy, "the practice of affixing the name of the scientist to all or part of what he has found": as in the Copernican system, Hooke's law, Halley's comet. (Don't be impatient, reader, I'll come to *On the Shoulders of Giants* in a minute.) There are indeed other forms of recognition: the award of a Nobel Prize, for instance, or the establishment of a research institute to further one's work. But the happy moral of Merton's story was "that scientists are governed by a socially induced love of honor rather than of gain"—a quotation I take not from the Address but from the book you are now holding. See page 160, whereon the discovery of the moral is congenially ascribed to Sir William Temple. A socially induced love of honor: and the history of dueling is sufficient to note the quarrels that are blown up upon that head. Now that dueling has gone out of fashion, its place has been taken by the learned paper which, when published, is accompanied by some rival scholar's "Comments on the Foregoing."

In the same lecture Merton turned to another motif in the sociology of science, "the socially enforced value of humility," according to which a scientist protests how little he has been able to do and how greatly he stands in debt to his precursors. E.g., Newton writing to Hooke, February 5, 1675/76: "If I have seen further it is by standing on ye sholders of Giants." In the lecture, Merton referred to this as "the epigram Newton made his own," a vigilant phrase disavowing any suggestion that Newton had invented the elegant thing. Clearly, Merton had been researching the matter, because even in his first published reference to it—"A Note on Science and Democracy" (1942)—he had already known that Newton's remark, whether we call it an epigram or an aphorism, was a standard phrase in 1675/76 and indeed, as Merton observed, "from at least the twelfth century." See page 1 of *OTSOG*, to give *On the Shoulders of Giants* the abbreviated form in which its claim to linguistic invention has been lodged.

Now to effect a swift transition from the Address to *OTSOG*. Suppose that in October 1957 Merton were to send a copy of his Address—either a typescript copy or an early galley of the *ASS* essay soon thereafter to appear—to his friend, the distinctive and distinguished Harvard historian Bernard Bailyn. Bailyn replies, a "thank-you" note containing a reference to Newton's epigram and attributing it, on the double authority of Gilson and Lavisse, to Bernard of Chartres. Merton replies in turn and so forth. But suppose further that Merton, having gotten his sober reflections on a matter of persistent interest to him off his chest in the Address, felt inclined to view the same matter in a genial, amused, whimsical spirit. The matter would remain with him as seriously as ever—how the growth of knowledge comes about, the relation between forgetting and remembering, the part played in knowledge by happy chance or serendipity, the biographical context in which scientific problems are tackled. But this matter is now viewed in a somewhat pipe-smoking haze of good fellowship: the merits of a comic sense of life—as distinct from its rival or Nietzschean tragic sense of life—are benignly pondered, with sundry reflections of an amiable kind. Bear in mind, though, that Merton is still a scholar; he has an interest—entirely social and honorable— in getting to the bottom of a question. What more congenial than that he should try to get to the bottom of the question at issue: who invented the aphorism of dwarfs-and-giants that Newton made his own?

But a further ingredient must be added. Our author has from time to time immersed himself in Burton's *Anatomy of Melancholy* and Sterne's *Tristram Shandy*, two works com-

293

patible only if the spirit of comedy suffuses them. It is possible to read the *Anatomy* in a Shandean spirit, now that our knowledge of inward desolations is even more detailed than Burton's: to read *Tristram Shandy* in a Shandean spirit is the only reasonable way to do it, otherwise the book appears—as it appeared to F. R. Leavis—pretentious and trifling. Sterne's procedure (imagine, by the way, the serendipity by which he has to be spoken of as stern while written of as Sterne) licenses Merton to digress as the spirit of travel strikes him. He is not obliged to take the shortest road to Loretto.

So I fancy that we are all set. We have a scholarly question: Who has the right of priority in the property of the dwarfs-and-giants? We have a sociologist's interest in the ways by which knowledge is acquired and transmitted—with gaps which may be called intermittences or intermissions. We have a humanist's concern with the vicissitudes of the reasoning process. We have a scholar in his room and occasionally making forays to the library at Columbia. Our author has three children who seem to be responsible for surrounding him with fifteen cats—hence, in the dedication of *OTSOG*, the allusion to "The Naming of Cats" in T. S. Eliot's *Old Possum's Book of Practical Cats*, where a cat is seen in a rapt contemplation of his name:

> His ineffable effable
> Effanineffable
> Deep and inscrutable singular Name.

What else? Nothing more is required than a good mood. So, after several years, a bundle of scholarly references becomes a surreptitious typescript which becomes, in 1965, a book, in the event recognized as a masterpiece of intellectual comedy— I must, after this flourish, give it its full title, *On the Shoulders of Giants*, and its subtitle, *A Shandean Postscript*. A postscript to what? My deduction is: to the script of the Presidential Address.

So we have an impeccably deployed intellectual exercise, tracking down the origin of an aphorism, going beyond—or rather, behind—Bernard of Chartres to the Roman grammarian Priscianus, a leap of six centuries, a sizeable intermittence. And we have digressions touching upon the following, *inter alia*: John Aubrey on eyes, Hooke on the merits of pursuing truth by intimate debate rather than by public dispute, Merton on the notable number of notable Johns in the history of science between A.D. 1100 and 1300, divers militants in the seventeenth-century Battle of the Books, Hakewill on plagiary, Mill (J.S.) on Bentham's later style, Macaulay's assault upon Temple, Merton on lost conversations, Priscianus on youth, John of Salisbury's self-depreciation; not to speak of such questions as, why did Voltaire publish in Holland rather than in France his *Élémens de la philosophie de Neuton,* and why did Jonathan Swift, having written *The Battle of the Books* in 1697–98 and delayed publishing it in deference to Temple's wishes, wait a further five years after Temple's death before (as A.C. Guthkelch has it) "disregarding them"?

But note how charmingly the official narrative—the detective story—and the digressions are choreographed. The interest of the narrative is historical, genetic: how did something come to be, and how should we interpret it in the concentrated light of its having come to be in that way? The interest of the digressions is intrinsic or, as we say, concentrated upon the 'thing in itself.' There is a difference, but it is one of entirely compatible manners. An interest in the intrinsic is rightly deemed to be an aesthetic interest, since it proposes no other purpose, aim, or end than rapt contemplation of the object. In this connection I recall that one of John Henry Cardinal Newman's discourses on university education is called "Knowledge its Own End," a formula as good as any to represent such an interest; though I don't recall that

Newman emphasized the aesthetic aspect of that knowledge or the economic aspect, my point being that the only people who take an interest in the intrinsic quality of an object are those who can afford to do so, that is, those who don't need to use it or otherwise have designs upon it. The present occasion, however, enables the reader to have the best of both interests: having bought *OTSOG* and therefore acquired 'the hard way' the right to enjoy its contents, he/she or she/he can indulge his/her or her/his sense of the intrinsic on the full assurance that none of these digressions can be put to the slightest use.

Talking thus of uselessness, I now add my own tuppence-worth, on five matters worthy of note in this context and probably in no other.

One: on Didacus Stella, Burton's authority for the aphorism, I have to report that *The Macmillan Book of Proverbs, Maxims, and Famous Phrases* gives Burton's man as Didacus Castellus and refers the reader to his (D.C.'s) *Tratado de Cuentas* (1551).

Two: in the only form in which the American people are likely to read the *Anatomy of Melancholy*, namely in the selection from it as made by Lawrence Babb and published by Michigan State University Press in 1965, the famous footnote now appears as: "In Luciano 10, Tome 2: "Pigmaei gigantum humeris impositi plusquam ipsi gigantes vident." Proof positive that Professor Babb didn't quote Didacus directly, any more than lazy Burton did. See page 258 of the present volume.

Three: the indignant wit referred to on page 163n herewith was Winston Churchill, his victim his wartime Cabinet colleague, the mild and somewhat diminutive Clement Attlee. (I could produce evidence if I had to.)

Four: on the footnote that sprawls from page 205 to 206. This note is insufficiently digressive, however. You will find that it quotes Newton as saying, a short while before his death:

> I do not know what I may appear to the world, but to myself I seem to have been only like a boy playing on the seashore, and diverting myself in now and then finding a smoother pebble or a prettier shell than ordinary, whilst the great ocean of truth lay all undiscovered before me.

Merton might 'of course' have noted that Newton's sentence is the source of W. B. Yeats's lines in the poem "At Algeciras— A Meditation upon Death":

> Often at evening when a boy
> Would I carry to a friend—
> Hoping more substantial joy
> Did an older mind commend—
> Not such as are in Newton's metaphor,
> But actual shells of Rosses' lovely shore.

Rosses: meaning Rosses Point, one of the two strands local to Yeats's Sligo, the other being Strandhill. Yeats's poem, by the way, is dated November 1928 as if to assert that he was ready to meditate upon death eleven years before he met it.

Five: Merton's dealing (pp. 232ff.) with peregrinity might have peregrinated even further. "Rabelais coined *pérégrinité* to denote the condition of a *peregrinus* or foreigner: a kind of feeling-out-of-place-ness." Perhaps he might have added a passage from T. S. Eliot's "Little Gidding," where the "familiar compound ghost" refers to

> the spirit unappeased and peregrine
> Between two worlds become much like each other . . .

and I, somewhat casually referred to on page 210 as "Denis the critic," might quote a passage from R. P. Blackmur's essay "Unappeasable and Peregrine: Behavior and the *Four Quartets*" (*Language as Gesture*), as follows:

In the Republic and the Empire, *peregrini* were, in Rome, citizens of any state other than Rome, with an implied membership in a definite community. The Shorter O.E.D. says of 'peregrine': one from foreign parts, an alien, a wanderer; and goes on to say that in astrology (that ironic refuge of Eliot as of Donne and of Dante) a peregrine is a planet situated in a part of the zodiac where it has none of its essential dignity. In Italian the meanings are similar, and the notion of pilgrim is a late development.—Have we not an expatriate looking for a *patria*—an American turned Anglican—a perpetual peregrine at Rome? To clinch it, let us look to Dante (*Purgatorio* XIII, 94–96):

> O frate mio, ciascuna è cittadina
> d'una vera città; ma tu vuo' dire
> che vivesse in Italia peregrina.

[O my brother, each one here is a citizen of a true city: but you mean one that lived in Italy while a pilgrim.]
... I do not think this is too much to pack into a word, but it is no wonder that it should take the attribute unappeasable, for it is the demands of the peregrine, whether outsider or pilgrim, that cannot be met. I will add that the peregrine is also a hawk or falcon found the world over but never at home: always a migrant but everywhere met; and, wherever found, courageous and swift.

I will add that I have replaced Blackmur's translation of the Dante lines by Charles S. Singleton's, for reasons quite good but not worth going into.

Now I revert from my digression to my narrative, such as it is. Mainly to append four further instances of the dwarfs-and-giants aphorism.

The first is Leslie Stephen, who said in his Introduction to *The Science of Ethics* (1882) that if giants had built a foundation for the subject of ethics, "even dwarfs may add something to the superstructure of the great edifice of science." This puts dwarfs on the shoulders of giants as anyone might climb a ladder or scaffold to raise a wall. I found the citation in Noel Annan's recently reissued *Leslie Stephen: The Godless Victorian.*

The second—Merton knows this one very well—is Lionel Trilling, who wrote in "Freud and Literature" (1940), one of the essays gathered in *The Liberal Imagination*:

> For psychoanalysis is one of the culminations of the Romanticist literature of the nineteenth century. If there is perhaps a contradiction in the idea of a science standing upon the shoulders of a literature which avows itself inimical to science in so many ways, the contradiction will be resolved if we remember that this literature, despite its avowals, was itself scientific in at least the sense of being passionately devoted to a research into the self.

The third is Harold Bloom, but I'm sheepish about leading him into this context; he doesn't use the aphorism directly. But his theory of poetry involves the modern poet choosing (or being fated to 'choose') a great precursor, and entering upon a relation to him such that it may indeed entail standing upon his shoulder, if only to complete the work the precursor left unfinished. Thus the poet Stevens in relation to Emerson; or Yeats in diverse relations to Blake and Nietzsche. I concede that special pleading is required here, but I am encouraged to force Bloom into the case by Merton's reference (p. 45) to "a motivated hostility toward a forerunner," a sentiment for which Bloom's theory allows, as in Blake's relation to Milton. And is not Bloom's famous theory of misreading allowed for in Merton's reference (p. 195) to Bernard and his colleagues in the twelfth century who "had to misinterpret Priscian fruitfully in order to arrive at their distinctive idea of the progress of knowledge"?

With the fourth I am on stronger ground or even wider

shoulders, though again only the idea of dwarfs-and-giants is retained and not the aphorism itself. Think of T. S. Eliot's essay "Tradition and the Individual Talent" (in *Selected Essays*). Is it not clear that Eliot's theme and Merton's theme are one and the same: the relation between present and past; a modern writer's recourse to Tradition, which requires "the historical sense" if he is to develop beyond his twenty-fifth year; and, more widely, the question of authority and how it is imposed in a particular art or science? Eliot runs the risk of implying that the best a modern writer can do is to clasp Tradition around the neck and hang on; but he allows, in the end, that the young writer may indeed develop his individual talent and help to purify the dialect of the tribe. Bear in mind, too, that Eliot was an American poet, and he knew that the Emersonian motive in American culture is commonly directed against the past and against any notion that we should try to learn from it. He knew, too, that poetry is not a community, as science is, and that an institutional or civic character—such as Merton attributes to science—is not to be found in poetry. As a result, Eliot had to define 'originality' more stringently, and discourage young poets from seeking it too directly.

So here is the quotation from "Tradition and the Individual Talent":

Someone said: "The dead writers are remote from us because we *know* so much more than they did." Precisely, and they are that which we know.

Finally, and in case I forget to mention it, I hope you have enjoyed *OTSOG* and now admire and love it as much as I do. It is one of the three books I most wish I had written; the other two being Kenneth Burke's *Towards a Better Life* and Italo Svevo's *The Confessions of Zeno*.

Denis Donoghue